A G

FEDERAL
AGENCY

ADJUDICATION

2ND EDITION

JEFFREY B. LITWAK

EDITOR

**Section of Administrative Law
and Regulatory Practice
American Bar Association**

16 15 14 13 12 5 4 3 2 1

Cataloging-in-Publication Data is on file with the Library of Congress

A Guide to Federal Agency Adjudication, 2nd Edition
Jeffrey B. Litwak
ISBN: 978-1-61438-537-0

CONTENTS

FOREWORD

To many people, the term "adjudication" or "trial" conjures up a vision of a judge and jury in a paneled court room with attorneys making eloquent arguments to the judge or engaging witnesses in emotional cross-examination. These representations come from television and movie dramas that bear little relevance to the daily lives of their audience. The vast majority of American citizens will never participate as a litigant, witness, or juror in a civil or criminal trial at the federal or state level of the legal process.

The entertainment industry has ignored the one area of adjudication that affects the lives of all our citizens, individual and commercial. Administrative adjudication before federal, and state, agencies covers almost all aspects of our activities as a people. It may not be as dramatic as the cases on "Law and Order," but its impact is more direct and more comprehensive than what is depicted on television. For example, administrative law judges (ALJs) decide over one million cases each year by applicants for Social Security Disability and Medicare benefits. ALJs and administrative judges decide claims of workplace discrimination, collective bargaining rights, utility regulation, and workers' compensation claims. Immigration judges preside over thousands of alien deportation hearings at the Department of Justice. In essence, administrative adjudications govern numerous areas of our lives, including health and safety, financial operations, environmental preservation, workplace conditions, and commercial operations.

This treatise provides an update of the latest developments in administrative adjudications. In addition, it demonstrates that the administrative process is governed by sound rules of fairness under the Administrative Procedure Act that protects the rights of participants and promotes efficiency in governmental processes. It is an invaluable tool for all members of the bar and the general public. The contributors and editors are to be commended for producing another invaluable edition.

John Vittone, Chief Judge, U.S. Department of Labor (retired)

PREFACE

This volume is intended as a handbook to assist government and private counsel engaged in administrative adjudication under the federal Administrative Procedure Act (APA).

The original 2003 edition of this book was an outgrowth of a study of the federal APA that was launched by the American Bar Association's (ABA) Section of Administrative Law and Regulatory Practice. That study resulted in the adoption of a "blackletter" summary of the law adopted by the Section's Council on November 3, 2001.[1] The study overview pointed out: "At present, there is no reasonably comprehensive, credible, and readily accessible statement of administrative law as it now exists." This has now changed. The Section of Administrative Law and Regulatory Practice now publishes and periodically updates a series of "guides" to the major administrative law topics: *A Guide to Federal Judicial and Political Review, A Guide to Federal Agency Rulemaking*, and this *Guide to Federal Agency Adjudication*.

Since the APA was adopted in 1946, many aspects of the administrative landscape have been transformed almost beyond recognition. Yet the core provisions of the APA relating to adjudication, rulemaking, and judicial review remain almost unchanged. Since 1946, rulemaking has become vastly more significant and judicial review of agency action has become considerably more available and more rigorous. Federal agency adjudication remains important today, affecting millions of people every year, although it is no longer the primary vehicle for articulation of government policy.

Today the great majority of "formal adjudications" under the APA consist of disputes about Social Security and other benefit programs. Such cases are critically important to the claimants and, in the aggregate, to the federal fisc. Many other federal agencies generate a relatively small number of decisions through the formal adjudicatory process. These include, but are by no means limited to, the long-established independent regulatory agencies such as the National Labor Relations Board (NLRB), Federal Energy Regulatory Commission (FERC), Federal Communications Commission (FCC), Federal Trade Commission (FTC), or the Securities and

---

1. The blackletter summary is available at 54 ADMIN. L. REV. 1 (2002). A revised blackletter summary of adjudication is in Appendix A.

Exchange Commission (SEC). Although these agencies decide fewer adjudicated cases than in earlier times, the cases they do decide are often very important to the general public and to regulated groups. They involve a range of significant disputes in federal labor law, energy law, communications law, consumer protection and antitrust, and securities law. In 2002, as the original *Guide to Federal Agency Adjudication* was being published, the Supreme Court found that adjudication under the APA is fundamentally identical to proceedings of the federal district courts; it held that states are immune from privately initiated federal administrative adjudicatory proceedings just as the states are immune from cases brought in court.[2]

A great deal of federal administrative adjudication, referred to by the misleading name "informal adjudication," is conducted partly or wholly outside the auspices of the APA. Immigration cases are not governed by the APA, nor are government contracts, equal employment, federal personnel, or security clearance disputes, to name just a few of the many classes of informal adjudication. For these cases, the evolving concepts of due process govern agency action.

In this second edition, we have retained the structure and much of the original text of the original edition, but we scoured each chapter for important changes and developments in the law. In addition to simply updating the law, we have expanded footnotes to give more depth and understanding to issues that require more than a single-sentence explanation. We have pointed out circuit splits and subjects that courts have not yet conclusively addressed. We have introduced issues associated with the 2007 amendments to the ABA Model Code of Judicial Conduct that apply the Model Code to members of the administrative law judiciary,[3] and the growing use of technology in adjudications.[4] And, we have added a chapter on Adjudication in the 2010 Model State APA (MSAPA),[5] which may be a predictor of shifts or trends (however slight) in federal agency adjudication.

As with the original edition, we arranged the present volume into 12 chapters:

---

2. Federal Maritime Comm'n v. S. Carolina State Ports Auth., 535 U.S. 743 (2002).
3. Model Code of Judicial Conduct, Application § I.B (2007). See Chapter 7 and Chapter 10, § 10.0621.
4. See Chapter 1, § 1.05, and Chapter 2, § 2.056.
5. Revised Model State Administrative Procedure Act (2010), available at http://uniformlaws.org/Act.aspx?title=State Administrative Procedure Act, Revised Model (last visited Jan. 10, 2012). See Chapter 12.

Chapter 1: Adjudication under the Administrative Procedure Act
Chapter 2: Hearings required by procedural due process
Chapter 3: The right to a hearing under the APA
Chapter 4: Pre-hearing requirements
Chapter 5: Hearing requirements
Chapter 6: Post-hearing requirements
Chapter 7: Integrity of the decisionmaking process
Chapter 8: Alternative dispute resolution
Chapter 9: Informal adjudication
Chapter 10: Administrative law judges
Chapter 11: Attorneys' fees under the Equal Access to Justice Act
Chapter 12: Adjudication under the 2010 Model State APA

Jeffrey B. Litwak edited the entire second edition and updated chapters 1, 2, 3, and 7. Litwak is General Counsel for the Columbia River Gorge Commission and an Adjunct Professor of Law at Lewis and Clark Law School.

Michael Asimow edited the original 2003 edition, wrote the original chapters 1, 7, 10, and 11, and updated chapters 6, 10, and 11. Asimow is Visiting Professor of Law, Stanford Law School, and Professor of Law Emeritus, UCLA School of Law.

Jack M. Beermann wrote the original chapter 4, most of the original chapter 9, and part of the original chapter 5, and updated chapters 4 and 5. Beermann is Professor of Law at Boston University School of Law.

Phyllis Bernard wrote the original chapter 8 and updated it. Bernard is Professor of Law at Oklahoma City University School of Law.

Alexia M. Emmermann wrote chapter 12. Emmermann is on the Insurance Counsel with the Nevada Division of Insurance and is a member of the ABA's Section of Administrative Law and Regulatory Practice State Administrative Law Committee.

Jeremy Hunt updated chapter 9. He is an associate with the office of William C. Connor, where he practices municipal and transactional law.

John Hardin Young wrote part of the original chapter 9 and updated it. Young is past chair of the ABA's Section of Administrative Law and Regulatory Practice, Counsel to Sandler, Reiff, Young & Lamb P.C., and adjunct professor at William & Mary Law School.

The original 2003 edition noted that errors and omissions are inevitable in a work of this scope with multiple authors. We did not find those promised errors, but offer the same disclosure about this 2012 edition. We also know that readers may disagree with some of the propositions discussed here. Even though virtually every sentence in this book finds its support in statutes, regulation, case law, or other authorities, we have included some opposing views and criticisms of those authorities. We continue to welcome your suggestions to improve the next editions. Finally, we remind our readers that the law is constantly evolving; thus we encourage users to update the research here. Please send any input to the above-named authors of the chapter in question with a copy to Jeffrey Litwak. The e-mail addresses of the authors are as follows:

Jeffrey B. Litwak: litwak@gorgecommission.org
Michael Asimow: asimow@law.stanford.edu
Jack M. Beermann: beermann@bu.edu
Phyllis Bernard: pbernard@okcu.edu
Alexia M. Emmermann: alexia.emmermann@gmail.com
Jeremy Hunt: jphunt+gfaa@gmail.com
John Hardin Young: young@sandlerreiff.com

All of us who collaborated on this book hope that you, the user, will find it helpful in your work of engaging in federal administrative adjudication.

Chapter 1

ADJUDICATION UNDER THE ADMINISTRATIVE PROCEDURE ACT

1.01 CHAPTER OVERVIEW

This chapter provides a brief legislative history of the federal Administrative Procedure Act[1] (APA), focusing on the adjudication provisions of that act. (§ 1.02) It surveys the various sources of law on which a private party can rely to obtain procedural protections from a federal agency. (§ 1.03) It then turns to defining "adjudication" under the APA. (§ 1.04)

---

1. 5 U.S.C. §§ 551–558. The APA is cited without the prefatory 5 U.S.C. in this book.

1.02 THE FEDERAL ADMINISTRATIVE PROCEDURE ACT (APA)

1.021 The Attorney General's Committee

The history of the APA[2] begins with President Franklin Roosevelt's appointment in 1939 of the Attorney General's Committee on Administrative Procedure. Roosevelt hoped that the committee would recommend moderate reforms and isolate those in Congress who wanted more radical reforms of administrative procedure.[3] Early in 1941, the Attorney General's Committee submitted its report.[4] This epochal document provided an overview of the administrative process as it then existed, a set of recommendations, and monographs on 27 agencies.

The committee crafted its recommendations by identifying the best practices then existing, rather than by attempting radical restructuring. It found that most of the problems with the adjudicatory process were concentrated in the economic regulatory agencies. The report seemed mostly satisfied with the highly informal procedures of benefit-granting agencies such as the Veterans Administration, Social Security, or federal workers' compensation.

The majority report called for relatively modest reforms in adjudication, rulemaking, and judicial review. It recognized the diversity of agencies and declined to recommend the mandatory separation of rulemaking, prosecution, and enforcement from adjudication.[5] It recommended elevating the status of hearing examiners but rejected the concept of a central panel because of the loss of the benefits of specializa-

---

2. The leading article on the political and legislative history of the APA is George B. Shepherd, *Fierce Compromise: The Administrative Procedure Act Emerges from New Deal Politics*, 90 Nw. U. L. Rev. 1557 (1996). *See also* WILLIAM F. FUNK ET AL., FEDERAL ADMINISTRATIVE PROCEDURE SOURCEBOOK, ch. 1 (4th ed. 2008), which contains a thorough bibliography.

3. *Shepherd, supra* note 2, at 1594–98. Undeterred by the appointment of the Attorney General's Committee, Congress passed the Walter-Logan Bill in 1940, but Roosevelt vetoed it. *Id.* at 1598–632. Walter-Logan would have rigidified the adjudication process; it would have subjected all federal adjudication to formal procedural rules and required three-member decisional panels.

4. U.S. Attorney General's Committee on Administrative Procedure, Final Report, S. Doc. No. 8, 77th Cong., 1st Sess. (1941). *See Shepherd, supra* note 2, at 1632–38.

5. *AG Final Report, supra* note 4, at 55–60. The two minority reports would have required external separation in many situations. *Id.* at 203–09, 248–50.

tion and expertise.[6] The committee recommended that hearing examiners be given substantial authority to regulate the hearing and be required to write a proposed decision that would become the final agency decision unless appealed by the agency heads. Legislative committees considered the proposed APA extensively in 1941, but the issue was set aside for the duration of World War II.

1.022 APA as compromise legislation

The legislation that ultimately passed Congress by unanimous vote in 1946 combined the approaches taken by the majority and moderate minority of the Attorney General's Committee. Virtually every provision in the bill involved compromise, and much of it was intentionally left ambiguous.[7]

The adjudication provisions of the APA were cautious and evolutionary. The APA provided for a rather formal hearing process, including the examination and cross-examination of witnesses.[8] It required an internal separation of functions between adjudicators and adversaries but left this provision subject to significant exceptions.[9]

The Act did not separate hearing examiners from the agencies for which they decided cases, but it sharply elevated their status and independence.[10] It required hearing examiners to prepare preliminary decisions and provided litigants a right to submit proposed findings, conclusions, and exceptions.[11] The examiners had to be organizationally independent within the agency hierarchy, meaning that persons engaged in investigation or prosecution could not supervise them. Ex parte contacts with hearing examiners were banned. Examiners would be hired, compensated, and promoted by the Civil Service Commission (CSC),[12] not by the employer agency. Examiners could be removed from office only for good cause and only after a hearing provided by the CSC.[13]

But note all of the things that the APA might have done but did not do. Its formal adjudication provisions apply only if some statute *other than the*

---

6. *Id.* at 47.
7. *Shepherd, supra* note 2, at 1649–75.
8. *See* Chapter 5 for discussion of the hearing process.
9. *See* Chapter 7, § 7.06.
10. *See* Chapters 7 and 10 for discussion of the various APA provisions that protect the independence of administrative law judges (ALJs).
11. APA § 557(b), (c). *See* Chapter 6, § 6.02.
12. The Office of Personnel Management (OPM) now carries out this function.
13. The Merit Systems Protection Board now discharges this process.

APA requires a hearing on the record.[14] As a result, the act imposes virtually no constraints on the vast area of informal adjudication, including a large number of benefits-related decisions.[15] In contrast, the rulemaking and judicial review provisions of the APA apply much more comprehensively. The APA validated the existing combined-function agencies, protected the policymaking function of the agency heads,[16] preserved the ability of agency heads to supervise investigation and select cases,[17] and failed to separate hearing officers from the agencies for which they decide cases. It did not prohibit ex parte contacts between outsiders and agency heads.[18]

In 1947, the Department of Justice published the *Attorney General's Manual on the Administrative Procedure Act* ("Attorney General's Manual"),[19] which is a leading reference source on the Act[20] and is cited often in this book.

---

14. *See* Chapter 3, § 3.01.
15. For discussion of informal adjudication and the meager procedural constraints imposed by the APA, *see* Chapter 9. For discussion of benefits-related decisions and due process, *see* Chapter 2, § 2.022.
16. *See* APA § 557(b): "On appeal from or review of the initial decision, the agency has all the powers which it would have in making the initial decision except as it may limit the issues on notice or by rule."
17. *See* APA § 554(d)(C), providing that separation of functions "does not apply . . . to the agency or a member or members of the body comprising the agency." This provision is discussed in Chapter 7, § 7.065.
18. In 1976, the APA was amended to include prohibitions on ex parte contact with all agency decisionmakers, both ALJs and agency heads. APA § 557(d); Government in the Sunshine Act, Pub. L. No. 94-409, § 4(a), 90 Stat. 1241 (1976). *See* Chapter 7, § 7.04.
19. Shepherd noted that affected parties scrambled during negotiations and after adoption of the APA to create legislative history—"to create a record that would cause future reviewing courts to interpret the new statute in a manner that would favor the party," Shepherd, *supra* note 2, at 1662—and that the Attorney General's Manual was one of those post-adoption documents, *id.* at 1666. The Attorney General's Manual is reproduced in WILLIAM F. FUNK, ET AL., FEDERAL ADMINISTRATIVE PROCEDURE SOURCEBOOK (4th ed. 2008), and at http://www.oalj.dol.gov/public/apa/references/reference_works/agtc.htm (last visited Jan. 7, 2012).
20. *But see* Shepherd, *supra* note 2, at 1682–83, concluding that the Supreme Court's deference to the Attorney General's Manual is suspect and that there is no reason to give more weight to the Attorney General's Manual than to other contrasting interpretations.

1.03 RIGHTS TO PROCEDURAL PROTECTION—SOURCES OF LAW

Clients facing adverse government action frequently wish to compel government agents to hear their side of the story before the government takes action. This subsection suggests different legal sources that might provide rights to private parties to require the government to provide adjudicatory procedural protections. Several of these sources of law may apply to a given case. Obviously, counsel should draw from all available sources in order to provide a client with maximum procedural protection.

First, the due process clauses of the Fifth and Fourteenth Amendments provide procedural protections when government action deprives a person of life, liberty, or property.[21] Precisely what form due process will take in a given case depends on a balancing of factors.[22]

Second, even when the formal adjudication provisions of the APA are inapplicable, the Act contains a number of procedural protections applicable to adjudication generally.[23]

Third, as noted in § 9.032, particular statutes may provide for hearings or other procedural protections even when due process or the APA does not apply. Thus a statute that calls for a "hearing," but not a "hearing on the record," still requires the agency to provide *some* kind of procedural protection.

Fourth, agency procedural regulations frequently confer procedural rights that the agency was not required to provide by statute or due process. Even though not legally required, the agency will be compelled to follow its procedural regulations if such regulations were provided for the protection of the public as distinguished from the convenience of the agency.[24] Conceivably, a court might require an agency to provide procedures that had become long-standing and well-settled customs but had never been codified in regulations.[25]

---

21. *See* Chapter 2 for discussion of due process; § 2.02 discusses deprivation of liberty and property and the predicates for application of due process.
22. *See* Chapter 2, §§ 2.04, 2.05.
23. *See* Chapter 9, §§ 9.03–9.06.
24. *See* Chapter 9, § 9.032.
25. *See* Vermont Yankee Nuclear Power Corp. v. NRDC, 435 U.S. 519, 542 (1978): "It might also be true, although we do not think the issue is presented in this case and accordingly do not decide it, that a totally unjustified departure from well-settled agency procedures of long standing might require judicial correction."

1.04 THE DEFINITION OF "ADJUDICATION" UNDER THE APA

Whether the APA's adjudication provisions apply depends on whether a particular dispute between a private party and the government is considered "adjudication." This question is resolved by considering the APA's definitional sections. Unfortunately, those sections were poorly drafted and cannot be literally applied.

Under the APA, "'adjudication' means agency process for the formulation of an order."[26] An "'order' means the whole or a part of a final disposition . . . of an agency in a matter *other than rule making but including licensing*."[27] Thus, adjudication becomes a residual category; it covers licensing and anything that is not rulemaking.

As a result, the definition of "rule" is the key to drawing the line between adjudication and rulemaking. A "'rule' means the whole or a part of an agency statement of general or particular applicability and future effect designed to implement, interpret, or prescribe law or policy."[28] "Rulemaking," in turn, "means agency process for formulating, amending, or repealing a rule."[29]

The definition of "rule" is problematic because of the words "or particular." In common usage, adjudication means agency action of particular or individualized applicability, while rulemaking means agency action of general applicability (often referred to as "quasi-legislative"). Yet the APA's definition classifies agency action of particular applicability and future effect as rulemaking.[30] Thus an agency order to a private party to

---

26. APA § 551(7).
27. APA § 551(6) (emphasis added).
28. APA § 551(4).
29. APA § 551(5).
30. This peculiar definition evidently was designed to make clear that future-directed individualized ratemaking would be treated as rulemaking rather than as adjudication. *See* Thomas D. Morgan, *Toward a Revised Strategy for Ratemaking*, 1978 U. ILL. L. FORUM 21, 50. Scholars have long discussed the confusion and suggested corrections. *See, e.g.*, Ronald M. Levin, *The Case for (Finally) Fixing the APA's Definition of "Rule,"* 56 ADMIN. L. REV. 1077 (2004). The ABA has also proposed eliminating the "or particular" language to avoid this conceptual problem. 106 ABA ANN. REP. 549, 783 (1981); 95 ABA ANN. REP. 548, 1025 (1970). The Administrative Conference of the United States agreed, with the understanding that a matter could be of general applicability even if it applied to a class consisting only of a single person since in the future the number of persons might increase. ACUS Statement 2, On ABA Resolution No. 1 Proposing

cease and desist from some kind of action would fall under the definition of "rule" (since it is action of particular applicability other than licensing and is of future effect). Yet such action has always been treated as adjudication under the APA since it tends to involve fact-finding relating to past action rather than policymaking.[31] In general, courts confronted with this dilemma analyze the particular dispute to see whether it better fits the categories of rulemaking or adjudication.[32]

There is a second problem with the definitions of "rule" and "order." Licensing is automatically treated as adjudication, yet the definition of "rule" significantly overlaps the definition of "license." A "'license' includes the whole or a part of an agency permit, certificate, approval, registration, charter, membership, statutory exemption or other form of permission."[33] "Licensing," in turn, "includes agency process respecting the grant, renewal, denial, revocation, suspension, annulment, withdrawal, limitation, amendment, modification, or conditioning of a license."[34]

"'Rule' . . . includes the approval or prescription for the future of rates, wages, corporate or financial structures or reorganizations thereof, prices, facilities, appliances, services, or allowances therefor or of valua-

---

to Amend the Definition of "Rule" in the Administrative Procedure Act. 38 Fed. Reg. 16,841 (June 27, 1973), *as amended*, 39 Fed. Reg. 23,045 (1974). *See also* JEFFREY S. LUBBERS, A GUIDE TO FEDERAL AGENCY RULEMAKING Pt. II, ch. 1(A) (5th ed. 2012).

31. *See Attorney General's Manual* at 15 (FTC or NLRB proceedings leading to issuance of orders to cease and desist from unfair labor practices or unfair methods of competition are adjudication, not rulemaking).

32. *See, e.g.,* Yesler Terrace Cmty. Council v. Cisneros, 37 F.3d 442, 448–49 (9th Cir. 1994). In *Yesler Terrace*, the Department of Housing and Urban Development (HUD) determined that Washington State's eviction process satisfied due process. The court held that HUD had engaged in rulemaking, not adjudication; its decision was invalid because it failed to provide notice and comment rulemaking procedures. The criteria were (1) the determination involved broad classes of unspecified individuals rather than specific individuals and; (2) the determination had no immediate effect on any specific individual but would have such an effect only after it was applied. *See also* MacLean v. Dep't of Homeland Security, 543 F.3d 1145, 1151–52 (9th Cir. 2008). In *MacLean*, TSA issued an order declaring that a particular text message contained sensitive information. The court concluded that the order was the result of an adjudication, reasoning that it was an agency process for the formulation of an order and did not affect the rights of a broad class of people.

33. APA § 551(8).

34. APA § 551(9).

tions, costs or accounting, or practices bearing on any of the foregoing."[35] Suppose a corporation cannot reorganize without agency permission, which the agency proposes to deny. Is the necessary permission a license or a rule? It is both, since "license" includes "permit . . . approval . . . or any other form of permission," while "rule" explicitly includes "approval of . . . corporate or financial structures or reorganizations."

Presumably, the explicit treatment of "reorganizations" as a "rule" trumps the more general treatment of approvals or permissions under the definition of "license."[36] Yet what about other forms of initial licensing that may also involve policy determinations, such as radio or television broadcasting or certificates of public convenience enabling a carrier to obtain monopoly rights to particular forms of transportation? Presumably, these are licenses, not rules, or the APA's definition of licensing would be stripped of all significance.[37]

Illustrations:

1. Agency A orders M to withdraw a particular food from the market. While the order has "particular applicability" and "future effect," it should be treated as adjudication rather than rulemaking.[38]

2. Agency B orders N to cut its price for a particular good by $1 per pound. This order is rulemaking rather than adjudication for purposes of the APA since the definition of "rule" specifically includes "prescription for the future" of "prices." If a statute provides for a "hearing on the record," the agency should treat the proceedings as formal rulemaking.[39] Due process might also apply to this proceeding since it may involve an individualized deprivation of property.[40]

---

35. APA § 551(4).
36. *Attorney General's Manual* at 14 (reorganizations and any similar types of decisionmaking should be treated as rules, not licenses).
37. *Id.* at 15–16 (radio licenses, certificates of public convenience and necessity, and airman certificates are treated as adjudication).
38. *Id.*
39. *See* APA § 553(c) (last sentence) (providing for formal rulemaking procedures when rules are required by statute to be made on the record after opportunity for an agency hearing).
40. *See* Chapter 2, §§ 2.022, 2.06.

3. Agency C denies O's application for permission to provide helicopter tours over a national park. The permission in question should be treated as a "license" rather than a "rule" and thus C should treat the dispute as adjudication rather than rulemaking.[41]

4. Agency D proposes to set permitted emissions of copper smelters in Z County. P operates the only copper smelter in Z County and opposed D's proposal. D should treat this dispute as rulemaking rather than adjudication.[42]

1.05 USE OF ELECTRONIC TECHNOLOGY IN ADJUDICATION

The last decade has shown an explosion in the use of technology in federal agency adjudication. Agencies continue to update and improve their procedures, allowing for electronic submission of documents and claims.[43] Digital recording of hearings allows citations to an exact point (hour, minute, and second) without need to produce a written transcript. Some agencies even steer claimants to file the first level of appeal via the Internet.[44] Many agencies also conduct video hearings before an administrative law judge (ALJ).[45] In 2011, the Administrative Conference of the United States produced a recommendation for agency use of video

---

41. *Attorney General's Manual* at 16.
42. Hercules, Inc. v. EPA, 598 F.2d 91, 118 (D.C. Cir. 1978); Anaconda Co. v. Ruckelshaus, 482 F.2d 1301, 1306 (10th Cir. 1973). *See* Chapter 2, § 2.06.
43. For example, the Social Security Administration has an "Electronic Records Express" program that allows claimants to file health and school records related to disability claims. *See* Social Security Admin., Pub. No. 05-10049, Use Electronic Records Express to Send Client Records (July 2010), *available at* http://www.ssa.gov/ere/index.html (last visited Jan. 7, 2012). All documents become part of a claimant's electronic folder, which may be downloaded and viewed at any time.
44. For example, Social Security claimants may request review of decisions about eligibility for disability benefits through an Internet appeals process. *See* https://secure.ssa.gov/apps6z/iAppeals/ap001.jsp (last visited Jan. 7, 2012).
45. *E.g.*, Social Security Admin., Pub. No. 70-067, Why You Should Have Your Hearing by Video (April 2008), *available at* http://www.socialsecurity. gov/appeals/odar_pubs/70-067.html (last visited Jan. 7, 2012). For a good description of video hearings in immigration cases, *see Developments in the Law—Access to Courts: Access to Courts and Videoconferencing in Immigration Court Proceedings*, 122 Harv. L. Rev. 1181 (2009).

hearings and issued a comprehensive report on this subject.[46] Despite this activity, there is little case law on use of video hearings to date.[47]

Perhaps as a predictor of where federal adjudication is going, the prefatory note to the 2010 Model State APA (MSAPA) states that it "is designed to . . . promote efficiency in agency proceedings by providing for extensive use of electronic technology."[48] For example, the MSAPA defines the terms "electronic" and "electronic record,"[49] allows agencies to satisfy the requirement to produce indices by providing a record that is searchable on the Internet,[50] allows electronic signatures,[51] specifically authorizes conducting hearings by electronic means,[52] and requires decisions to be prepared electronically.[53]

As agencies experiment with more and different uses of electronic technology, practitioners must monitor new requirements for the agencies they practice before and assure that their own technology is fully compatible with the agencies' technology.

---

46. Administrative Conference of the United States, Recommendation No. 2011-4, Agency Use of Video Hearings: Best Practices and Possibilities for Expansion (June 17, 2011). This report and the project documents are available at http://www.acus.gov/research/the-conference-current-projects/video-hearings/ (last visited Jan. 7, 2012).
47. *See* Chapter 2, § 2.056 for discussion of video hearings and due process.
48. *See* Model State APA (2010) (MSAPA) Prefatory Note, Chapter 12, § 12.02.
49. *Id.* at §§ 102(8), (9).
50. *Id.* at § 102, cmt.
51. *Id.* at 8, § 801.
52. *Id.* at § 403(e).
53. *Id.* at § 403(j).

Chapter 2

HEARINGS REQUIRED BY
PROCEDURAL DUE PROCESS

2.01 BASIC PRINCIPLES

Both the Fifth Amendment (applicable to the federal government) and the Fourteenth Amendment (applicable to the states) provide that "no person . . . [shall] be deprived of life, liberty, or property without due process of law."[1] Essentially, the due process clauses provide *procedural* protections for private individuals and business interests.[2] The requirement of due process attaches only to "state action," meaning actions taken by government entities, rather than to actions taken by private entities.[3] In order to conclude that a person is entitled to procedural due process, and to determine what process is due, the courts must determine the following:

- that there exists a constitutionally protected interest (namely life, liberty, or property) (§ 2.02)
- that government action has "deprived" a person of such an interest (§ 2.03)
- when due process must be provided (§ 2.04)
- what process must be provided (§ 2.05)
- that the state has acted through adjudication rather than legislative-type action such as rulemaking (§ 2.06).

To maintain a colorable due process claim, the plaintiff must exhaust administrative remedies.[4] A due process hearing is required only to prove a fact or set of facts relevant to the inquiry at hand.[5]

---

1. On due process, *see generally* RICHARD J. PIERCE, JR., ADMINISTRATIVE LAW TREATISE, ch. 9 (5th ed. 2010); JERRY L. MASHAW, DUE PROCESS IN THE ADMINISTRATIVE STATE 107–53 (1985); Edward L. Rubin, *Due Process and the Administrative State*, 72 CALIF. L. REV. 1044, 1130–78 (1984).
2. Substantive, as opposed to procedural, due process concerns the level of justification the state must establish before depriving a person of life, liberty, or property. The subject of substantive due process is beyond the scope of this book.
3. *See infra* § 2.033 (addressing actions by quasi-governmental entities). Am. Mfrs. Mut. Ins. Co. v. Sullivan, 526 U.S. 40 (1999) (workers' compensation insurer not a state agent merely because of state regulation and, therefore, not subject to due process obligations).
4. Leavell v. Ill. Dep't of Natural Res., 600 F.3d 798, 807 (7th Cir. 2010). *But see* Keating v. Neb. Pub. Power Dist., 562 F.3d 923, 929 (8th Cir. 2009) (noting "it is not necessary for a litigant to have exhausted available postdeprivation remedies when the litigant contends that he was entitled to predeprivation process") (emphasis omitted).
5. Conn. Dep't of Pub. Safety v. Doe, 538 U.S. 1 (2003) (no due process hearing required to establish whether plaintiff is currently dangerous prior to placing plaintiff on registry of all sex offenders because "dangerousness" was not relevant under Connecticut's Megan's Law statute).

2.02 CONSTITUTIONALLY PROTECTED INTERESTS

Procedural due process requires that a person asserting a right to protection must claim deprivation of an interest in "life, liberty, or property." In administrative adjudication, property and liberty are almost always the substantive interests involved. The right to life is seldom asserted.[6]

Persons entitled to due process include organizations outside of the United States but with sufficient connection to the United States.[7]

2.021 General rule

The rights that are protected by procedural due process may be derived from a variety of sources. In the case of property, the right or entitlement must be grounded outside the U.S. Constitution, which does not itself create property rights. Sources of protected property rights include state or federal statutes as well as common law. Liberty interests may be grounded in state or federal statutes, but they can also be grounded in constitutional provisions.

2.022 Property rights

Property rights are created by rules or understandings that stem from an independent source of law, such as a state statute. These sources must support a claim of legal *entitlement* to a particular interest or benefit.[8] If the decision to provide a particular benefit or status is discretionary with government officials (as in the case of employment at will), it is not treated as property.[9] The term "property" includes traditional property

---

6. *See, e.g.*, Woodard v. Ohio Adult Parole Auth., 107 F.3d 1178, 1186–88 (6th Cir. 1997) (death row inmate had possibly valid claim of life and liberty interests in clemency process), *rev'd* 523 U.S. 272 (1998).

7. Nat'l Council of Resistance of Iran v. Dep't of State, 251 F.3d 192 (D.C. Cir. 2001) (citing Mathews v. Eldridge, an organization with a sufficient connection to the United States has the right to be heard at a meaningful time and manner before being deprived of a protected property or liberty interest).

8. Board of Regents v. Roth, 408 U.S. 564, 577–78 (1972) ("Property interests, of course, are not created by the Constitution. Rather, they are created and their dimensions are defined by existing rules or understandings that stem from an independent source such as state law—rules or understandings that secure certain benefits and support claims of entitlement to those benefits.").

9. *Id.*

rights (such as personal[10] or real property or money[11]), as well as "new" property rights (statutory entitlements that lack many elements of traditional property, such as assignability).

New property rights can be derived not only from statutes but also from express or implied contracts between the individual and the government[12] or agency decisional practices.[13] If an independent source of law creates a property right as defined above, the holder of that right is entitled to the protections provided by due process, not to some lower level of protection provided by the statute in question.[14] The idea that some statutory entitlements are mere "privileges," rather than "rights," has been repudiated.[15]

Entitlements that are treated as property include the following:

---

10. *See, e.g.,* Shaul v. Cherry Valley-Springfield Cent. Sch. Dist., 363 F.3d 177, 187 (2d Cir. 2004) (government's retention of lawfully seized property could require due process) (citing United States v. David, 131 F.3d 55, 59 (2d Cir. 1997) (entertaining due process challenge to government delay in forfeiting or returning seized property)).
11. *See, e.g.,* Burns v. Pa. Dep't of Corr., 544 F.3d 279, 288 (3d Cir. 2008) (Department of Corrections' assessment of an inmate's account for medical and other expenses was similar to a money judgment that reduced the economic value of that account was a deprivation of a protected property).
12. *See* Perry v. Sindermann, 408 U.S. 593 (1972) (right to governmental employment based on implied contract, which the Court described as "written or unwritten state or local government policies or from 'mutually explicit understandings' between a government employer and employee"); Hennigh v. City of Shawnee, 155 F.3d 1249 (10th Cir. 1998) (collective bargaining agreement containing a "for cause shown" restriction on terminating employment created property interest); Baraka v. McGreevey, 481 F.3d 187, 206–07 (3d Cir. 2007) (no mutual understanding to $10,000 honorarium in appointment as New Jersey Poet Laureate). For further discussion of contract rights as property, *see* text at notes 25–26.
13. *See* Furlong v. Shalala, 156 F.3d 384, 395 (2d Cir. 1998) (rights to payment for service arising out of consistent pattern of ALJ decisions).
14. Cleveland Bd. of Educ. v. Loudermill, 470 U.S. 532, 541 (1985); Club Misty, Inc. v. Laski, 208 F.3d 615, 619 (7th Cir. 2000) (liquor license that is revocable only for cause is an interest in property despite fact that statute provides for procedures that do not satisfy due process). *Loudermill* overrules Arnett v. Kennedy, 416 U.S. 134 (1974). A plurality of justices had held in *Arnett* that an employee must take "the bitter with the sweet," meaning that the statute creating the property right could also define the procedural protections for that right.
15. Board of Regents v. Roth, 408 U.S. 564, 571 (1972).

- welfare benefits[16]
- essential public utility services[17]
- occupational licenses[18]
- public employment[19]
- public education[20]
- the right to contract with government[21]
- the right to make use of an agency's adjudicatory process to remedy a legal wrong[22]
- revocation of parole or probation[23]

Whether a particular claim is an entitlement or is instead at the discretion of state agents is a difficult issue requiring an examination of the factual context.[24] In order to create a property interest, the statute or other source of law must contain *substantive* protections for the interest (such as

---

16. *See, e.g.,* Goldberg v. Kelly, 397 U.S. 254 (1970) (Aid to Families with Dependent Children benefits); Mathews v. Eldridge, 424 U.S. 319 (1976) (Social Security disability benefits).
17. Memphis Light, Gas & Water Div. v. Craft, 436 U.S. 1 (1978).
18. Barry v. Barchi, 443 U.S. 55 (1979) (horsetrainer's license).
19. *Loudermill,* 470 U.S. 532 (civil servant who could be discharged only for cause). A public employee may also be deprived of property if stripped of the benefits of the job to which he is entitled (even though the employee is not discharged). *See* Wozniak v. Conry, 236 F.3d 888, 890 (7th Cir. 2001) (tenured professor deprived of teaching and research opportunities).
20. Goss v. Lopez, 419 U.S. 565 (1975) (elementary education).
21. *See, e.g.,* Pataula Elec. Membership Corp. v. Whitworth, 951 F.2d 1238, 1243–44 (11th Cir. 1992) (state law requiring the award of public contracts to the "lowest responsible bidder" represents a rule or understanding sufficient to create a property interest).
22. Logan v. Zimmerman Brush Co., 455 U.S. 422, 428–37 (1982) (agency destroyed employee's right to obtain relief from employment discrimination by scheduling conference after deadline).
23. Morrissey v. Brewer, 408 U.S. 471 (1972); Gagnon v. Scarpelli, 411 U.S. 778 (1973).
24. *See* Bishop v. Wood, 426 U.S. 341 (1976) (upholding lower court decision that policeman who was a "permanent employee" was mere employee at will and thus lacked a property interest in his job); Stehney v. Perry, 101 F.3d 925, 936 (3d Cir. 1996) (no constitutionally protected property interest in a security clearance or a job requiring a security clearance); Town of Castle Rock v. Gonzales, 545 U.S. 748 (2005) (preprinted text of restraining order mirroring statute that used terms such as "every reasonable means" and "would be impractical" did not make enforcement of restraining order mandatory).

a requirement that discharge from employment can occur only for cause), not merely *procedural* protections for an interest that can be terminated in the state's discretion.[25]

Although contract rights between a private party and government may be interests in property,[26] due process requirements are satisfied if the rights can be protected through ordinary breach of contract litigation in court.[27]

Illustrations:

1. Worker receives benefits under statute entitling disabled workers to such benefits. Agency proposes to terminate the payments since it determined that Worker is no longer disabled. Worker has a property right in the disability payments that is protected by due process.[28]

2. Homeless Family challenges procedures used to allocate emergency shelter assistance. Neither a city ordinance nor an administrative rule prescribes the standards for making allocations, and agency does not follow any consistent practice. Family has no property interest sufficient to trigger due process.[29]

3. Security Guard, a "classified civil servant" under state law, is dismissed for dishonesty. State law provides that no classified civil servant may be removed except for specified causes such as incompetence or dishonesty or any other failure of good behavior. The statute also provides that a dismissed civil servant is entitled

25. Bunger v. Univ. of Okla. Bd. of Regents, 95 F.3d 987, 990–91 (10th Cir. 1996) (tenure procedures specified in faculty handbook not sufficient to create a property interest); *see also Town of Castle Rock*, 545 U.S. at 764 (2005) (no property right to seeking an arrest warrant authorized in a restraining order because that "would be an entitlement to nothing but procedure").
26. Brock v. Roadway Express, 481 U.S. 252, 260 (1987) (employer's contract right to discharge an employee for cause is an interest in property).
27. Lujan v. G&G Fire Sprinklers, Inc., 532 U.S. 189, 196–97 (2001).
28. Mathews v. Eldridge, 424 U.S. 319 (1976) (Social Security disability payments); Goldberg v. Kelly, 397 U.S. 254 (1970) (claim for welfare benefits treated as property).
29. Washington Legal Clinic for the Homeless v. Barry, 107 F.3d 32, 36–38 (D.C. Cir. 1997).

to administrative review of the dismissal, but such procedures do not satisfy the requirements of due process. Security Guard has a property interest in his position. The statutory review procedures cannot limit the underlying property right, which is created by the "for cause" terms of the statute, or diminish the extent of protections provided by due process.[30]

4. State University denies tenure to Professor. A University faculty code provides certain formal procedures for making tenure decisions. It also requires that candidates for tenure show outstanding ability in teaching or research. Teacher does not have a property interest in the procedures alone, and the guidelines provide no significant substantive limitations on officials' discretion.[31]

5. State College refuses to renew Teacher's contract. The standards for renewal set out in the Faculty Guide fail to provide any significant substantive limitation on officials' discretion, but in actual practice College has always renewed contracts if a teacher's services were satisfactory. These practices create an implied contract right to tenure, which, in turn, creates an entitlement protected by due process.[32]

6. A state statute requires that general contractors and subcontractors pay prevailing wages on government construction jobs. If a subcontractor fails to do so, the state subtracts the wage underpayment from the amount payable to the general contractor. The general contractor, in turn, is expected to subtract such amount from its payments to the subcontractor. Agency believes that Subcontractor underpaid its workers $135,000, so it subtracted this amount from its payments to General Contractor, which, in turn, reduced its payment to Subcontractor by $135,000. No hearing was provided before such withholding occurred. Subcontractor denies that it failed to pay prevailing wages. While the right to payment may be a property right, Subcontractor's claim can be

---

30. Cleveland Bd. of Educ. v. Loudermill, 470 U.S. 532 (1985); Greenwood v. New York, 163 F.3d 119, 122–23 (2d Cir. 1998) (psychiatrist's clinical privileges, grounded in clinic bylaws, treated as property right).
31. Goodisman v. Lytle, 724 F.2d 818, 821 (9th Cir. 1984).
32. Perry v. Sindermann, 408 U.S. 593 (1972).

asserted in normal state court breach of contract litigation. Consequently, due process does not require that Agency provide Subcontractor with a hearing.[33]

7.   Insurance Company is lowest bidder on a public contract to administer public insurance, but State Contracting Authority selects another bidder pursuant to an explicit discretionary power to reject any bid. Insurance Company has no protected interest.[34]

8.   A classification plan states that Collections Officers must possess a "Bachelor in Business Administration or related fields from an accredited institution"; however, a job announcement states, "The required academic preparation may be substituted by additional experience in the Collections area." Plaintiffs hired with the additional job experience, but not the required bachelor degree, have no property interest in continued employment because they are not lawfully hired pursuant to the classification plan.[35]

2.023 Liberty interests

Liberty interests are derived from positive law sources (such as state or federal statutes) as well as from rights provided in the Constitution (such as the right of freedom of speech provided by the First Amendment). The term liberty

denotes not merely freedom from bodily restraint but also the right of the individual to contract, to engage in any of the common occupations of life, to acquire useful knowledge, to marry, establish a home and bring up children, to worship God accord-

33. Lujan v. G&G Fire Sprinklers, Inc., 532 U.S. 189 (2001).
34. United of Omaha Life Ins. Co. v. Solomon, 960 F.2d 31 (6th Cir. 1992). *See also* Morley's Auto Body, Inc. v. Hunter, 70 F.3d 1209 (11th Cir. 1995) (wrecker service companies have no property interest in remaining on county sheriff's wrecker rotation call list); Indep. Enters., Inc. v. Pittsburgh Water & Sewer Auth., 103 F.3d 1165 (3d Cir. 1996) (construction company had no property right in procedures requiring agency to award contract to lowest bidder; such procedures exist only for benefit of public).
35. Costa-Urena v. Segarra, 590 F.3d 18 (1st Cir. 2009).

ing to the dictates of his own conscience, and generally to enjoy those privileges long recognized . . . as essential to the orderly pursuit of happiness by free men.[36]

The term also includes a right to be free from unjustified intrusions on personal security and punishment.[37]

Parties frequently assert liberty interests in connection with a discharge from public employment accompanied by a false and stigmatic public statement about the discharged employee.[38] The discharged employees are entitled to a hearing at which they can attempt to clear their names.[39] Some circuits have held that a plaintiff must request a name-clearing hearing prior to filing suit.[40] There is no specific form

---

36. Bd. of Regents v. Roth, 408 U.S. 564, 572 (1972), quoting Meyer v. Nebraska, 262 U.S. 390, 399 (1923) (a substantive due process case).

37. Ingraham v. Wright, 430 U.S. 651, 674 (1977) (corporal punishment of school children implicates a liberty interest under due process, although state tort law provides all the process that is due).

38. *See Bd. of Regents*, 408 U.S. at 572–75. The information must be publicly disclosed by the government as opposed to being privately communicated to the employee. Bishop v. Wood, 426 U.S. 341, 348–49 (1976). It is unclear whether the employer is considered to have disclosed the information merely because it is placed in a personnel file and thus might be disclosed to a future employer who requests the information. *See* Donato v. Plainview-Old Bethpage Cent. Sch. Dist., 96 F.3d 623, 631–32 (2d Cir. 1996) (information placed in claimant's employment file is a sufficient publication because future employers will ask to see the file); Olivieri v. Rodriguez, 122 F.3d 406, 408–10 (7th Cir. 1997) (department might not disclose the information if future employers asked for it; information disclosed by the employee himself does not count as disclosure). Finally, the information must be stigmatic in the sense that it would impede future employment. *See Donato*, 96 F.3d at 630 (statements that seriously disparaged professional fitness were stigmatizing even though they did not implicate moral character).

39. In order to trigger a name-clearing hearing, the employee must allege that the stigmatizing information is false. Codd v. Velger, 429 U.S. 624, 627–28 (1977); *but see* Graham v. City of Philadelphia, 402 F.3d 139 (3d Cir. 2005) (probationary police officer terminated following arrest was not entitled to a name-clearing hearing after his acquittal at trial because the trial satisfied the requirements of due process).

40. *See, e.g.*, Winskowski v. City of Stephen, 442 F.3d 1107, 1112 (8th Cir. 2006).

required to request a hearing, and courts may interpret communications liberally as hearing requests.[41]

However, a state official who defames a person, but does not do so in connection with other government action (such as discharging the person from employment), does not infringe a liberty interest. This is the so-called "stigma-plus requirement."[42] Claims of stigma unaccompanied by the plus factor must be rectified, if at all, under state defamation law rather than through a name-clearing hearing required by due process. Posttermination statements may be "in the course of the termination"[43] if there is a temporal nexus between the stigma and the government action, but there is no bright-line test.[44]

---

41. *See, e.g.,* Greene v. Street, No. 10-4529, 2011 U.S. Dist. LEXIS 67018, at *16 (E.D. Pa. June 22, 2011) (surviving a motion to dismiss was a letter from plaintiff's attorney that did "not specifically state that Plaintiff sought an opportunity to defend his reputation against false accusations made by Defendants, [but referred] to an 'unfortunate salvo of attacks' against Plaintiff, raise[d] concerns about public statements made by Defendant Street, and include[d] an offer to meet with the Board to resolve any problems associated with Plaintiff's employment").

42. *See* Paul v. Davis, 424 U.S. 693, 701–02, 710–11 (1976). (Plaintiff must establish not only that the government made a derogatory and false statement about him but also must show some tangible and material state imposed burden or alteration of his or her status, or a right in addition to the stigmatizing statement.) *But see* Siegert v. Gilley, 500 U.S. 226 (1991) (voluntary resignation from employment accompanied by stigmatic letter in file does not meet stigma-plus requirement).

43. Campanelli v. Bockrath, 100 F.3d 1476, 1482 (9th Cir. 1996) (citing Paul v. Davis, 424 U.S. at 710).

44. *Siegert,* 500 U.S. at 234 (alleged defamation must be "uttered incident to the termination"); Hadley v. County of Du Page, 715 F.2d 1238, 1246 (7th Cir. 1983) (in order for slur on reputation to give rise to a liberty interest it must occur at or near the time of termination since that is when the liberty interest arises); *Campanelli,* 100 F.3d at 1483 (rejecting bright-line test and holding that a seven- to nine-day interval between termination and publication of stigmatizing statement survived a Rule 12(b)(6) motion; Tibbetts v. Kulongoski, 567 F.3d 529 (9th Cir. 2009) (16 months between a termination of employment and governor's press release with "stigmatizing facts" was clearly outside of any temporal nexus; 19-day interval "presents a more difficult question," and concluding governor was entitled to qualified immunity because the parameters of temporal nexus are not clearly established by case law).

Prisoners who are deprived of physical liberty by the criminal justice system have very limited liberty rights.[45] A prisoner's liberty interest is infringed only if the action in question would inevitably affect the duration of the prisoner's sentence[46] or if it involves some restraint that "imposes atypical and significant hardship" going beyond the ordinary incidents of prison life.[47]

---

45. Sandin v. Conner, 515 U.S. 472, 483–84 (1995) (due process protection extends only to deprivations that "impose[] atypical and significant hardship on the inmate in relation to the ordinary incidents of prison life"). *Sandin* overruled prior cases that found infringement of liberty interests in cases of prison discipline or in cases where a statute or regulation created some kind of entitlement. *See, e.g.,* Hewitt v. Helms, 459 U.S. 460 (1983). Thus, the post-*Sandin* cases reject application of due process to routine disputes involving prisoners. *See, e.g.,* Wagner v. Hanks, 128 F.3d 1173, 1175 (7th Cir. 1997) ("under *Sandin* the key comparison is between disciplinary segregation and nondisciplinary segregation rather than between disciplinary segregation and the general prison population"; conditions of discretionary segregation against which the plaintiff's confinement is to be judged are not necessarily those of the prison in which the plaintiff is incarcerated, but rather those of the most restrictive prison in the state penal system). Dominique v. Weld, 73 F.3d 1156 (1st Cir. 1996) (loss of work privileges not violation of liberty interest); Frazier v. Coughlin, 81 F.3d 313 (2d Cir. 1996) (confinement in special housing unit not violation of liberty interest); Crowder v. True, 74 F.3d 812 (7th Cir. 1996) (administrative detention not violation); Mitchell v. Dupnik, 75 F.3d 517 (9th Cir. 1996) (inspection of legal papers not violation).
46. *Sandin* approved the result, although not the reasoning, in Wolff v. McDonnell, 418 U.S. 539 (1974). *Wolff* held that due process applied to a prison disciplinary hearing. Under *Sandin,* the key fact in *Wolff* was that the disciplinary proceeding could result in the loss of good time credits and thus inevitably prolong the prison term. *Sandin,* 515 U.S. at 472–73.
47. *See* Wilkinson v. Austin, 545 U.S. 209 (2005) (transfer of a prisoner to the Ohio State Penitentiary (OSP), a supermax prison, deprived the prisoner of a liberty interest due to conditions of OSP, which included a prohibition on all human communication, cell light on all day and night, and 23 hours per day in cell, but the court concluded the procedure for transfer out of supermax confinement, which occurs after the first 30 days, and then only annually using multistep reviews, was sufficient). *See also* Vitek v. Jones, 445 U.S. 480 (1980) (transfer from prison to mental hospital); Washington v. Harper, 494 U.S. 210 (1990) (involuntary administration of psychotropic drugs).

Courts are often reluctant to find "new" liberty interests, especially where the plaintiff may be a public figure, or a highly publicized figure.

Illustrations:

9. Police Chief circulates flyer containing photos of active shop-lifters, causing severe reputational injury to X, whose photo was included. Chief's action does not deprive X of liberty in the absence of an additional adverse effect, such as foreclosure of employment opportunities.[48]

10. Staff Psychiatrist is deprived of clinical staff privileges based on false, stigmatizing information. The information is disseminated to other hospitals. The stigma accompanied by the deprivation of staff privileges is sufficient to create a liberty interest.[49]

11. Probationary Police Officer is dismissed and his file, containing true but derogatory material, is shown to a subsequent employer. No liberty interest has been violated.[50]

12. Prisoner is placed in solitary confinement as a punishment for misconduct. This restraint was within the range of disciplinary action normally expected during long-term confinement in prison. Since the confinement neither inevitably extended the duration of his sentence nor imposed an unexpected restraint (like transfer to a mental hospital), it did not infringe a liberty interest.[51]

13. Candidate for public office had no liberty interest in private information involving investigation of attorney ethics and state laws.[52]

---

48. Paul v. Davis, 424 U.S. 693, 701 (1976) (plaintiff must resort to state defamation remedies rather than obtain a due process–based name-clearing hearing).
49. Greenwood v. New York, 163 F.3d 119, 123–24 (2d Cir. 1998).
50. Codd v. Velger, 429 U.S. 624 (1977) (if a due process hearing is to serve any useful purpose, there must be some factual dispute between an employer and a discharged employee that has significant bearing on employee's reputation).
51. *Sandin*, 515 U.S. 472.
52. Wolfe v. Schaefer, 619 F.3d 782 (7th Cir. 2010).

14. Plaintiff committed a heinous crime involving a sexual organ of the victim; he was acquitted of sexual assault but convicted of kidnapping and first-degree assault and sentenced to prison. No liberty interest invoked when corrections official assigned plaintiff a high "sexual offense treatment needs score."[53]

2.03 DEPRIVATION

2.031 What constitutes a deprivation?

A deprivation must be targeted to the individual claiming the interest. An individual may not maintain a due process violation for government actions that affect the general population.[54] Not every government action adversely affecting a protected property or liberty interest amounts to a "deprivation."[55] The due process clause is not implicated by "random and unauthorized" acts, i.e., negligent acts of an official causing unintended loss of or injury to a protected interest.[56] The Seventh Circuit sometimes

---

53. Vega v. Lantz, 596 F.3d 77 (2d Cir. 2010).
54. *See, e.g.,* Harrington v. County of Suffolk, 607 F.3d 31 (2d Cir. 2010) (no constitutionally protected property interest in an adequate police investigation because it confers a benefit that is merely discretionary and it confers a benefit on the public generally rather than creating an individualized entitlement). *But see* Thompson v. District of Columbia, 530 F.3d 914 (D.C. Cir. 2008) (deprivation of a property interest when government transferred plaintiff from an employment position protected from discharge by cause to a position already scheduled to be eliminated through a reduction in force, which does not trigger due process protections because it applies across the board, not to individualized conduct).
55. Deprivation must be "direct" as opposed to "indirect and incidental." *See* O'Bannon v. Town Court Nursing Ctr., 447 U.S. 773 (1980) (government decertifies a nursing home, forcing the patients to move; this action deprived the nursing home but not the patients of a property interest).
56. *See* Daniels v. Williams, 474 U.S. 327 (1986). *See also* Seamons v. Snow, 84 F.3d 1226, 1234 (10th Cir. 1996) (nondeliberate tolerance of private harassment by school officials does not constitute a "deprivation"); Leavell v. Ill. Dep't of Natural Res., 600 F.3d 798 (7th Cir. 2010) (failure to give prehearing notice was random and unauthorized, and no due process deprivation when plaintiff failed to argue that postdeprivation remedies did not satisfy due process); Dahl v. Rice County, 621 F.3d 740 (8th Cir. 2010) (no due process hearing required before sheriff struck deputy sheriff because there was no policy authorizing the sheriff to assault employees, and evidence showed that the sheriff merely "lost his temper").

asks whether the deprivation was predictable.[57] Minor missteps in a due process hearing may not rise to a due process violation.[58] An individual's own action cannot cause a deprivation by the government; however, a deprivation might occur if the government coerced an individual's action. A deprivation of property need not be permanent.[59] Whether there has been a deprivation of a protected interest is a fact-specific inquiry.

Illustrations:

15. City Police Commander's choice to retire early in lieu of awaiting the outcome of a continuing investigation so that he could retain lifetime health insurance coverage does not deprive him of a liberty or property interest. However, there are some situations in which a person coerced into resigning could demonstrate that he left his employment involuntarily.[60]

---

57. *See* Easter House v. Felder, 910 F.2d 1387, 1400 (7th Cir. 1990); Germano v. Winnebago County, 403 F.3d 926 (7th Cir. 2005).

58. Energy W. Mining Co. v. Oliver, 555 F.3d 1211, 1219 (10th Cir. 2009) (due process clause does not protect against missteps; "[i]ts interest is only in whether an adjudicative proceeding as a whole is sufficiently fair and reliable that the law should enforce its result").

59. Kuck v. Danaher, 600 F.3d 159 (2d Cir. 2010) (finding procedural due process violation for 14- to 20-month wait for appeal hearing of denial of gun license; the complaint plausibly alleged a practice of delaying appeals, the delay was considerable and affected a significant number of applicants, and the government failed to give a reason tied to its safety interest that justified the delays); Shaul v. Cherry Valley-Springfield Cent. Sch. Dist., 363 F.3d 177 (2d Cir. 2004) (school district's ongoing retention of lawfully seized personal property could require due process) (citing United States v. David, 131 F.3d 55, 59 (2d Cir. 1997) (entertaining a due process challenge to government delay in forfeiting or returning seized property).

60. Knappenberger v. City of Phoenix, 566 F.3d 936, 941 (9th Cir. 2009). This is often a difficult claim to establish. *See, e.g.,* Mountain High Knitting, Inc. v. Reno, 51 F.3d 216, 219–20 (9th Cir. 1995). In *Mountain High Knitting,* appellants who held green cards but were listed on a "no-match letter" from the Immigration and Naturalization Service (INS) argued that the letters coerced the employer into suspending or firing them without due process. The court held, however, that the letter directed the employer only to comply with its preexisting obligations and informed the company of statutory penalties).

16. Individual X visited park every day to watch the sunset and stayed in his car. When another person reported that X was watching the park with binoculars, police discovered that X was a convicted child molester. No deprivation of liberty or property interest when government excluded him from city parks without any process.[61]

17. No deprivation of property for cancellation of a $10 park recreation permit of a person who had been lurking around a city-owned swimming pool and staring at children because it was de minimis, but exclusion from all parks deprived plaintiff of a liberty interest in right to visit a public place.[62]

2.032 Denial of application as deprivation

State action that terminates an entitlement such as welfare payments is a deprivation of property. However, it is not clear whether the denial of an application for the same benefit is a deprivation. The Supreme Court has never held that an applicant for public benefits possesses a property interest protected by due process,[63] but every federal circuit court that has

---

61. Brown v. Michigan City, 462 F.3d 720 (7th Cir. 2006).
62. Kennedy v. City of Cincinnati, 595 F.3d 327 (6th Cir. 2010) (citing City of Chicago v. Morales, 527 U.S. 41 (1999)).
63. *See* Am. Mfrs. Mut. Ins. Co. v. Sullivan, 526 U.S. 40, 58–61 (1999) (alternative holding). *American Manufacturers* concerned a workers' compensation scheme that entitled claimants to payment of their reasonable and necessary medical expenses. Under the scheme, employers could contest this obligation pending an administrative review. The plurality opinion held that an employee had no property interest in such payments until his right to them was already established. The case may mean that an application as opposed to termination of benefits does not trigger due process. On the other hand, it may simply mean there is no due process right to actually receive benefits during the time that an application is being considered by the agency. The latter interpretation of the case, obviously, is much narrower than the former. *See also* Lyng v. Payne, 476 U.S. 926, 942 (1986) (potential applicants who did not receive notice of the availability of a farm loan program would not be entitled to reopening the program because applicants for benefits as distinct from those already receiving benefits do not have a legitimate claim of entitled protected by the due process clause).

considered the question has concluded that an applicant for benefits may possess a property interest in the receipt of welfare benefits.[64]

Where courts have concluded that an application for an entitlement creates a property interest, the courts have focused on whether there is discretion in determining eligibility or discretion to revoke the entitlement.[65]

Illustration:

18. State law provides that persons with income below a certain level are entitled to receive welfare benefits. Mary applies for benefits but is rejected because the agency determines that her income is too high. Mary disputes this conclusion. Mary is not entitled to a due process hearing because she has not been "deprived" of property.[66] However, if Mary were granted benefits, but the benefits were later terminated because it was discovered that her income

---

64. Cushman v. Shinseki, 576 F.3d 1290, 1298 (Fed. Cir. 2009) (application for veterans' benefits is a matter of statutory entitlement); Kapps v. Wing, 404 F.3d 105, 115 (2d Cir. 2005) (discussing reasoning and listing numerous cases); Hamby v. Neel, 368 F.3d 549 (6th Cir. 2004) (Tennessee citizens had right to apply for an enroll in "TennCare" benefits program pursuant to state statute and, thus, a legitimate claim of entitlement giving rise to property right). *But see* Edwards v. Shinseki, 582 F.3d 1351, 1356–58 (Fed. Cir. 2009) (Judge Rader writing separately questioning whether veterans' benefits are similar to Social Security benefits). For a stimulating discussion of this subject, *see* Jeffrey S. Lubbers, *Giving Applicants for Veterans' and Other Government Benefits Their Due (Process)*, 35 ADMIN. & REG. L. NEWS 16 (Spring 2010).

65. *See, e.g.*, Shanks v. Dressel, 540 F.3d 1082 (9th Cir. 2008) (opponents to a development proposal had no property interest in denial of permit because the regulations at issue gave significant discretion to the city in deciding whether to issue or deny the permit).

66. *Am. Mfrs. Mut. Ins.*, 526 U.S. at 58–61. However, this result has not yet been definitively established. It is possible that *American Manufacturers* will ultimately be understood to hold only that Mary need not receive benefits during the period between her application and the hearing, but not that the state can deny her a hearing altogether. *See supra* note 63. In any event, a hearing would probably be required in this situation by statute or regulations even if one would not be required by due process.

was too high, Mary would have a right to a due process hearing in connection with this termination.[67]

2.033 Deprivation by quasi-governmental entities

Due process may apply to nongovernmental organizations that fulfill traditional government responsibilities.[68]

2.04 WHEN PROCESS IS DUE

Once it is determined that a person claims deprivation of a protected substantive right, it must be determined whether due process should be provided *before or after* the deprivation occurs (§ 2.04) and what particular procedures are constitutionally required (§ 2.05).

Judicial *balancing* of three factors determines both the "when" and the "what procedure" issues: (1) the degree of potential deprivation to be suffered by the private party,[69] (2) the fairness and reliability of existing procedures, and the probable value of additional procedural safeguards, and (3) the government's interest in resisting these safeguards.[70] These are often referred to as the *Mathews* factors and the process involved as *Mathews* balancing.

The general rule is that due process must be provided *before* the deprivation of liberty or property occurs,[71] but there are numerous exceptions

---

67. Goldberg v. Kelly, 397 U.S. 254 (1970).
68. *See, e.g.*, Thomas M. Cooley Law Sch. v. Am. Bar Ass'n, 459 F.3d 705 (6th Cir. 2006) (due process and some provisions of the APA applied to the ABA when fulfilling its accreditation function delegated under the Higher Education Act of 1965). *See also* Paul R. Verkuil, *Privatizing Due Process*, 57 Admin. L. Rev. 963 (2005).
69. In some cases, the court must balance the interests of several private parties. *See* Brock v. Roadway Express, Inc., 481 U.S. 252 (1987). *Roadway Express* involved a statute protecting trucking employees from retaliatory discharge if they complained about unsafe trucks. Under the statute, if the secretary determined that there was reasonable cause to believe that a retaliatory discharge had occurred, the employer could not discharge the employee until after a hearing. In determining whether the statute denied due process to the employer, the Court had to balance the private interests of both the employer and employee.
70. Mathews v. Eldridge, 424 U.S. 319, 334–35 (1976).
71. *See* Zinermon v. Burch, 494 U.S. 113, 132 (1990) ("In situations where the State feasibly can provide a predeprivation hearing before taking

to this rule. Some situations present true exigent circumstances: The government is permitted to act first and provide a meaningful hearing later, even though there is a serious risk of error. Such situations tend to occur in cases of public health or safety,[72] environmental harm,[73] or financial emergencies.[74]

In many situations, such as discharge of government employees for cause, due process allows for some sort of informal probable-cause-type procedure before the government discharges the employee, followed by a due process hearing within a reasonable time after discharge.[75] The predischarge procedure serves as an "initial check against mistaken decisions—essentially a determination of whether there are reasonable grounds to believe that the charges against the employee are true and support the proposed action."[76] Prior to discharge, government employees must receive oral or written notice of the charges against them, an explanation of the employer's evidence, and an opportunity to present their side of the story—orally or in writing.[77] In case of true exigent circumstances, however, an employer can suspend the employee without

---

property, it generally must do so regardless of the adequacy of a postdeprivation tort remedy to compensate for the taking.").

72. Ewing v. Mytinger & Casselberry, Inc., 339 U.S. 594 (1950) (misbranded drugs); N. Am. Cold Storage Co. v. Chicago, 211 U.S. 306 (1908) (food held in cold storage and believed to be rotting); Catanzaro v. Weiden, 140 F.3d 91 (2d Cir. 1998) (summary destruction of collapsing building—court should review whether a bona fide emergency existed); Spinelli v. City of New York, 579 F.3d 160, 171–75 (2d Cir. 2009) (seizure of gun dealer's inventory because of multiple security lapses).

73. Hodel v. Va. Surface Mining Ass'n, 452 U.S. 264 (1981).

74. FDIC v. Mallen, 486 U.S. 230 (1988) (suspension of banking executive under indictment for felony involving dishonesty).

75. Cleveland Bd. of Educ. v. Loudermill, 470 U.S. 532 (1985). The same principle applies to government action that prevents an employer from discharging an employee for cause. The agency must provide prereinstatement procedures that establish an initial check against a mistaken decision, and a full due process hearing must follow expeditiously. *Roadway Express*, 481 U.S. at 259; Riggins v. Goodman, 572 F.3d 1101, 1110 (10th Cir. 2009) (due process satisfied by providing police officer who suffered psychotic episodes three-step process prior to final termination decision).

76. *Roadway Express*, 481 U.S. at 269.

77. *Id.* at 264.

any prior procedures.[78] It appears that the employer is not required to pay the employee during the suspension period (the period of time between the initial and final discharge decision).[79]

Illustrations:

19. Jane and her children are receiving welfare benefits based upon her very low income. Agency seeks to terminate the benefits because it determines that her income has risen. Jane is entitled to a hearing before termination of benefits. Balancing the three factors, Jane's need is dire, and termination of the payments would cause great financial distress; the issues are factual, and witness credibility may well be critical; the government has a strong interest in halting payments before the hearing because the ability to delay termination will cause many persons to request a hearing even when they are certain to lose; moreover, the government is unlikely to be able to recoup benefits to which Jane is not entitled.[80]

20. Ted receives federal benefits based on his work-related disability. These payments do not depend on Ted's income or financial need. Agency believes that Ted is no longer disabled. Ted is not entitled to a hearing before termination of benefits. Balancing the three factors, Ted may not have a dire need for the income since the program is not need-based, the issues are likely to be based on medical reports rather than credibility determinations, and the government has a strong interest in resisting a prior hearing for the same reasons given in the previous illustration.[81]

21. Police Officer is dismissed for dishonesty in filling out his employment application. Prior to dismissal, he is informed in writing of the reasons for discharge, shown the evidence on which the Department relies, and given a chance to tell his side of the story in writing. If he continues to assert that the Department

---

78. Gilbert v. Homar, 520 U.S. 924 (1997) (campus policeman suspected of drug offenses).
79. *Id.* at 925.
80. Goldberg v. Kelly, 397 U.S. 254 (1970).
81. Mathews v. Eldridge, 424 U.S. 319 (1976).

is mistaken, he is entitled to a full posttermination hearing. Police Officer has received due process.[82]

2.05 WHAT PROCESS IS DUE

2.051 *Mathews v. Eldridge* framework

Early due process cases contain a fixed list of procedural protections required by due process:

- The hearing must be at a reasonable time and conducted in a meaningful manner.
- Timely and adequate notice must be provided.
- The private party must have an opportunity to confront adverse witnesses and to present their own arguments and evidence orally.
- There is a right to retained counsel.
- The decisionmaker's conclusion must rest solely on the legal rules and evidence adduced at the hearing.
- The decisionmakers must state the reasons for their determination and indicate the evidence upon which they relied.
- An impartial decisionmaker is essential.[83]

Later, the Supreme Court abandoned this approach to prescribing the elements of a due process hearing. Now, its approach is wholly contextual. If due process applies, the person deprived of liberty or property "must be given *some* kind of notice and afforded *some* kind of hearing."[84]

---

82. Cleveland Bd. of Educ. v. Loudermill, 470 U.S. 532 (1985).
83. *Goldberg*, 397 U.S. at 271; Withrow v. Larkin, 421 U.S. 35 (1975).
84. Goss v. Lopez, 419 U.S. 565, 579 (1975) (emphases in original). Nevertheless, some of these concepts are still applicable. For example, an agency cannot "change theories midstream," Rodale Press, Inc. v. FTC, 407 F.2d 1252, 1256 (D.C. Cir. 1968); or issue a decision based on a theory not raised at the administrative hearing, NLRB v. Homemaker Shops, Inc., 724 F.2d 535, 544 (6th Cir. 1984), Bendix Corp. v. FTC, 450 F.2d 534, 542 (6th Cir. 1971). Surprisingly, there are still cases involving the need to provide some kind of notice and opportunity for hearing. *See, e.g.*, Humphries v. County of Los Angeles, 554 F.3d 1170 (9th Cir. 2009) (violation of due process where California did not provide any obvious procedure for removing name from child abuse registry; the agency that originally listed plaintiffs could notify the registry, but there was no means to require the agency to do so).

2.052 "Some kind of notice"

With respect to notice, courts do not follow the *Mathews v. Eldridge* framework. Instead, courts consider whether the notice was "reasonably calculated under all the circumstances to apprise" the party of the pendency and nature of the proceedings.[85]

2.053 "Some kind of hearing"

With respect to the hearing, the courts employ the three-factor *Mathews* balancing test to decide whether a particular procedural protection sought by the plaintiff must be provided by the government. This requires a case-specific assessment of the relevant factors and precludes broad generalizations, sometimes with the result that individuals are not entitled to the traditional elements of due process.

Illustrations:

22. Agency seeks to reduce benefits received by Veteran because it believes that his physical condition is improving. By statute, lawyers are not permitted to appear in hearings held by Agency,

---

85. Dusenbery v. United States, 534 U.S. 161 (2002) (holding that the test in Mullane v. Cent. Hanover Bank & Trust Co., 339 U.S. 306, 314 (1950), should be applied in determining the adequacy of notice, not the three-factor balancing test of Mathews v. Eldridge). In *Dusenbery*, the issue was whether a letter sent to petitioner in prison by certified mail was adequate notice of a pending forfeiture action. The Court held that this procedure was "reasonably calculated under all the circumstances" to give notice, even if the prison failed to deliver the letter to petitioner. *See* also Ho v. Donovan, 569 F.3d 677, 680–81 (7th Cir. 2009) (no due process violation when agency provided defendant with four notices and defendant chose not to open them; the court rejected defendant's defense that she generally mistrusts all governments, stating "conscious avoidance of information is a form of knowledge"). *But see* Jones v. Flowers, 547 U.S. 220 (2006) (notice of tax foreclosure not sufficient when notice of sale was sent by certified mail and returned as unclaimed (even when homeowner's ex-wife and children still lived in the house); the Court concluded that when the state was informed that its notice did not reach the intended recipient, it must take additional reasonable steps to give notice). The notice requirement under due process seems to be the same as the notice requirement under the APA. For a discussion of notice under the APA, *see* Chapter 4, §§ 4.01 and 4.02.

but lay representatives are permitted to appear. While Veteran's interest in resisting reduction of benefits is quite substantial, the availability of lay representation is adequate to safeguard these interests in the great majority of cases. Agency has an interest in keeping veterans' benefits hearings informal and nonadversarial and in protecting veterans from claims for attorneys' fees. The exclusion of lawyers from agency hearings does not violate due process.[86]

23. Plaintiff was not entitled to a due process hearing to establish whether he is currently dangerous prior to placing him on a registry of all convicted sex offenders because placement on the registry was tied to conviction of a sexual offense, not to "dangerousness."[87]

24. Defendant bypassed her opportunity to be heard when she walked out of a hearing after administrative law judge (ALJ) denied a motion for continuance.[88]

25. Applicant's due process rights were violated when an immigration judge bullied the applicant. On review, the court introduced the case as follows: "The case now before us exemplifies the 'severe wound . . . inflicted' when not a modicum of courtesy, of respect, or of any pretense of fairness is extended to a petitioner and the case he so valiantly attempted to present. Yet once again,

---

86. Walters v. Nat'l Ass'n of Radiation Survivors, 473 U.S. 305, 323–24 (1985). *Walters* involved a statute that permitted attorneys to appear, but limited their fees to $10. Only four justices concurred in this holding; two others indicated that there might be a "special circumstances" rule in which due process would require that lawyers be allowed to appear in cases of unusual difficulty. *See also* Osteen v. Henley, 13 F.3d 221 (7th Cir. 1993) (no right to representation by counsel in student disciplinary hearing). Note that *Walters* involved an application for benefits, rather than a reduction in benefits, and the Supreme Court has never determined that due process applies to applications. *See supra* § 2.032.
87. Conn. Dep't of Pub. Safety v. Doe, 538 U.S. 1 (2003). *See also* Wozniak v. Conry, 236 F.3d 888 (7th Cir. 2001) (tenured college professor barred from teaching classes and lost research funding after refusing to submit required grading materials; professor refused opportunities to submit a written explanation and was not entitled to an oral hearing because no disputed material facts were at issue).
88. Ho v. Donovan, 569 F.3d at 680–81.

under the 'bullying' nature of the immigration judge's questioning, a petitioner was ground to bits."[89]

2.054 Evidence in due process hearings

Courts generally review evidentiary issues in administrative hearings under the *Mathews v. Eldridge* standard; however, courts may not use *Mathews* for basic issues of fairness.

Illustrations:

26. City's administrative hearing process for revocation of liquor license requiring club to request that the Mayor issue a subpoena for witnesses to appear provided a reasonable balance under *Mathews v. Eldridge*; there was no right for defendant to subpoena its own witnesses and compel testimony at hearing.[90]

27. Bureau of Immigration Appeals (BIA) must give notice to an applicant before taking official notice of a key fact; mere opportunity for rebuttal through a motion to reopen is insufficient under *Mathews v. Eldridge* because the decision to grant the motion is discretionary and the filing of the motion did not stay the effect of the order of removal. Only the BIA's good faith would prevent the applicant from being removed before the motion was decided.[91]

28. Social Security Claimant could not afford to see a doctor. ALJ acknowledged there was insufficient medical evidence in the record and claimant requested that the Social Security Administration provide a medical exam. ALJ ordered the exam. After

---

89. Cham v. Attorney General, 445 F.3d 683 (3d Cir. 2006). Impartiality is covered in Chapter 7, § 7.049.

90. Foxy Lady, Inc. v. City of Atlanta, 347 F.3d 1232 (11th Cir. 2003).

91. Burger v. Gonzalez, 498 F.3d 131 (2d Cir. 2007). The Second Circuit's decision follows decisions by the Ninth and Tenth Circuits. Getachew v. INS, 25 F.3d 841 (9th Cir. 1994); De la Llana-Castellon v. INS, 16 F.3d 1093 (10th Cir. 1994). It is contrary to decisions of the Fifth, Seventh, and D.C. Circuits. Gutierrez-Rogue v. INS, 954 F.2d 769 (D.C. Cir. 1992); Rivera-Cruz v. INS, 948 F.2d 962 (5th Cir. 1991); Kaczmarczyk v. INS, 933 F.2d 588 (7th Cir. 1991). *See* Michael Asimow, *Adjudication, in* DEVELOPMENTS IN ADMINISTRATIVE LAW AND REGULATORY PRACTICE 2007–2008, 5 n.6 (Jeffrey S. Lubbers ed., 2009).

receiving the report of the exam, ALJ did not give Claimant an opportunity to respond to a post-hearing medical report. This denied Claimant due process.[92] This evidentiary issue was not reviewed under the *Mathews* test.

29. Applicant's due process rights were violated when the BIA based its decision almost entirely on unreliable and untrustworthy evidence.[93] This evidentiary issue was not reviewed under the *Mathews* test.

30. Where national security is a concern, notice satisfying due process does not require disclosure of classified portions of an administrative record submitted to the court in camera and ex parte (not reviewed under *Mathews*);[94] however, pursuant to *Mathews*, the government must provide the unclassified information in a timely manner to allow the defendant sufficient opportunity to rebut the information.[95]

2.055 Due process protections for students

Like other situations in which parties contest the ingredients of a due process hearing, the nature of due process provided to students depends heavily on the circumstances. In the case of expulsion of a student for disciplinary reasons (such as cheating or fighting), schools must provide the full panoply of procedural protections if there is a dispute as to the material facts. In the case of brief suspensions from school for disciplinary reasons, however, the courts require only an abbreviated procedure: Students must receive oral or written notice of the charges against them and, if they deny them, an explanation of the evidence against them and an opportunity to present their side of the story. The student has no right to call his or her own witnesses or retain counsel or confront adverse witnesses.[96]

---

92. Yount v. Barnhart, 416 F.3d 1233 (10th Cir. 2005). *See supra* § 2.032 for discussion of due process for public benefit applicants generally.
93. Ezeagwuna v. Ashcroft, 325 F.3d 396, 408 (3d Cir. 2003).
94. Nat'l Council of Resistance of Iran v. Dep't of State, 251 F.3d 192, 208–09 (D.C. Cir. 2001).
95. People's Mojahedin Org. of Iran v. U.S. Dep't of State, 613 F.3d 220 (D.C. Cir. 2010).
96. Goss v. Lopez, 419 U.S. 565, 581–83 (1975) (involving suspension of up to 10 days).

Finally, in cases of dismissal based on academic rather than disciplinary reasons, it is likely that due process calls for no hearing at all.[97]

Illustrations:

31. Medical Student is not allowed to graduate from Medical School based on recommendations of examining physicians and a review of her performance by a council of faculty and students. Although Student's interest in a full hearing is substantial, the nature of the decision, involving academic and professional judgments of performance, is not suited to adversarial type procedures. School has a substantial interest in maintaining informality in its academic decisionmaking. Student's dismissal from School without a formal hearing did not violate due process.[98]

32. Medical Student is expelled from Medical School following guilty plea to felony drug charge. After arrest (but before guilty plea), School sent a letter to Student notifying Student of suspension "until all external investigations/hearings [were] completed" and right to internal investigation. Student requested and School granted internal hearing after guilty plea. Student was provided adequate notice and opportunity to be heard.[99]

2.056 Due process issues with video teleconference hearings

Complaints of due process violations have followed the use of video teleconference hearings.[100] The use of video conferencing does not violate the statutory right to representation even though it separates attorneys from their clients.[101] Courts have concluded that petitioners must

---

97. Bd. of Curators of the Univ. of Mo. v. Horowitz, 435 U.S. 78 (1978). *Cf.* Regents of the Univ. of Mich. v. Ewing, 474 U.S. 214 (1985) (substantive due process review of university dismissal of student for academic deficiency; even assuming a protected property interest, academic judgments of fitness to remain student are owed great deference).

98. *Bd. of Curators*, 435 U.S. at 86–91.

99. Flaim v. Med. Coll. of Ohio, 418 F.3d 629 (6th Cir. 2005).

100. Reported circuit court opinions have involved immigration cases; 8 U.S.C. § 1229a(b)(2)(A)(iii) specifically authorizes removal hearings by video teleconference.

101. Rapheal v. Mukasey, 533 F.3d 521, 531 (7th Cir. 2008).

demonstrate that a video hearing caused prejudice or that problems with video equipment disadvantaged the petitioner.

Illustrations:

33. Video hearing "provided the petitioner with an 'opportunity to be heard at a meaningful time and in a meaningful manner,' under *Mathews v. Eldridge* even though the three-hour hearing 'was plagued by communication problems.'" Specifically, Petitioner's damaged mouth and teeth made him unable to speak clearly, and the court reporter noted "indiscernible" on the transcript 132 times; Petitioner also had difficulty understanding questions from his attorney.[102]

34. Claim that a video hearing prevented Petitioner from proving homosexuality by having the Immigration Judge observe his physical stature in person did not present a due process violation under *Mathews v. Eldridge* because petitioner did not show prejudice.[103]

35. There was no due process violation when video equipment malfunctioned, producing a transcript with 418 separate notations that the recording was indiscernible, and when Petitioner failed to challenge Immigration Judge's summary of the evidence.[104]

2.057 When other remedies may satisfy due process

In a number of situations, the Supreme Court has ruled that state tort or contract remedies provide all of the process that is due. Consequently, an agency need provide no hearing at all. In the case of random or unauthorized deprivations of property by officials such as prison guards, a prior hearing is obviously impossible; the Court has ruled that state court tort remedies suffice.[105] Similarly, the Court ruled that a school does not

---

102. Rusu v. INS, 296 F.3d 316 (4th Cir. 2002).
103. Eke v. Mukasey, 512 F.3d 372 (7th Cir. 2008).
104. Clark v. Holder, 424 Fed. App'x 526 (6th Cir. 2011).
105. Hudson v. Palmer, 468 U.S. 517 (1984); Parratt v. Taylor, 451 U.S. 527 (1981), *overruled on another ground by* Daniels v. Williams, 474 U.S. 327 (1986). *See also supra* § 2.031 for additional discussion of random and unauthorized acts.

need to provide prior procedure before administering corporal punishment to a student, even though it would be feasible to provide some sort of prepunishment hearing; tort remedies for excessive force will suffice.[106] Similarly, the right to receive damages for breach of contract by the state is a property interest, but due process requires only the availability of a state court contract action.[107]

2.06 ADJUDICATION RATHER THAN QUASI-LEGISLATIVE ACTION

Due process does not apply when courts characterize agency action as quasi-legislative rather than adjudicative.[108] In general, quasi-legislative action is applicable to a class of persons, while adjudication is targeted at specific persons.[109] Persons adversely affected by such action must resort to political, rather than legal, remedies. Since courts consider administrative rulemaking quasi-legislative, an agency engaged in rulemaking is not constitutionally required to provide any procedure to those adversely

---

106. Ingraham v. Wright, 430 U.S. 651 (1977). The Court balanced the *Mathews* factors, placing particular emphasis on the burden that a prior hearing requirement would place on the school.

107. Lujan v. G&G Fire Sprinklers, Inc., 532 U.S. 189 (2001). *See also supra* § 2.022 (text at notes 26–27).

108. Interport Pilots Agency, Inc. v. Sammis, 14 F.3d 133, 142 (2d Cir. 1994) (policy statement by Board of Commissioners of Pilots of the State of New York was legislative in nature, not adjudicative and, therefore, was not subject to notice and hearing requirements of due process clause).

109. United States v. Fla. E. Coast Ry, 410 U.S. 224, 246 (1973) ("While the line dividing them may not always be a bright one, these decisions represent a recognized distinction in administrative law between proceedings for the purpose of promulgating policy-type rules or standards, on the one hand, and proceedings designed to adjudicate disputed facts in particular cases on the other."). Grand River Enter. Six Nations, Ltd. v. Pryor, 425 F.3d 158 (2d Cir. 2005) (escrow accounts required by Master Settlement Agreement and adopted as statutes were legislative preconditions for the privilege of engaging in future cigarette sales in the individual states and substantially different in kind from individual prejudgment deprivation of property). Individualized ratemaking is often considered quasi-legislative for some purposes, see Chapter 1, § 1.04 n. 30, but it appears that it is treated as adjudicative for due process purposes. *See, e.g.,* Ohio Bell Tel. Co. v. Pub. Util. Comm'n, 301 U.S. 292, 300 (1937).

affected by the rule.[110] Of course, state and federal administrative procedure statutes typically provide for advance notice and comment before
adoption of rules, but these procedures are required by statute, not by due
process.

Courts have relied on various criteria in drawing the line between
general and particular action. The size of the class of persons affected
is relevant, with large-size classes indicating that the action is legislative.[111] Nevertheless, agency action that purports to be directed at a class
is rulemaking, even if that class consists of only a single party, provided
that others might conceivably join the class at a later time.[112] Whether

---

110. Modern cases that draw the distinction between quasi-legislative and
    adjudicative action frequently hark back to two old cases relating to Col-
    orado property taxation. In Bi-Metallic Inv. Co. v. State Bd. of Equaliza-
    tion, 239 U.S. 441 (1915), the Court held that Denver taxpayers were not
    entitled to a hearing with respect to a general increase in the valuation
    of Denver property. The Court distinguished Londoner v. Denver, 210
    U.S. 373 (1908), where one of the issues was the benefit that a particular
    taxpayer would derive from street improvements. In *Bi-Metallic*, Justice
    Holmes wrote: "Where a rule of conduct applies to more than a few
    people it is impracticable that every one should have a direct voice in its
    adoption. . . . In Londoner v. Denver . . . [a] relatively small number of
    persons was concerned, who were exceptionally affected, in each case
    upon individual grounds." *Bi-Metallic*, 239 U.S. at 445–46. For examples
    of modern cases relying on the *Bi-Metallic/Londoner* distinction, see
    Minn. State Bd. for Cmty. Coll. v. Knight, 465 U.S. 271, 283–85 (1981);
    Vermont Yankee Nuclear Power Corp. v. Natural Res. Def. Council, Inc.,
    435 U.S. 519, 542 (1978); *Fla. E. Coast Ry.*, 410 U.S. at 244–45.
111. *See e.g., Bi-Metallic*, 239 U.S. at 445 (action generally affecting "more than
    a few people" is legislative).
112. *See* Quivira Mining Co. v. NRC, 866 F.2d 1246, 1261–62 (10th Cir. 1989)
    (due process inapplicable to generally stated rule involving only sin-
    gle regulated party); Philly's v. Byrne, 732 F.2d 87, 92–93 (7th Cir. 1984)
    (power of voters to declare a precinct "dry" does not violate due pro-
    cess rights of single liquor licensee in precinct since action is general in
    nature); Anaconda Co. v. Ruckelshaus, 482 F.2d 1301, 1306–07 (10th Cir.
    1973) (air pollution rule concerning emissions in a particular county that
    affected only single company is rulemaking). *Philly's* was distinguished
    in Club Misty, Inc. v. Laski, 208 F.3d 615, 617–22 (7th Cir. 2000), in which
    the voters were empowered to revoke the license of a particular licensee
    rather than declare the entire precinct dry; such action would be consid-
    ered adjudication rather than rulemaking.

the agency proceeding involves primarily "legislative facts" (facts that do not concern a specific party) or "adjudicative facts" (facts that concern only a specific party) also plays an important role (although this distinction is more important in deciding what kind of hearing is required than whether a hearing is required at all).[113] Also important is whether the action sets policy for the future as opposed to imposing legal consequences based on facts that occurred in the past.[114]

Illustrations:

36. Congress enacts a statute that lowers from 20 percent to 18 percent the amount of a household's earned income that could be disregarded for purposes of determining food stamp eligibility. The statute lowers benefits to many families. The state welfare agency made numerous errors in computing the reduced benefits. Recipients are not entitled to notice and a hearing with respect to the reduction in benefits occurring by reason of the new statute, but they are entitled to a hearing if they claim that the agency has erroneously computed their benefits.[115]

37. By statute, only an "Alaskan air carrier" may operate charter flights in Alaska. Air Co. is not an Alaskan air carrier, but Agency grants Air Co. an exemption that allows it to fly Alaskan charters. Air Co. contracts to provide charter flights for Oil Co. within Alaska in competition with Tundra Co., a certificated carrier that provides scheduled flights. Agency revokes Air Co.'s exemption, finding that Tundra Co.'s service was adequate to meet Oil Co.'s needs and that the charters would divert excessive revenue from Tundra Co. Due process requires that Agency provide Air Co. with a hearing, because Agency's decision is adjudicative rather than legislative. Agency's order concerns a single airline; the

---

113. *See, e.g.*, Ohio Bell Tel. Co. v. Pub. Util. Comm'n, 301 U.S. 292, 300–06 (1937) (use of judicial notice to find facts concerning the value of specific utility's property, based on various undisclosed indexes or other sources of information, violated due process).

114. *See, e.g.*, Prentis v. Atl. Coast Line Co., 211 U.S. 210, 226–27 (1908) (judicial inquiry declares liability based on past facts and existing laws while legislation looks to the future and changes existing conditions by making a new rule).

115. Atkins v. Parker, 472 U.S. 115 (1985).

issues in controversy involve "adjudicative facts" that are particular to Air Co., Oil Co., and Tundra Co.[116]

38. Developer purchases 50 acres of land on which to build condominiums. Township approves Developer's plan and grants building permits for part of the development. Later, it denies a permit for additional development because the original zoning plan had been changed to reduce the allowable density. Procedural due process is inapplicable, because the zoning change was legislative rather than adjudicative action.[117]

39. In response to complaints about Main St. nightclubs, Mayor and City Council refuse to renew business licenses of two nightclubs located there. Insofar as the decision focused not on violations by a particular licensee, but on general conditions on Main St., the action might be considered a legislative action. Insofar as only two licensees are affected by the decision, it could be considered adjudicative.[118]

---

116. Alaska Airlines, Inc. v. Civil Aeronautics Bd., 545 F.2d 194 (D.C. Cir. 1976).
117. Rogin v. Bensalem Twp., 616 F.2d 680, 692–95 (3d Cir. 1980), *cert. denied*, 450 U.S. 1029 (1981).
118. Richardson v. Town of Eastover, 922 F.2d 1152, 1158–61 (4th Cir. 1991) (not necessary to decide classification since owner's ability to argue to City Council provided due process). It is often difficult to decide whether particular local land use planning decisions are legislative or adjudicative in nature, or whether there is a property right at stake, or whether there has been a deprivation of that right. Moreover, the decisions are often highly political in character, making it difficult to achieve fair hearings or find unbiased decisionmakers. Thus, courts find it difficult to decide whether due process applies and, if so, what process is due. It is possible that the Supreme Court will hold that procedural due process does not apply even to individualized land use planning disputes, if the applicant can argue in court that a taking has occurred and if local courts provide judicial review of the reasonableness of the decision. *See* River Park, Inc. v. City of Highland Park, 23 F.3d 164, 165–67 (7th Cir. 1994). This development would parallel several decisions that local courts provide all the process that is due in government contract disputes or in the cases of certain torts. *See supra* § 2.05.

Chapter 3

THE RIGHT TO A HEARING UNDER THE APA

3.01 THE "ON THE RECORD" REQUIREMENT
3.02 HEARINGS REQUIRED BY DUE PROCESS
3.03 AGENCY ACTION EXCEPTED FROM ADJUDICATION REQUIREMENTS

3.01 THE "ON THE RECORD" REQUIREMENT

The APA specifies various procedural requirements that must be provided in a formal adjudication. These provisions are set forth in sections 554, 556, and 557 of the APA and in the provisions relating to administrative law judges (ALJs).[1] However, the APA formal adjudication provisions are not applicable unless the APA is triggered.[2] In this respect, the adjudication sections differ from the informal rulemaking sections of the act, which are automatically applicable to all cases of federal agency rulemaking unless specifically excepted.[3]

The triggering mechanism for the APA's formal adjudication sections is contained in section 554(a), which provides: "This section applies, according to the provisions thereof, in every case of adjudication required by statute to be determined *on the record after opportunity for an agency hearing.*"[4] (emphasis added)

---

1. In addition, prevailing parties are entitled in some circumstances to recover attorneys' fees under the Equal Access to Justice Act (EAJA) when the APA formal adjudication provisions apply. *See* Chapter 11 (discussing attorneys' fees under the EAJA).
2. If the APA formal adjudication provisions are not triggered, the proceeding is considered to be informal adjudication. Many fewer procedural protections are applicable. *See* Chapter 9 (discussing informal adjudication).
3. APA § 553(a).
4. The definition of "adjudication" in this section is discussed in Chapter 1, § 1.04. The term "record" means that the trier of fact is confined to

41

If a statute concerns adjudication and specifically calls for a "hearing on the record," it triggers the APA adjudication provisions.[5] However, many statutes involving adjudications call for a "hearing" or a "public hearing" but fail to use the magic words "on the record." Unfortunately, present case law supports several different approaches to the problem.[6]

The prevailing methodology at this time is for courts to apply *Chevron*[7] in interpreting section 554(a). Since a statute that calls for a "hearing" but fails to use the words "on the record" is ambiguous with respect to whether the APA applies, the court must defer to a reasonable agency interpretation of the statute. If the agency has interpreted the statute so that the APA is not triggered, and there are no indications that this approach is unreasonable, the court must defer to the agency's interpretation.[8]

---

considering the record compiled at the hearing rather than considering matters outside of the record.

5. If the statute calls for rulemaking, the presence of "hearing on the record" language triggers formal rulemaking, meaning that sections 556 and 557 of the APA would apply. *See* APA § 553(c) ("When rules are required by statute to be made on the record after opportunity for an agency hearing, sections 556 and 557 of this title apply instead of this subsection.").

6. For a brief discussion of the three approaches, *see* Cooley R. Howarth, Jr., *Restoring the Applicability of the APA's Adjudicatory Procedures*, 56 ADMIN. L. REV. 1043 (2004).

7. Chevron U.S.A. Inc. v. Natural Res. Def. Council, Inc., 467 U.S. 837 (1984).

8. Dominion Energy Brayton Point v. Johnson, 443 F.3d 12 (1st Cir. 2006). In *Dominion Energy*, the court noted that it had anticipated its decision in a prior decision, Citizens Awareness Network v. United States, 391 F.3d 338 (1st Cir. 2004), and stated that Nat'l Cable & Telecomm. Ass'n v. Brand X Internet Serv., 545 U.S. 967 (2005) demanded that it reevaluate pre-*Chevron* precedent in light of *Chevron*. This *Chevron* approach started with Chemical Waste Mgmt., Inc. v. EPA, 873 F.2d 1477, 1480–83 (D.C. Cir. 1989) (no presumption that "public hearing" means "on the record" hearing). The court in *Chemical Waste* announced that it would refuse to follow a prior circuit opinion containing dictum that relied on Seacoast Anti-Pollution League v. Costle, 572 F.2d 872 (1st Cir.), *cert. denied*, 439 U.S. 824 (1978). *Chemical Waste*, 873 F.3d at 1481–83 (citing Union of Concerned Scientists v. NRC, 735 F.2d 1437, 1444 n.12 (D.C. Cir. 1984)). *See also* Crestview Parke Care Ctr. v. Thompson, 373 F.3d 743 (6th Cir. 2004); Sibley v. Dep't of Educ., 913 F. Supp. 1181, 1186 n.3 (N.D. Ill. 1995), *aff'd without op.*, 111 F.3d 133 (7th Cir. 1997) (deferring to agency's interpretation that stat-

Some courts have held that, at least in adjudicative licensing cases involving sharply disputed factual questions, there is a presumption that a statutory reference to a "hearing" or "public hearing" means a hearing conforming to the APA. The First Circuit, which once had the leading case for this approach, *Seacoast Anti-Pollution League v. Costle,* has now changed its approach to apply *Chevron* to the question.[9] Other courts, however, still apply the presumption.[10]

Still other courts have declined to apply such a presumption; thus, in the absence of a clear requirement in the legislative history that the APA should apply, the courts would not require the agency to comply with the APA.[11]

---

ute granting employees a "hearing" to challenge salary offset does not require hearing on the record).

9.   *Seacoast,* 572 F.2d at 875–78. *Dominion Energy,* 443 F.3d at 17, expressly overruled *Seacoast.*

10.   Aageson Grain & Cattle v. USDA, 500 F.3d 1038 (9th Cir. 2007); Five Points Rd. Joint Venture v. Johanns, 542 F.3d 1121 (7th Cir. 2008). Pre-*Dominion Energy* cases include: Lane v. USDA, 120 F.3d 106 (8th Cir. 1997) (hearings provided by USDA's National Appeals Division are covered by APA since statute intended formal hearings and exclusive record); Marathon Oil Co. v. EPA, 564 F.2d 1253, 1260–64 (9th Cir. 1977); Steadman v. SEC, 450 U.S. 91, 96 n.13 (1981) (absence of words "on the record" does not prevent application of APA to licensee sanction case, citing *Seacoast* with approval). *Aageson, Five Points,* and *Lane* all involve the right to award of attorneys' fees under the EAJA for hearings at the agency level, which requires that the hearings be covered by the APA. *See* Chapter 11, § 11.04.

11.   *See* City of West Chicago v. Nuclear Regulatory Comm'n, 701 F.2d 632, 644–45 (7th Cir. 1983) (requirement of "a hearing" for nuclear licensing cases does not trigger an APA-type hearing absent "clear intent" in the legislative history supporting such a requirement). *But see Citizens Awareness Network,* 391 F.3d at 350 (petitioners argued that the term "a hearing" requires that licensing hearings be formal, on-the-record hearings under the APA § 556(d), and therefore that hearings designated as "informal" in Nuclear Regulatory Commission (NRC) rules were required to provide for discovery and opportunity for the parties to cross-examine witnesses). In the course of oral argument, NRC counsel represented that the new rules were equivalent to the APA in certain respects. *Id.* at 351. The court, based on this representation, upheld the new rules in question, finding they had a rational basis, that they "[met] the APA requirements for on-the-record adjudications," and that, "[t]hough the Commission's new rules may approach the outer bounds of what is permissible under

Note that the Seventh Circuit has decisions that subscribe to all of the approaches. None of the decisions reconciles any other. Not surprisingly, some courts seem to try to avoid the problem.[12]

In cases of rulemaking, if a statute calls for a hearing "on the record" the agency must engage in "formal rulemaking," which embodies most of the provisions applicable to formal adjudication. However, the Supreme Court has made clear that there is a strong presumption against interpreting an ambiguous statute to call for formal rulemaking.[13]

Illustrations:

1. A statute provides that Agency can recover civil penalties from airlines that fail to follow regulations relating to servicing aircraft. The statute provides that Agency must provide a "hearing" before assessing such penalties. Agency adopts regulations providing that agency attorneys rather than ALJs will serve as fact-finders in its civil penalty hearings. In determining whether these regulations are valid, a court would most likely review the statute under a *Chevron* analysis, in which case the court would likely conclude the regulations are valid. If, however, the court adopted the *Seacoast* presumption (and assuming the civil pen-

---

the APA, . . . the statute [is] sufficiently broad to accommodate them." *Id.* at 351, 355. In reaching this ruling, however, the court also stated that, "[should the agency's administration of the new rules contradict its present representation or otherwise flout [the principle that cross-examination must be available when 'required for a full and true disclosure of the facts,' as provided at APA § 556(d)], nothing in this opinion will inoculate the rules against future challenges." *Id.* at 354.

12. *See, e.g., Citizens Awareness Network*, 391 F.3d at 348 (stating that "for years the courts of appeals have avoided the question" whether 42 U.S.C. § 2239, which uses the term "a hearing," requires formal adjudication, and also declining to address the question because the procedures at issue complied with the APA adjudication requirements).

13. *See* United States v. Fla. E. Coast Ry., 410 U.S. 224, 238 (1973) (holding that a statutory mandate that railroad rates applicable to entire industry be made "after hearing" did not mean an "on the record" hearing governed by the APA). *See also* Bell Tel. Co. of Penn. v. FCC, 503 F.2d 1250, 1263–68 (3d Cir. 1974) ("opportunity for hearing" does not trigger the evidentiary requirements of the APA in case involving determination of general policy, regardless of whether it is classified as rulemaking or adjudication).

alty cases present sharply disputed factual questions), the rules would be invalid.

2. A statute provides that, "after opportunity for public hearing," Agency can establish rates for the reimbursement of private parties who operate federal prisons. Agency adopts the rates applicable to all private prison operators by using informal rulemaking procedures under section 553 of the APA. Agency refuses to permit cross-examination of witnesses as provided in section 556(d) of the APA. Because rulemaking rather than adjudication is involved, the presumption is that the statute calls for informal rather than formal rulemaking. The rates are validly adopted.

3.02 HEARINGS REQUIRED BY DUE PROCESS

A problem arises when no statute calls for an adjudicatory hearing "on the record." As a result, the APA's formal adjudication provisions are not triggered.[14] However, because the federal government's action would deprive a person of an interest in liberty or property, procedural due process applies.[15] Normally, this determination would require a *Mathews v. Eldridge* analysis of what procedural protections are required and when the required hearing should occur.[16]

In an early case, *Wong Yang Sung v. McGrath*,[17] the Supreme Court held that the APA formal adjudication provisions are triggered when a hearing is compelled by procedural due process. However, Congress acted immediately to overturn *Wong Yang Sung* by amending the applicable statute to provide that the APA should not apply to deportation cases.[18]

---

14. *See supra* § 3.01.
15. *See* Chapter 2, § 2.02.
16. *See* Chapter 2, §§ 2.04, 2.05.
17. 339 U.S. 33 (1950). *Wong Yang Sung* involved a proposed deportation of an alien. The Court held that due process requires a hearing in this situation, and the hearing must observe APA requirements. The Court refused to "attribute to Congress a purpose to be less scrupulous about the fairness of a hearing necessitated by the Constitution than one granted as a matter of expediency." *Id.* at 50.
18. Supplemental Appropriation Act of 1951, 64 Stat. 1048, P.L. 82-843. The Court sustained the constitutionality of this amendment. Marcello v. Bonds, 349 U.S. 302, 306–307 (1955).

Nevertheless, it remains possible that *Wong Yang Sung* could apply to matters other than deportation, with the result that the APA's formal adjudication provisions would apply to hearings required by due process. However, subsequent decisions indicate that this is unlikely, and that the Court would decline to follow *Wong Yang Sung* if the issue is squarely presented to it. For example, *Wong Yang Sung* seems inconsistent with *Mathews v. Eldridge*, the decision holding that the requirements of due process are wholly contextual;[19] *Wong Yang Sung* would impose all of the rigid APA formal adjudication provisions, including the requirement that hearings be conducted by ALJs, regardless of whether *Mathews* balancing would require anything close to such formality. With few post-*Mathews* exceptions,[20] lower court cases have consistently ruled that *Wong Yang Sung* does not require application of the APA in situations where due process calls only for informal hearings.[21]

---

19. *See* Chapter 2, §§ 2.04, 2.05.
20. Aageson Grain & Cattle, 500 F.3d 1038, 1043–44 (9th Cir. 2007) (citing *Wong Yang Sung* in support of conclusion that a requirement for an "evidentiary hearing" requires compliance with section 554(a)); Collord v. Dep't of Interior, 154 F.3d 933 (9th Cir. 1998) (applying *Wong Yang Sung* for the limited purpose of saying that a hearing could be said to be "subject to" the APA for purposes of allowing a winning litigant to claim fees under the EAJA). The EAJA is discussed in Chapter 11.
21. *See* Greene v. Babbitt, 64 F.3d 1266, 1274–75 (9th Cir. 1995) (indicating that formal hearing provisions of the APA should be followed, based on *Mathews* analysis, but failing to mention *Wong Yang Sung*); Chemical Waste Mgmt., Inc. v. EPA, 873 F.2d 1477, 1483–85 (D.C. Cir. 1989) (only informal procedures required for orders requiring corrective action following release of hazardous waste); City of West Chicago v. NRC, 701 F.2d 632, 644 n.11 (7th Cir. 1983) (*Wong Yang Sung* limited to cases where due process requires formal hearing); Girard v. Klopfenstein, 930 F.2d 738, 742–43 (9th Cir. 1991) (purporting to distinguish *Wong Yang Sung*, but suggesting also that it did not survive *Mathews*); Clardy v. Levi, 545 F.2d 1241, 1246 (9th Cir. 1976) (declining to apply APA to prison disciplinary cases to which due process applied). *See* Robert E. Zahler, Note, *The Requirement of Formal Adjudication Under Section 5 of the Administrative Procedure Act*, 12 HARV. J. ON LEGIS. 194, 218–41 (1975).

Illustration:

3. The facts are the same as Illustration 1 except that the statute empowering Agency to collect civil penalties does not make any reference to hearings. The assessment of a civil penalty entails a deprivation of property, and Agency must observe due process. However, Agency will not be required to use ALJs to preside over hearings in civil penalty cases.

3.03 AGENCY ACTION EXCEPTED FROM ADJUDICATION REQUIREMENTS

Section 554(a) explicitly exempts a number of classes of adjudicatory matters from the formal adjudication provisions of the APA even if statutes applicable to those matters call for a hearing on the record:

*   matters subject to a subsequent trial of the law and the facts de novo in a court[22]
*   the selection or tenure of an employee, except an ALJ appointed under 5 U.S.C. § 3105[23]

---

22. Arwady Hand Truck Sales, Inc. v. Vander Werf, 507 F. Supp. 2d 754, 760 (S.D. Tex. 2007) ("Because the Court has the discretion to conduct a trial de novo of the ATF's denial [of federal firearms license], the underlying ATF hearing is a matter to which the APA adjudication procedures do not apply.") (citation omitted); Traveler Trading Co. v. United States, 713 F. Supp. 409 (Ct. Int'l Trade 1989) (because agency decision is subject to de novo review before the Court of International Trade, the APA did not apply to its proceedings). *See* also Attorney General's Manual at 43 (no need for full administrative hearing where party aggrieved has right to full judicial retrial).
23. Hoska v. U.S. Dep't of Army, 694 F.2d 270 (D.C. Cir. 1982). *See also* Attorney General's Manual, at 44 (selection and control of personnel traditionally regarded as a discretionary function).

- proceedings in which decisions rest solely on inspections, tests, or elections[24]
- the conduct of military or foreign affairs functions[25]
- cases in which an agency is acting as an agent for a court[26]
- certification of worker representatives[27]

---

24. *See* Door v. Donaldson, 195 F.2d 764 (D.C. Cir. 1952); Attorney General's Manual at 44–45 (reason for exemption is that determinations based on inspections and tests are matters of judgment that are not suitable for consideration in formal hearings). In *Door*, the court held that the determination of whether films were obscene did not fall under this exception since such determinations were based on more than "physical facts as to which there is little room for difference of opinion, or else upon technical facts like the quality of tea or the conditions of airplanes, as to which administrative hearings have long been thought unnecessary." *Door*, 195 F.2d at 766.
25. Ass'n of Civilian Technicians, Inc. v. United States, 603 F.3d 989 (D.C. Cir. 2010) (discharge of National Guardsmen involves conduct of military functions that is not subject to the requirements for adjudication under the APA); Haire v. United States, 869 F.2d 531 (9th Cir. 1989) (agency determinations involving the violation of export regulations prohibiting export of certain semiconductors are exempt from the APA since they involve a military or foreign affairs function).
26. Apparently, the rationale for this exemption is that in such cases, the matter would be retried de novo in court. Administrative Procedure Act, Legislative History 202, S. Doc. No. 248, 79th Cong., 2d Sess. (1946). *See* Comm'r v. Neal, 557 F.3d 1262, 1283 (11th Cir. 2009) (citing S. Rep. No. 79-752, at 221 (1945) to explain that tax functions of the Internal Revenue Service are exempt from formal adjudications that require notice, a hearing, and creation of a record because they are matters subject to a subsequent trial of the law and facts de novo in any court).
27. The rationale of the exception is that certification decisions "rest so largely upon an election or the availability of an election" that a hearing would be inappropriate. Attorney General's Manual, at 46.

Chapter 4

PRE-HEARING REQUIREMENTS

4.01 SUMMARY OF BASIC REQUIREMENTS

This chapter considers a number of important pre-hearing issues. The APA requires that a party receive adequate notice of the matters of fact and law asserted so the party can prepare for the hearing. (§ 4.02) The APA does not provide for discovery, but it is available under the rules of many agencies. (§ 4.03) Subpoenas are quite important in administrative practice, both as a method for the agency to gather information and for private parties to assure that witnesses and documents will be available at the hearing. (§ 4.04) In order to protect their interests, parties may seek to intervene in pending adjudicative cases. (§ 4.05) Because the APA requires that "due account shall be taken of the rule of prejudicial error," agency pre-hearing procedural errors are ordinarily grounds for reversal only if they actually harm the subject of the agency hearing. (§ 4.06)

4.02 NOTICE

Section 554(b) of the APA contains a detailed provision requiring agencies to give notice of formal adjudications.[1]

---

1. APA § 554(b) provides: "Persons entitled to notice of an agency hearing shall be timely informed of

   (1) the time, place, and nature of the hearing;

4.021 "Persons entitled to notice of an agency hearing"

The APA's notice provision applies to "persons entitled to notice of an agency hearing." The APA does not identify which "persons" are entitled to notice, and there is little authority on the issue. Other sources, including the agency's procedural regulations, as well as due process norms and general principles of procedural fairness, must be analyzed to determine who is entitled to notice of agency hearings.

The term "persons entitled to notice" includes the parties to the proceeding and any other person entitled to notice by statute or rule.[2] In addition, due process requires agencies to provide notice to others whose legal rights or interests may be affected by agency adjudication.[3] However, for nonparties with an interest in the proceedings who fail to intervene as parties, a notice published in the *Federal Register* may satisfy the notice requirement.[4]

---

    (2) the legal authority and jurisdiction under which the hearing is to be held; and

    (3) the matters of fact and law asserted.

"When private persons are the moving parties, other parties to the proceeding shall give prompt notice of issues controverted in fact or law; and in other instances agencies may by rule require responsive pleading. In fixing the time and place for the hearings, due regard shall be had for the convenience and necessity of the parties or their representatives."

2. General procedural norms reflected in the Federal Rules of Civil Procedure provide that parties to the controversy are entitled to notice. *See* Fed. R. Civ. P. 4. Further, an agency must give notice to anyone entitled to notice by way of another statute. *See* Pinkett v. United States, 105 F. Supp. 67, 71 (D. Md. 1952) (interested parties entitled to notice under § 205(e) of the Interstate Commerce Act were also afforded the procedural protections of APA § 554).

3. "Reasonable notice to interested persons that their legally protected interests may be adversely affected by administrative action is a requirement of due process, the Interstate Commerce Act, the APA, and the Commission's own rules." N. Ala. Express, Inc. v. United States, 585 F.2d 783, 786 (5th Cir. 1978). *See also* Chi., Milwaukee, St. Paul & Pac. R.R. Co. v. United States, 585 F.2d 254, 260 (7th Cir. 1978) (fundamental fairness in administrative proceeding requires notice clearly informing party of the proposed action and the basis for the action).

4. *N. Ala. Express*, 585 F.2d at 789. *See also* Buckner Trucking, Inc. v. United States, 354 F. Supp. 1210, 1219 (S.D. Tex. 1973) (approving notice to interested nonparties via publication in the Federal Register).

4.022 Sufficiency of notice

Section 554(b) of the APA requires agencies to give notice "of the time, place, and nature of the hearing; the legal authority and jurisdiction under which the hearing is to be held; and the matters of fact and law asserted."

The third of these items is most important. Both due process and the APA require that parties to administrative hearings be given sufficient notice to litigate adequately the issues involved in the hearing. The notice requirement is satisfied "[a]s long as a party to an administrative proceeding is reasonably apprised of the issues in controversy and is not misled."[5] In order to be sufficient, notice of an issue must be more than a passing reference in a brief concerning related matters.[6] Note also that statutes that apply to particular agencies may require greater notice and a specific form.[7]

4.023 Prejudice requirement

In order to prevail on a claim of inadequate notice, a party must establish prejudice from the lack of notice in terms of an inability to prepare

---

5. Savina Home Indus., Inc. v. Sec'y of Labor, 594 F.2d 1358, 1365 (10th Cir. 1979). *See also* Long v. Bd. of Governors of the Fed. Reserve Sys., 117 F.3d 1145, 1158 (10th Cir. 1997) (applying *Savina* standard and holding that notice was adequate where agency notice proposed penalty of $300,000 and assessed penalty of $717,941 after hearing); Bos. Carrier, Inc. v. ICC, 746 F.2d 1555, 1559–60 (D.C. Cir. 1984) (notice must be sufficient to alert party to "subjects that would be examined at the . . . hearing" but agency not required to provide bill of particulars); Akers Motor Lines, Inc. v. United States, 286 F. Supp. 213, 224–25 (W.D.N.C. 1968) (notice pleading is sufficient in administrative proceedings and the particularization required in common law pleading is not necessary). For a case finding notice insufficient under these principles, *see* NLRB v. United Aircraft Corp., 490 F.2d 1105, 1111–12 (2d Cir. 1973) (employer was not adequately notified that contents of particular letter would be basis for finding of unfair labor practice and therefore was deprived of opportunity to prepare potentially meritorious defense).
6. Wyoming v. Alexander, 971 F.2d 531, 542 (10th Cir. 1992).
7. *See* Mayfield v. Nicholson, 444 F.3d 1328 (Fed. Cir. 2006) (38 U.S.C. § 5103(a) imposes specific notice requirements in certain veterans' claims proceedings).

adequately for the hearing.[8] The purpose of the notice requirement in administrative proceedings is to allow the party to prepare for the hearing, know the relevant issues, and have the means to prepare an adequate defense.[9] Thus, if a party alleging inadequate notice is not prejudiced in terms of preparing for the hearing, the results of the hearing will not be disturbed.[10]

Illustration:

1. On March 1, Company promised its workers a pay raise to take effect on June 1. On May 1, Union was certified to represent the workers. Company failed to pay the increase. On July 10, it retroactively paid the increase but wrote a letter to the workers blaming Union for the delay. Agency issued a complaint stating that nonpayment of the raise on June 1 was an unfair labor practice. The complaint made no reference to the July 10 letter and there was no testimony about it at the hearing. The NLRB ruled that nonpayment of the raise on June 1 was not an unfair labor practice, but sending the July 10 letter was an unfair labor practice. A court could hold that Agency failed to provide adequate notice to Company and that the failure to do so was prejudicial.[11]

4.024 APA notice and due process

Proper notice is an essential element of due process.[12] Courts often equate the requirements of the APA's notice provisions with the require-

---

8. Shinseki v. Sanders, 556 U.S. 396 (2009); Conway v. Principi, 353 F.3d 1369 (Fed. Cir. 2004).
9. Rapp v. Office of Thrift Supervision, 52 F.3d 1510, 1520 (10th Cir. 1995); NLRB v. Johnson, 322 F.2d 216, 219 (6th Cir. 1963), *cert. denied*, 376 U.S. 951 (1964).
10. *See* Duane v. Dep't of Defense, 275 F.3d 988, 993–96 (10th Cir. 2002) (party was adequately apprised of issues at hearing to present its defense); *Long*, 117 F.3d at 1158 (10th Cir. 1997) ("To establish a due process violation, an individual must show he or she has sustained prejudice as a result of the allegedly insufficient notice."); *United Aircraft*, 490 F.2d at 1112 n.9 (party prejudiced by inadequate notice where it "may well have been able to introduce persuasive evidence in support of its claim" but did not due to lack of notice).
11. *United Aircraft*, 490 F.2d at 1111–12.
12. *See, e.g.,* Mullane v. Cent. Hanover Trust Co., 339 U.S. 306, 313 (1950) ("there can be no doubt that at a minimum [due process] requires that

ments of due process.[13] The principles developed in cases relying on due process seem identical to those developed in cases relying more directly on the APA.[14] Due process requires that a notice be "reasonably calculated under all the circumstances to apprise" a person of the pendency of proceedings[15] and the nature of those proceedings. In particular, agencies must inform parties of the issues that will be addressed and resolved at the hearing.[16] Agencies must give advance notice of the theory on which a case is to be tried.[17]

---

deprivation of life, liberty, or property by adjudication be preceded by notice and opportunity for hearing appropriate to the nature of the case"); Goss v. Lopez, 419 U.S. 565, 579 (1975) (person deprived of liberty or property "must be given *some* kind of notice and afforded *some* kind of hearing") (emphasis in original). *See* Chapter 2, § 2.052.

13. For example, in *Long*, 117 F.3d at 1158, the court referred to the APA and due process notice requirements interchangeably.

14. For example, the Fifth Circuit has stated that "in the administrative context, due process requires that interested parties be given a reasonable opportunity to know the claims of adverse parties and an opportunity to meet them." N. Alabama Express, Inc. v. United States, 585 F.2d 783, 786 (5th Cir. 1978). Both due process and the APA are satisfied if the party understood the issues and was given full opportunity to justify its conduct. Golden Grain Macaroni Co. v. FTC, 472 F.2d 882, 885 (9th Cir. 1972), *cert. denied*, 412 U.S. 918 (1973).

15. Dusenbery v. United States, 534 U.S. 161 (2002), relying on *Mullane*, 339 U.S. at 314. For further discussion of notice and due process, *see* Chapter 2, § 2.05.

16. Pub. Serv. Comm'n of Ky. v. FERC, 397 F.3d 1004, 1012 (D.C. Cir. 2004) (notice was inadequate because it failed to apprise parties of the methodology the agency intended to apply to reach decision); St. Anthony Hosp. v. U.S. Dep't of Health and Human Servs., 309 F.3d 680 (10th Cir. 2002) (notice adequately informed subject of proceeding of issues involved).

17. Bendix Corp. v. FTC, 450 F.2d 534, 542 (6th Cir. 1971) ("an administrative agency must give a clear statement of the theory on which a case will be tried"); Rodale Press, Inc. v. FTC, 407 F.2d 1252, 1256 (D.C. Cir. 1968) ("an agency may not change theories in midstream without giving respondents reasonable notice of the change").

4.025 Notice of time, place, and nature of the hearing

The APA requires that the party entitled to notice shall be timely informed of the time, place, and nature of the hearing.[18] It also states that in fixing the time and place for hearings, due regard shall be had for the convenience and necessity of the parties or their representatives.[19]

These provisions grant discretion to an agency to choose the time and place of the hearing in a way that is convenient for both the agency and the parties. It does not specify the period of notice, but does require that notice be "timely." Whether notice is timely depends on the circumstances, including the urgency of the situation and the complexity of the issues involved.[20] Generally, notice is timely if the individual has enough time to adequately prepare for the hearing.[21]

4.026 Notice of the legal authority and jurisdiction under which the hearing is to be held

The APA requires the agency to include in its notice the authority from which it derives its legal powers and jurisdiction in the particular instance.[22] This notice should allow the parties to ascertain the relevant legal issues that they should address at the hearing.[23]

4.027 Fair warning requirement

Due process requires that a statute and agency regulations give fair warning that a particular conduct is illegal. Even though an agency's interpretation of the statute may pass muster under *Chevron*,[24] if the legal standard is so indefinite that it fails to give fair warning, the agency will

---

18. APA § 554(b)(1), quoted in note 2.
19. APA § 554(b), quoted in note 2.
20. Department of Justice, *Attorney General's Manual on the Administrative Procedure* Act 46–47.
21. Wolff v. McDonnell, 418 U.S. 539, 564 (1974) (regarding timeliness of notice in the context of a prison disciplinary hearing).
22. APA § 554(b)(2), quoted in note 1.
23. Attorney General's Manual at 47.
24. Chevron U.S.A. v. NRDC, 467 U.S. 837, 844 (1984) (requiring courts to defer to agency's reasonable interpretation of ambiguous statute).

be precluded from imposing sanctions on a regulated party that has relied in good faith on a reasonable but different interpretation.[25]

4.028 When private persons are the moving parties

The APA notice provides specially for situations in which private persons rather than an agency are the moving parties.[26] When a private party is the moving party, the responding agency must still give notice of the disputed issues so that the private party will know which issues will be in controversy at the hearing.[27]

4.029 Special notice requirements for the withdrawal, suspension, revocation, or annulment of a license

Section 558(c) of the APA provides special requirements concerning notice in licensing cases.[28] This provision is applicable both to formal

---

25. PMD Produce Brokerage Corp. v. USDA, 234 F.3d 48, 51–54 (D.C. Cir. 2000) (overturning dismissal of internal agency appeal because party had relied on reasonable interpretation of unclear regulation); United States v. Chrysler Corp., 158 F.3d 1350 (D.C. Cir. 1998) (overturning recall order because of lack of notice of agency's interpretation of safety standards); Gen. Elec. Co. v. EPA, 53 F.3d 1324 (D.C. Cir. 1995) (overturning monetary penalty because agency did not provide notice of its interpretation of unclear regulations). *But see* Abhe & Svoboda, Inc. v. Chao, 508 F.3d 1052 (D.C. Cir. 2007) (prior unpublished agency decision provided fair warning of legal requirements).
26. Language following APA § 554(b)(3), quoted in note 1.
27. Attorney General's Manual at 47.
28. APA § 558(c) provides: "Except in cases of willfulness or those in which the public health, interest, or safety requires otherwise, the withdrawal, suspension, revocation, or annulment of a license is lawful only if, before the institution of agency proceedings therefor, the licensee has been given—
    (1) notice by the agency in writing of the facts or conduct which may warrant the action; and
    (2) opportunity to demonstrate or achieve compliance with all lawful requirements. When the licensee has made timely and sufficient application for a renewal or a new license in accordance with agency rules, a license with reference to an activity of a continuing nature does not expire until the application has been finally determined by the agency."

and informal adjudication and is discussed in the chapter on informal adjudication.[29]

4.0210 Method of service of notice

The APA makes no specific provision for the method of service of process. Therefore, assuming due process is satisfied by adequate notice, other statutes or agency rules may govern the precise method for service of process in agency proceedings.[30]

4.03 DISCOVERY

4.031 Discovery not required in agency proceedings

Neither the APA nor the Constitution requires discovery in administrative proceedings.[31] Therefore, discovery is normally unavailable in

---

See generally Buckingham v. USDA, 603 F.3d. 1073 (9th Cir. 2010) (applying APA § 558(c) to the revocation of a grazing permit); Finer Foods Sales Co., Inc. v. Block, 708 F.2d 774, 778 (D.C. Cir. 1983); ("flagrant and repeated" violations are willful, thus excusing agency from special notice requirement for license revocation).

29. *See* Chapter 9, § 9.06 (concerning licensing). Note that before these special notice requirements apply, a determination must be made that the challenged government action actually implicates a license. The APA defines license as "an agency permit, certificate, approval, registration, charter, membership, statutory exemption or other form of permission." APA § 551(8). The courts have taken divergent approaches to determining when a license exists. *Compare* Horn Farms, Inc. v. Johanns, 397 F.3d 472 (7th Cir. 2005) (eligibility for farm subsidy not a license since subject was still free to engage in farming), *with* New York Pathological & X-Ray Labs., Inc. v. INS, 523 F.2d 79 (2d Cir. 1975) (eligibility to conduct medical exams to certify health of applicants for permanent resident status is license subject to special APA notice requirements even though physician still able to conduct other medical exams).

30. Olin Indus., Inc. v. NLRB, 192 F.2d 799 (5th Cir., 1951), *cert. denied*, 343 U.S. 919 (1952).

31. *See* Kenrich Petrochemicals, Inc. v. NLRB, 893 F.2d 1468, 1484 (3d Cir.), *vacated & reheard en banc but not in pertinent part*, 907 F.2d 400 (3d Cir.), *cert. denied*, 498 U.S. 981 (1990), citing NLRB v. Valley Mold Co., 530 F.2d 693, 695 (6th Cir.), *cert. denied*, 429 U.S. 824 (1976) (no constitutional or APA requirement); Frilette v. Kimberlin, 508 F.2d 205, 208 (3d Cir. 1974) (en banc), *cert. denied*, 421 U.S. 980 (1975) (no APA requirement).

administrative hearings without a statute or agency provision requiring or allowing discovery.[32] Numerous court decisions leave it to the discretion of the agency whether to allow discovery and, if so, to what extent,[33] and the denial of discovery will not, except in "the most extraordinary circumstances," result in the overturning of an agency decision.[34]

4.032 Agencies may allow discovery

Agencies may, if governing statutes allow, provide for discovery.[35] Some agencies, such as the U.S. Department of Agriculture (USDA), provide for discovery and incorporate other federal statutes and rules in the administration of discovery.[36] Agencies may also grant or deny discovery on a discretionary basis if agency rules do not provide for discovery.[37]

---

32. Citizens Awareness Network, Inc. v. United States, 391 F.3d 338, 350 (1st Cir. 2004) (agency not required to allow discovery and therefore has the power to eliminate it by amending rule that previously allowed discovery); *Frilette*, 508 F.2d at 208; Moore v. Adm'r, Veterans Admin., 475 F.2d 1283, 1286 (D.C. Cir. 1973) ("in absence of special statutory provision, and in absence of special administrative regulation, no procedure for discovery is normally available in a federal administrative proceeding"). *But see* Water Transp. Ass'n v. ICC, 722 F.2d 1025, 1032 (2d Cir. 1983) (requiring ICC to allow discovery where statute requires the disclosure of certain information in agency proceedings).
33. *See* Hi-Tech Furnace Sys., Inc. v. FCC, 224 F.3d 781, 787–90 (D.C. Cir. 2000) (absent statute or agency rule providing for discovery, party to agency proceeding not entitled to compel answers to interrogatories directed to opposing party). *Hi-Tech* held that agency decisions to deny discovery requests are reviewable under a deferential abuse of discretion standard.
34. Trailways Lines v. ICC, 766 F.2d 1537, 1546 (D.C. Cir. 1985).
35. *See* Pac. Gas & Elec. Co. v. FERC, 746 F.2d 1383, 1387–88 (9th Cir. 1984). *But see* Fed. Mar. Comm'n v. Anglo-Canadian Shipping Co., 335 F.2d 255 (9th Cir. 1964) (agency lacked statutory authority to provide for discovery).
36. *See* 7 C.F.R. § 1.141(h)(1)(iii) (applying Jencks Act, 18 U.S.C. § 3500, to discovery of statements by government witnesses in USDA proceedings); McClelland v. Andrus, 606 F.2d 1278, 1286 n.50 (D.C. Cir. 1979) (listing agencies that provide for discovery); Fairbank v. Hardin, 429 F.2d 264, 268 (9th Cir.), *cert. denied*, 400 U.S. 943 (1970).
37. *See* NLRB v. Robbins Tire & Rubber Co., 437 U.S. 214, 237 n.16 (1978) (noting that all circuits except one hold that prehearing discovery in unfair labor practice proceedings is up to the discretion of the NLRB). *See also* Darrell Andrews Trucking, Inc. v. Fed. Motor Carrier Safety Admin., 296

4.033 Due process may require discovery

An agency's discovery rules must satisfy the requirements of due process.[38] Due process requires that discovery be allowed to the extent necessary for parties to prepare for trial reasonably and adequately.[39] The issue of whether due process requires an agency to provide an opportunity for discovery would be analyzed under the usual three-factor *Mathews* test.[40]

4.034 Subpoenas as discovery

Subpoenas are a possible method of discovery.[41] However, their utility is limited since materials subpoenaed by private parties need not be

---

F.3d 1120, 1134 (D.C. Cir. 2002) (where no agency rule requires discovery, decision whether to provide it is entrusted to discretion of agency); J.H. Rutter-Rex Mfg. Co., Inc. v. NLRB, 473 F.2d 223, 230 (5th Cir.), *cert. denied*, 414 U.S. 822 (1973) (holding that the board may provide information and documents in some instances and not in others within its prerogative); *Trailways Lines*, 766 F.2d at 1546 ("The conduct and extent of discovery in agency proceedings is a matter ordinarily entrusted to the expert agency in the first instance and will not, barring the most extraordinary circumstances, warrant the Draconian sanction of overturning a reasoned agency decision.").

38. *McClelland*, 606 F.2d at 1285–86 (in personnel dispute party had due process right to examine a report on agency personnel practices commissioned for this very case); NLRB v. Valley Mold Co., 530 F.2d 693, 695 (6th Cir.), *cert. denied*, 429 U.S. 824 (1976) (no due process right to take depositions of employees in back pay dispute since they can be cross-examined at the hearing). *See also* Communist Party of U.S. v. Subversive Activities Control Bd., 254 F.2d 314, 328 (D.C. Cir. 1958) (applying Jencks Act and requiring discovery of government witness statements to provide subject of administrative hearing with due process).

39. *See* Standard Oil Co. v. FTC, 475 F. Supp. 1261, 1274–89 (N.D. Idaho 1979) (no right to concurrent discovery in massive antitrust case but ALJ violated due process by completely cutting off private party's discovery of documents in agency file).

40. *See* Chapter 2, § 2.053. In Sw. Airlines Co. v. TSA, 554 F.3d 1065, 1074 (D.C. Cir. 2009), the court held that due process did not require discovery during the agency proceeding without applying *Mathews*. Rather, the court concluded that the complaining party did not show a need for the information sought that was comparable to the urgent need established in *McClelland*.

41. *See* 4, § 4.04 for discussion of subpoenas and the restrictions on their use.

made available prior to the hearing.[42] APA § 556(c)(4) allows a hearing officer to take depositions "when the ends of justice would be served." However, this section was not intended to make depositions generally available to nonagency litigants, but merely to grant authority to hearing officers to take depositions to preserve testimony.[43]

4.035 FOIA and discovery

The Freedom of Information Act (FOIA) is another avenue for providing agency litigants with agency records, and its procedures may provide a partial substitute for discovery.[44]

4.036 Sanctions for noncompliance with discovery orders

If an agency statute or rule provides for discovery and a party fails to comply with a valid discovery request, the party may be ordered to comply. If the party still fails to comply, agency rules may prescribe procedural sanctions, including finding against the party[45] or drawing an adverse inference on matters related to disobeyed discovery orders.[46]

4.04 ADMINISTRATIVE SUBPOENAS

4.041 APA provisions regarding subpoenas

Section 555(d) of the APA, which is applicable to both formal and informal adjudication, provides a right for parties to demand that an

---

42. Seth D. Montgomery, Note, *Discovery in Federal Administrative Proceedings*, 16 STAN. L. REV. 1035, 1042 (1964).
43. *Id.* at 1043.
44. 5 U.S.C. § 552(a)(3). *See generally* Edward A. Tomlinson, *Use of the Freedom of Information Act for Discovery Purposes*, 43 MD. L. REV. 119 (1984). Detailed treatment of FOIA and its exceptions is beyond the scope of this book.
45. Genentech, Inc. v. Int'l Trade Comm'n, 122 F.3d 1409, 1418 (Fed. Cir. 1997).
46. *See* Int'l Union, UAW v. NLRB, 459 F.2d 1329 (D.C. Cir. 1972).

agency issue legally authorized subpoenas on a statement or showing of general relevance and reasonable scope.[47] This provision does not grant an agency or a private party the power to issue a subpoena but only to issuance of subpoenas authorized by law.[48] It allows private parties to take advantage of an agency's statutory subpoena power, according to applicable rules.[49] Thus, agency subpoenas are available to private parties to the same extent that they are available to agency representatives. A party may secure both subpoenas ad testificandum (compelling a witness to appear and testify at the hearing) and duces tecum (compelling production of documents).[50] However, an agency should not issue a subpoena to a private party that appears to be so irrelevant or unreasonable that a court would refuse to enforce it.[51]

---

47. APA § 555(d) provides: "Agency subpoenas authorized by law shall be issued to a party on request, and, when required by rules of procedure, on a statement or showing of general relevance and reasonable scope of the evidence sought. On contest, the court shall sustain the subpoena or similar process or demand to the extent that it is found to be in accordance with law." *See also* Attorney General's Manual at 67.

48. APA § 555(c) provides: "Process, requirement of a report, inspection, or other investigative act or demand may not be issued, made, or enforced except as authorized by law."

49. The ability to subpoena witnesses is not an absolute right in an administrative hearing. Instead, it depends on the terms of the agency's rules. *See, e.g.,* Butera v. Apfel, 173 F.3d 1049, 1057–59 (7th Cir. 1999). In *Butera,* the Social Security Administration's rule allowed witness subpoenas if reasonably necessary for full presentation of a party's case. The court upheld the ALJ's decision refusing an applicant's request that he issue a subpoena to physicians who had examined applicant. The applicant had failed to show why he needed to cross-examine the physicians. The court noted that cross-examination is not an absolute right under the APA but must be provided only when required for a full and true disclosure of the facts. APA § 556(d). *See* Chapter 5, § 5.08.

50. Attorney General's Manual at 67.

51. *Id.* at 68. *See* Morell E. Mullins, Manual for Administrative Law Judges 42–49 (Interim Internet ed. 2001), for discussion of numerous issues relating to discovery and subpoenas from the perspective of ALJs. This seminal work is available at http://www.oalj.dol.gov/public/apa/references/reference_works/malj_navigation.htm (last visited Jan. 9, 2012). A reformatted version was published at 23 Pepp. J. Nat'l Ass'n Admin. L. Judges 1 (2004).

Section 556(c) of the APA provides that presiding officers in formal adjudications may issue subpoenas authorized by law.[52] This section of the APA does not grant any subpoena or discovery powers to an agency, but merely transfers the powers that the agency does possess to the administrative law judge (ALJ) or other presiding officer.[53]

4.042 Judicial enforcement of agency subpoenas

Typically, federal agency subpoenas are enforced by a federal district court on the application of the party, usually the agency, seeking to enforce the subpoena.[54] The proceeding is adversarial in character and is generally decided based on documents submitted to the court.[55]

4.0421 *Early cases on subpoena power*

Early cases indicated that agency subpoenas would be enforced only where the agency could show that the material sought would include "evidence" of a statutory violation; "fishing expeditions" were prohibited.[56] In practice, this meant that before an agency could issue an enforceable subpoena, it would have to establish probable cause to believe that a violation of law had occurred.

---

52. APA § 556(c) provides: "Subject to published rules of the agency and within its powers, employees presiding at hearings may . . . (2) issue subpoenas authorized by law."
53. Attorney General's Manual at 74.
54. ICC v. Brimson, 154 U.S. 447 (1894), indicated that an agency could not be given power to enforce its own subpoenas. It is unclear whether this decision would be followed today if Congress chose to give an agency power to enforce its own subpoenas. The APA seems to assume that a court order is necessary to enforce a subpoena. *See* APA § 555(d), which provides: "On contest, a court shall sustain the subpoena or similar process or demand to the extent that it is found to be in accordance with law. In a proceeding for enforcement, the court shall issue an order requiring the appearance of the witness or the production of the evidence or data within a reasonable time under penalty of punishment for contempt in case of contumacious failure to comply."
55. The adversarial proceeding may take the form of an evidentiary hearing, oral arguments without taking evidence, or decision on papers submitted by the parties. FTC v. Atl. Richfield Co., 567 F.2d 96, 106 n.22 (D.C. Cir. 1977). Enforcement proceedings often take the form of a summary action under Rule 81(a)(3) of the Federal Rules of Civil Procedure.
56. FTC v. Am. Tobacco Co., 264 U.S. 298, 305–06 (1924).

4.0422 *Judicial rejection of limitations on subpoena power*

During the 1940s and 1950s, the Court eliminated the requirement that agencies establish probable cause before issuing a subpoena. Thus, an agency could determine whether it had jurisdiction through the inspection of documents "not plainly incompetent or irrelevant to any lawful purpose" of the agency.[57] The Court likened the investigative function of the agency to a grand jury investigation, where the proceeding does not require a finding of probable cause.[58] It recognized that agencies needed to gather evidence in order to locate violations, or merely confirm that there are none.[59] It ruled that the Fourth Amendment prohibition on unreasonable search and seizure did not apply to a subpoena in the same way that it would apply to a physical search; the Constitution required little more than that "the disclosure sought shall not be unreasonable."[60]

4.043 Contemporary statements of agency subpoena power

Under current law, the agency's subpoena power is extremely broad. In order to obtain enforcement of a subpoena, the agency must show that (1) the investigation is being conducted pursuant to a legitimate purpose, (2) the information sought is relevant to the inquiry,[61] (3) the information sought is not already within the agency's possession, and (4) the required administrative steps have been followed.[62] The courts will also require that the demand not be too indefinite or unreasonably broad or burdensome.[63] Finally, a court will refuse to enforce an agency subpoena if

---

57. Endicott Johnson Corp. v. Perkins, 317 U.S. 501, 509 (1943).
58. Okla. Press Publ'g Co. v. Walling, 327 U.S. 186, 216 (1946).
59. United States v. Morton Salt Co., 338 U.S. 632, 642–43 (1950).
60. *Okla. Press*, 327 U.S. at 208.
61. Courts defer to agency determinations of relevance unless they are "obviously wrong." FTC v. Invention Submission Corp., 965 F.2d 1086, 1089 (D.C. Cir. 1992). Particular statutes may impose a stricter relevance standard. *See* EEOC v. Shell Oil Co., 466 U.S. 54, 64 (1984) (EEOC subpoena must be relevant to the specific charge that has been filed and is under investigation which is much narrower than plenary subpoena authority enjoyed by most agencies); EEOC v. Quad/Graphics, Inc., 63 F.3d 642, 644–48 (7th Cir. 1995) (describing EEOC's subpoena authority and applying *Shell Oil Co.*); EEOC v. Wash. Suburban Sanitary Comm'n, 631 F.3d 174, 180 (4th Cir. 2011) (same).
62. United States v. Powell, 379 U.S. 48, 57–58 (1964).
63. *See* § 4.046.

enforcement would be an abuse of the court's process because, for example, the subpoena was issued merely to harass the recipient or pressure the recipient in an unrelated proceeding.[64]

4.044 Refusal to comply with agency subpoena

While an ALJ[65] may not compel a private party to comply with a subpoena, some courts have allowed the ALJ to visit adverse consequences on a party who unjustifiably refuses to comply. For example, the ALJ may refuse to allow the subpoena recipient to cross-examine witnesses with regard to issues that might have been resolved by complying with the subpoena.[66] Similarly, the agency or ALJ may apply the adverse inference rule, which assumes that records not produced are unfavorable to the party required to produce them.[67] However, other courts have indicated that because the recipient of a subpoena cannot challenge the subpoena in court until the agency brings a petition for enforcement, adverse consequences may not attach to the failure to comply with a subpoena until after a judicial enforcement order has been entered and disobeyed.[68] This

---

64. *Powell*, 379 U.S. at 58; FTC v. Bisaro, 2010 WL 4910268, at *7–8, *magistrate's recommendation adopted*, 757 F. Supp. 2d 1 (D.D.C. 2010).
65. "ALJ" in this context refers either to an ALJ or to the agency itself, depending on who is presiding over the hearing.
66. *See* Atl. Richfield Co. v. DOE, 769 F.2d 771, 792–93 (D.C. Cir. 1984); NLRB v. C.H. Sprague & Son Co., 428 F.2d 938, 942 (1st Cir. 1970). But *See* NLRB v. Int'l Medication Sys., Ltd., 640 F.2d 1110 (9th Cir. 1981), *cert. denied*, 455 U.S. 1017 (1982) (refusing to allow agency to limit cross-examination because of noncompliance with subpoena that agency had not sought to enforce in court).
67. Int'l Union, UAW v. NLRB, 459 F.2d 1329, 1335–36 (D.C. Cir. 1972). Similarly, an agency might withhold future benefits such as additional contracts or impose other sanctions. Uniroyal, Inc. v. Marshall, 482 F. Supp. 364 (D.D.C. 1979) (debarment).
68. *See* Shea v. Office of Thrift Supervision, 934 F.2d 41 (3d Cir. 1991) ("The subpoenaed party faces actual harm only after a successful enforcement action has been brought and, as a result of such action, the subpoenaed party has been ordered to comply."); Stryker Corp. v. U.S. Dep't of Justice, 2009 WL 424323, at *2 (D.N.J. Feb. 18, 2009) (same).

approach seems more in line with the weight of precedent, which holds that prior to a judicial subpoena enforcement proceeding, the failure to comply with a subpoena is neither an act of contempt nor ripe for judicial review[69] and the agency cannot compel the party to comply with the subpoena until after it brings the subpoena enforcement proceeding.[70] This also means that a party served with a subpoena cannot ask a court to quash the subpoena until the agency brings the enforcement proceeding.[71] A court order enforcing a subpoena is final and thus appealable.[72] If a party persists in refusing to comply with a subpoena after a judicial decision enforcing it, the party may be held in contempt.

4.045 Issues that cannot be litigated in subpoena enforcement proceedings

Subpoena enforcement proceedings are not the proper forum in which to litigate questions of agency jurisdiction or coverage under a

---

69. Schulz v. IRS, 395 F.3d 463 (2d Cir. 2005) (no case or controversy presented by motion to quash agency subpoena until agency seeks judicial order of enforcement; subpoena recipient may not be held in contempt until court issues enforcement order).
70. *See* Mobil Exploration & Producing U.S., Inc. v. Dep't of Interior, 180 F.3d 1192 (10th Cir. 1999).
71. "Where an agency must resort to judicial enforcement of its subpoenas, courts generally dismiss anticipatory actions filed by parties challenging such subpoenas as not being ripe for review because of the availability of an adequate remedy at law if, and when, the agency files an enforcement action." *In re* Ramirez, 905 F.2d 97, 98–99 (5th Cir. 1990) (citing Reisman v. Caplin, 375 U.S. 440 (1964); Atl. Richfield Co. v. FTC, 546 F.2d 646, 648–49 (5th Cir. 1977)).
72. Reisman v. Caplin, 375 U.S. 440 (1964). *See also Schulz*, 395 F.3d 463 (failure to obey agency subpoena may have no penal consequences until court orders enforcement after agency petition).

statute[73] or to litigate the strength of the agency's case[74] or whether the respondent has a defense.[75] There are good reasons for this rule of long standing:

- Allowing the jurisdictional question to be litigated at the subpoena stage creates undue delay and prevents the administrative agency from resolving investigations promptly.
- An individual is not adversely affected at the subpoena enforcement stage but only at the stage at which the agency takes some substantive action.
- In order to determine a jurisdictional issue, a court must examine the facts of the case and would often have to conduct a trial, thus contravening the congressional desire to have the controversy investigated and decided by an agency rather than a court.[76]

---

73. United States v. Sturm, Ruger & Co., Inc., 84 F.3d 1, 5 (1st Cir. 1996), *cert. denied*, 519 U.S. 991 (1996) ("We have repeatedly admonished that questions concerning the scope of an agency's substantive authority to regulate are not to be resolved in subpoena enforcement proceedings."). Nevertheless, if the subpoena discloses on its face that the agency is seeking information concerning a matter over which it plainly has no jurisdiction, the court may quash the subpoena. FTC v. Ken Roberts Co., 276 F.3d 583, 584 (D.C. Cir. 2002) ("unless it is patently clear that an agency lacks the jurisdiction that it seeks to assert" court will enforce subpoena—but the court carefully considered the jurisdictional challenge before deciding to enforce it); Reich v. Great Lakes Indian Fish & Wildlife Comm'n, 4 F.3d 490, 491–92 (7th Cir. 1993). One court has held that the court will resolve both statutory questions of agency jurisdiction that are not clear on their face as well as First Amendment issues in a subpoena enforcement proceeding where these claims are otherwise ripe for review and the subpoena imposes a substantial burden. Commodity Trend Serv., Inc. v. CFTC, 233 F.3d 981, 986–95 (7th Cir. 2000). This decision seems questionable in light of Supreme Court authority precluding judicial review of such issues at the subpoena enforcement stage.
74. *See* EEOC v. Shell Oil Co., 466 U.S. 54, 70–72 (1984).
75. EEOC v. A.E. Staley Mfg. Co., 711 F.2d 780, 788 (7th Cir. 1983), *cert. denied*, 466 U.S. 936 (1984).
76. *See* Bernard Schwartz, Administrative Law, § 3.12 at 134–136 (3d ed. 1991).

4.046 Issues that can be litigated in subpoena enforcement proceedings

Under current law, a party subject to a subpoena can raise various defenses in the subpoena enforcement proceeding. Fundamentally, the limitation on the agency's subpoena power is the "reasonableness" requirement of the Fourth Amendment.[77] Courts tend to be unsympathetic to attempts by parties subject to subpoenas to resist the demands for information and to be deferential to the agency's decision to seek a subpoena.[78] Appellate courts treat quite deferentially the decisions of trial courts that have enforced subpoenas.[79]

- A court will consider a party's argument that the investigation is not being conducted for a legitimate purpose. An investigation conducted for an illegitimate purpose such as harassment would be an abuse of process.[80]

---

77. *See* Okla. Press Publ'g Co. v. Walling, 327 U.S. 186, 208 (1946) (stating that as far as administrative subpoenas are concerned, "the gist of the [Fourth Amendment] protection is in the requirement that the disclosure sought shall not be unreasonable [in scope].").

78. *See In re* Office of Inspector Gen. R.R. Ret. Bd., 933 F.2d 276, 277 (5th Cir. 1991) (holding that judicial review in a subpoena enforcement proceeding is limited and to be handled summarily). *But see* United States v. Witmer, 835 F. Supp. 208, 220 (M.D. Pa. 1993), *aff'd without op.*, 30 F.3d 1489 (3d Cir. 1994) (holding that a court must do more than "rubber stamp" the issuance of an administrative subpoena).

79. Dow Chem. Co. v. Allen, 672 F.2d 1262, 1267 (7th Cir. 1982) (burdensomeness decision reviewed under abuse of discretion standard).

80. *A.E. Staley Mfg.*, 711 F.2d at 788 (abuse of process consists of wrongful conduct by the government, improper purpose of the government, or a purpose outside of agency's proper jurisdiction); SEC v. Wheeling-Pittsburgh Steel Co., 648 F.2d 118 (3d Cir. 1981) (improper interference by Senator on behalf of competitor influenced SEC to launch investigation). Similarly, if the agency engages in fraud or trickery, its subpoena could be an abuse of process. SEC v. ESM Gov't Sec., Inc., 645 F.2d 310, 317 (5th Cir. 1981) (fraud, deceit, or trickery in the context of the investigation constitutes an abuse of process). The opposing party has the burden of proving abuse of process or the unlawfulness of the subpoena and the party must establish facts that raise doubts about an agency's good faith before being permitted to conduct discovery. *See* United States v. Wilson, 864 F.2d 1219, 1222 (5th Cir.), *cert. denied*, 492 U.S. 918 (1989); SEC v. Dresser Indus., Inc., 628 F.2d 1368, 1390 (D.C. Cir.), *cert. denied*, 449 U.S. 993 (1980).

- A court will consider a party's argument that the face of the subpoena discloses that the information sought concerns a type of matter over which the agency has no jurisdiction and thus no power to investigate.[81]
- A court will consider a party's argument that the information is not relevant to the agency's inquiry. However, a court will not overturn the agency's determination of relevancy unless it is "obviously wrong" or "clearly erroneous."[82] Since the agency need not propound a narrowly focused theory of its case during the investigation stage, the relevance of the request may be measured only against the general purposes of the investigation.[83]
- A court will consider arguments that the information sought by a subpoena is privileged.[84]
- A court may refuse to enforce a subpoena, or may modify or exclude portions of the subpoena, if enforcement would be unreasonable or cause an undue burden. Undue burden or unreasonableness of a subpoena is extremely difficult to establish, given that every subpoena is a burden on its recipient. Production of documents is not an undue burden unless it would cause a serious hindrance or disruption to the normal operations of the business.[85]

---

81. *See* Reich v. Great Lakes Indian Fish & Wildlife Comm'n, 4 F.3d 490 (7th Cir. 1993). The same court also held that it could resolve both statutory questions of agency jurisdiction that are not clear on their face as well as First Amendment issues in a subpoena enforcement proceeding where these claims are otherwise ripe for review and the subpoena imposes a substantial burden. Commodity Trend Serv., Inc. v. CFTC, 233 F.3d 981, 986–95 (7th Cir. 2000). This latter decision seems questionable in light of Supreme Court authority precluding judicial review of such issues at the subpoena enforcement stage.
82. Linde Thomson Langworthy Kohn & Van Dyke, P.C. v. Resolution Trust Corp., 5 F.3d 1508, 1516 (D.C. Cir. 1993), citing FTC v. Invention Submission Corp., 965 F.2d 1086, 1089 (D.C. Cir. 1992) and FTC v. Lonning, 539 F.2d 202, 210 n.14 (D.C. Cir. 1976).
83. FTC v. Texaco, Inc., 555 F.2d 862, 874 (D.C. Cir.), *cert. denied*, 431 U.S. 974 (1977).
84. *See* § 4.049.
85. *See* EEOC v. United Air Lines, 287 F.3d 643, 648 (7th Cir. 2002) (refusing to enforce subpoena when subject asserted that it would take "approximately '5.5 employees working 2000 hours apiece for an entire year' to comply with the subpoena"); Civil Aeronautics Bd. v. Hermann, 353 U.S. 322 (1957) (upholding subpoena for all books, records and documents of an airline and its stockholders for period of 38 months); EEOC v. Bay

Rule 45(c) of the Federal Rules of Civil Procedure, while not directly applicable to administrative proceedings, may be referred to by courts to determine the standards for modifying and enforcing subpoenas.[86] Rule 45(c) declares that a subpoena may be modified where it subjects a person to undue burden.

Illustrations:

2. Agency, which regulates and licenses stockbrokers, issues a subpoena to Broker. Broker is a small stock brokerage business employing three people. The subpoena has been issued in full compliance with Agency's rules. Agency suspects, but has no probable cause to believe, that Broker might have illegally "churned" the accounts of customers whose accounts it managed (that is, engaged in many trades simply to generate commissions). The subpoena covers the record of past trades of six customers. A court will enforce this subpoena since the investigation is conducted pursuant to a legitimate purpose, the information sought is relevant to the inquiry, the information is not already within the agency's possession, and the required administrative steps have been followed. An agency need not have probable cause to believe a violation has occurred but can investigate on suspicion or simply to ascertain that no violation has occurred.

3. Assume the same facts as Illustration 2 except that Broker is a commodities broker. Agency has no jurisdiction over commodities brokers. A court might refuse enforcement of this summons

---

Shipbuilding Corp., 668 F.2d 304, 313 (7th Cir. 1981) (respondent must show subpoena would threaten normal operation of business); EEOC v. Md. Cup Corp., 785 F.2d 471, 477 (4th Cir), *cert. denied*, 479 U.S. 815 (1986) (failure to show that subpoena was unduly burdensome in light of normal operating costs and that gathering information would threaten normal business operations). Courts are skeptical about exaggerated claims of the cost of compliance. *See* EEOC v. Quad/Graphics, Inc., 63 F.3d 642, 648–49 (7th Cir. 1995). *See also* U.S. Dep't of Educ. v. NCAA, 481 F.3d 936 (7th Cir. 2007) (burden of loss of confidentiality of information outweighed by department's investigatory needs).

86. SEC v. Arthur Young & Co., 584 F.2d 1018, 1033 n.123 (D.C. Cir. 1978), *cert. denied*, 439 U.S. 1071 (1979). *See also Md. Cup Corp.*, 785 F.2d at 477 (noting that some courts apply Rule 45 by analogy but that it would not be warranted here where the notes to the Federal Rules state that they do not apply under the National Labor Relations Act).

since it is possible to ascertain from the face of the subpoena that the agency has no jurisdiction.[87]

4. Assume the same facts as Illustration 2 except that Broker asserts that it can prove that it has no managed accounts and trades for customers only on their request. The court will enforce the subpoena because it will not consider possible defenses on the merits during subpoena enforcement proceedings.

5. Assume the same facts as Illustration 2 except that Broker asserts that Broker owes $100,000 to Ken, the agency employee who is supervising the investigation against Broker. Broker asserts that Ken is trying to force Broker to pay this debt by investigating Broker's business. Assuming that Broker sustains the burden of proving these facts, a court might refuse to enforce the subpoena because it could be considered an abuse of process and thus not issued for a legitimate purpose.

6. Assume the same facts as Illustration 2 except that the subpoena demands all of the books and records of Broker, including the records of all stock trades for the last three years. The books and records are to be brought to Agency's office. A court could hold that this subpoena is unduly burdensome since compliance with it would make it nearly impossible for Broker to continue in business. The court might scale down the information demanded by the subpoena and enforce it as reduced.[88]

4.047 Private party use of agency subpoena power

Although agencies have discretion over whether to allow a private party to make use of agency subpoena power,[89] the ability of parties

---

87. Reich v. Great Lakes Indian Fish & Wildlife Comm'n, 4 F.3d 490, 492 (7th Cir. 1993).
88. EEOC v. Ford Motor Credit Co., 26 F.3d 44, 46–47 (6th Cir. 1994) (limiting time period from 12 years to three years because information sought at beginning of period was of tenuous relevance and full compliance would be very costly).
89. Holly Hill Farm Corp. v. United States, 447 F.3d 258 (4th Cir. 2006). In *Holly Hill*, the court held that the denial of a subpoena to have seven agency officials testify was not an abuse of discretion because the agency sent other witnesses whose testimony, together with the documentary evidence, was sufficient to disclose the relevant facts.

to an agency proceeding to compel the production of evidence and the testimony of witnesses may be vital to the fairness of the proceeding. If a party has been denied access to information or cross-examination of witnesses, the party has not had a fair chance to prove its version of the case.[90] While an agency's lack of subpoena power is not by itself a violation of due process, if the failure to issue a subpoena prevents a party from obtaining favorable witnesses or documents, there may be a violation of due process.[91]

4.048 Subpoenas directed at nonparties

Administrative subpoenas may validly require information and documents from third parties who are not within the regulatory jurisdiction of the agency investigation as long as the information meets the usual standard of reasonableness and relevance.[92]

---

90. *See* Grimm v. Brown, 291 F. Supp. 1011, 1014 (N.D. Cal. 1968), *aff'd*, 449 F.2d 654 (9th Cir. 1971) (quoting Powhatan Mining Co. v. Ickes, 118 F.2d 105 (6th Cir. 1941)). Because of the emphasis on the fairness of the hearing, the failure of an agency to issue subpoenas is only a reversible error when it deprives the party of relevant and substantial evidence, and when that deprivation is determined to be prejudicial. *See* NLRB v. Seine & Line Fishermen's Union, 374 F.2d 974, 981 (9th Cir), *cert. denied*, 389 U.S. 913 (1967); Passmore v. Astrue, 533 F.3d 658 (9th Cir. 2008) (no absolute right to subpoena physician in Social Security disability case; due process requires subpoena only when necessary for full presentation of evidence). *But see* Lidy v. Sullivan, 911 F.2d 1075, 1077 (5th Cir. 1990) (due process provides an absolute right to subpoena physician whose written report has been admitted into evidence).
91. Henley v. United States, 379 F. Supp. 1044, 1048 (M.D. Pa. 1974) (citing De-Long v. Hampton, 422 F.2d 21, 24–25 (3d Cir. 1970)).
92. *See* SEC v. Jerry T. O'Brien, Inc., 467 U.S. 735, 742 (1984) (agency not required to inform target of investigation that subpoenas have been issued to third parties).

4.049 Assertion of privilege in subpoena proceedings

Agencies and courts accept privileges recognized in other areas of law in subpoena proceedings. Thus the attorney-client,[93] work-product,[94] and marital communication privileges[95] are all applicable. The Fifth Amendment's protection against self-incrimination provides a defense against administrative subpoenas.[96] The Supreme Court declined to recognize any peer review privilege that would protect documents related to college or university tenure and other similar deliberations from agency subpoenas.[97] Government agencies may be able to claim executive privilege to protect the deliberative process.[98]

ALJs and agencies may resolve privilege claims, but if a private party refuses to produce documents, an agency may not require the party to submit the documents for in camera inspection to determine the validity of the privilege claim.[99] Rather, only an Article III court may require production for in camera inspection, and only when necessary to resolve the privilege claim.[100]

---

93. *See* Upjohn Co. v. United States, 449 U.S. 383, 389–97 (1981) (attorney-client privilege applies in tax investigation subpoena proceeding to communications between attorneys and corporate employees below the control-group level).

94. *Id.* at 398–99 (allowing work product privilege in tax summons enforcement proceeding).

95. SEC v. Lavin, 111 F.3d 921, 925 (D.C. Cir. 1997).

96. Detailed analysis of the Fifth Amendment privilege is beyond the scope of this book.

97. Univ. of Pa. v. EEOC, 493 U.S. 182, 201–02 (1990).

98. Detailed analysis of executive privilege or other privileges unique to government is beyond the scope of this book. The numerous authorities involving executive privilege under the FOIA's exception for "inter-agency or intra-agency memorandums or letters which would not be available by law to a party other than an agency in litigation with the agency" are relevant to subpoena enforcement proceedings. 5 U.S.C. § 552(b)(5).

99. NLRB v. Interbake Foods, LLC, 637 F.3d 492, 497–501 (4th Cir. 2011).

100. *Id.* at 498–503, stating in part, "[w]hen refusal to comply with a subpoena and the Board's order to produce documents is based on the attorney-client or work-product privilege, the Board's recourse is to apply to the district court for an order enforcing the subpoena."

4.05 INTERVENTION IN AGENCY PROCEEDINGS

4.051 APA provisions relating to intervention

No provision in the APA establishes standards for intervention or defines the rights of intervenors after intervention is allowed. Section 551(3) defines the term "party" and suggests that intervenors may be considered parties where they are "properly seeking and entitled as of right to be admitted as a party."[101] That section also suggests that an intervenor can be admitted as a party for limited purposes. As with many APA provisions, this statute most likely refers to specific agency statutes and rules and their requirements for intervention.

Section 554(c)[102] provides for informal settlement or adjustment of controversies as an alternative to formal adjudicatory proceedings. The provision does not focus on the fact that interested parties may participate in hearings, but does provide that "all interested parties" have an opportunity to take part in informal settlement proceedings.[103]

Section 555(b)[104] is the provision most often invoked in intervention cases. It provides that an "interested person" may "appear" in an agency

---

101. APA § 551(3) provides: "'party' includes a person or agency named or admitted as a party, or properly seeking and entitled as of right to be admitted as a party, in an agency proceeding, and a person or agency admitted by an agency as a party for limited purposes."

102. APA § 554(c) provides: "The agency shall give all interested parties opportunity for (1) the submission and consideration of facts, arguments, offers of settlement, or proposals of adjustment when time, the nature of the proceeding, and the public interest permit; and (2) to the extent that the parties are unable so to determine a controversy by consent, hearing and decision on notice and in accordance with sections 556 and 557 of this title."

103. Attorney General's Manual at 48. *See* N.Y. State Dep't of Law v. FCC, 984 F.2d 1209, 1218–19 (D.C. Cir. 1993) (this provision leaves agency with substantial discretion concerning settlement discussions and does not automatically require notice to all interested parties of pending settlement discussions).

104. APA § 555(b) provides: "So far as the orderly conduct of public business permits, an interested person may appear before an agency or its responsible employees for the presentation, adjustment, or determination of an issue, request, or controversy in a proceeding, whether interlocutory, summary, or otherwise, or in connection with an agency function."

proceeding "so far as the orderly conduct of public business permits." It is unclear whether this provision authorizes full-fledged intervention by any interested party, since it provides only for a right to "appear."[105]

Absent a statute or rule providing for a right to intervene, the question of intervention is left to the agency's discretion.[106]

4.052 Intervention through agency statutes or rules

Agency-specific statutes or agency rules usually govern intervention issues.[107] If a particular statute or rule sets standards for intervention, courts generally review an agency's denial of leave to intervene for abuse of discretion. An agency can properly deny intervention when other parties adequately represent the would-be intervenor's interests, when intervention would unduly broaden the issues considered, when intervention

---

105. "This provision is not to be construed as requiring an agency to give notice of its proposed action and to invite appearances by interested persons." Instead, APA § 555(b) provides for informal appearance by parties with an opportunity to discuss issues and decisions with responsible members of the agency. Further, there is no need to provide an opportunity for even an interested party to present an argument that has already been raised or proposed. Attorney General's Manual at 63. Similarly, *see* David L. Shapiro, *Some Thoughts on Intervention Before Courts, Agencies, and Arbitrators*, 81 HARV. L. REV. 721, 766 (1968), arguing that § 555(b) does not confer all the rights of parties but may present an opportunity to be heard if worthwhile to the proceeding.

106. *See* FCC v. Pottsville Broad. Co., 309 U.S. 134, 138 (1940) (observing, in pre-APA case, that intervention and similar questions were left to Commission). *See also* Am. Trucking Ass'n v. United States, 627 F.2d 1313 (D.C. Cir. 1980). *But see* Nat'l Welfare Rights Org. v. Finch, 429 F.2d 725 (D.C. Cir. 1970) (finding that party has right to intervene even in absence of any statute permitting intervention).

107. *See, e.g.*, National Labor Relations Act § 10(b); 29 U.S.C. § 160(b) ("In the discretion of the member, agent, or agency conducting the hearing or the Board, any other person may be allowed to intervene in the said proceeding and to present testimony"). The agency statutes governing intervention are often vague and imprecise in defining the procedural requirements for intervention and the extent of intervenors' rights. RICHARD J. PIERCE, JR., ADMINISTRATIVE LAW TREATISE § 16.10 at 1202 (5th ed. 2010).

would obstruct or overburden the proceedings, or when intervention would fail to assist the agency's decisionmaking.[108]

Typical intervention rules require consideration of some or all of the following factors: (1) the nature of the petitioner's right under the statute, if any, to be made a party to the proceeding, (2) the nature and extent of the property, financial, or other interest of the petitioner, (3) the effect of the order that may be entered in the proceeding on petitioner's interest, (4) the availability of other means whereby the petitioner's interest may be protected, (5) the extent to which petitioner's interest will be represented by existing parties, (6) the extent to which petitioner's participation may reasonably be expected to assist in the development of a sound record, and (7) the extent to which participation will broaden the issues or delay the proceeding.[109] Some agency rules are much less specific concerning the grounds for intervention, implying that general standards derived from civil procedure may inform agency intervention practice.[110]

4.053 Interested persons

Many statutes or rules allow "interested persons" to intervene, or require an agency to grant a hearing upon the request of any person "whose interest may be affected by the proceeding." These statutes and

---

108. *See, e.g.,* Union of Concerned Scientists v. NRC, 920 F.2d 50, 53–56 (D.C. Cir. 1990); *Am. Trucking,* 627 F.2d at 1319–20; S.C. Loveland Co., Inc. v. United States, 534 F.2d 958, 963 (D.C. Cir. 1976).

109. In *Am. Trucking,* 627 F.2d at 1322–23, the court characterized the now abolished Interstate Commerce Commission's (ICC's) intervention rule at issue in that case, which required consideration of the factors listed in text, as similar to the intervention rules of other agencies.

110. For example, the ICC's successor agency, the Surface Transportation Board, has promulgated a much less detailed intervention rule than the ICC rule examined in *Am. Trucking. See* 49 C.F.R. § 1113.7. Under the current rule, the petition to intervene 'must set forth the grounds for the proposed intervention, the position and interest of the petitioner in the proceeding, and whether petitioner's position is in support of or in opposition to the relief sought." *Id.* § 1113.7(b). The rule does not contain much in the way of a substantive standard, stating only that "[l]eave to intervene will be granted only when the petitioner addresses issues reasonably pertinent to the issues already presented and which do not unduly broaden them." *Id.* § 1113.7(f). The lack of an affirmative statement of the grounds for intervention implies that the agency must look to general legal principles for guidance on when to allow a putative party to intervene.

rules may be interpreted to provide for intervention either as of right or at the discretion of the agency. Generally, a person is "interested" if an agency decision will affect his or her legal or financial interests.[111]

The *Ashbacker* doctrine expands the right to participate in agency proceedings to competitors where agency action in favor of one applicant is either legally or effectively determinative of a competing application by a competitor.[112] Under *Ashbacker*, the agency must hold a comparative hearing in which both applicants are heard, effectively allowing intervention into proceedings that would preclude the approval of a competitor's application. However, the scope of this doctrine is narrow, applying only when a statute like the provisions of the Communications Act at issue in *Ashbacker* explicitly provides that an application may not be denied without a full hearing on the merits of the application and where granting one competitor's application effectively forecloses a positive decision on the other competitor's application.

Courts differ on the relationship between the right to intervene in an agency proceeding and standing to seek judicial review of an agency decision. Parties who do not have standing for judicial review purposes might be allowed or entitled to intervene in agency proceedings if they establish a sufficient interest under governing statutes or rules.[113] The law is clear that a party allowed to intervene in an agency proceeding does not automatically have standing to seek judicial review of the agency decision.[114] Some decisions say that parties entitled to seek judicial review of an agency action are automatically considered "interested persons" for

---

111. *See, e.g.,* Nichols v. Bd. of Trs., 835 F.2d 881, 896 (D.C. Cir. 1987) (beneficiaries of ERISA plan possessed an interest in a proceeding that might reduce their benefits). *See generally* Alleghany Corp. v. Breswick & Co., 353 U.S. 151, 173 (1957) (while "interest" may be defined as a legal right or interest that will be injuriously affected by an order, the definition is not easily applied and must always take into account the context of the situation and of the parties); *Am. Trucking,* 627 F.2d at 1319 (no ready and convenient definition in the case law).

112. Ashbacker Radio Corp. v. FCC, 326 U.S. 327 (1946).

113. *See Nichols,* 835 F.2d at 896, n.108; Ecee, Inc. v. FERC, 645 F.2d 339, 349 (5th Cir. 1981); Koniag, Inc. v. Andrus, 580 F.2d 601, 606 (D.C. Cir. 1978).

114. *See* Fund Democracy, LLC v. SEC, 278 F.3d 21, 27 (D.C. Cir. 2002) ("Because agencies are not constrained by Article III, they may permit persons to intervene in the agency proceedings who would not have standing to seek judicial review of the agency action.").

purposes of intervention.[115] However, more recent cases cast doubt on the idea that standing to seek review automatically confers a right to intervene. If an agency interprets the statute to exclude as intervenors some persons who might have standing, and if that interpretation is reasonable, the court is obliged by *Chevron*[116] to defer to this interpretation.[117]

Because reviewing courts normally consider only those issues that have been litigated before the agency, interested persons must intervene in the agency to ensure that their issues will be aired on judicial review.[118]

4.054 The rights of intervenors

Under APA § 555(b), a party is entitled to appear only "so far as the orderly conduct of public business permits." Therefore, it is open to agencies to provide hearing rights that are less comprehensive than those enjoyed by the original parties.[119] Thus the agency has authority to ensure orderly procedure by promulgating rules limiting both the number of intervenors and the nature of their participation.[120] The agency can prevent an intervenor from enlarging the scope or altering the nature of

---

115. Office of Comm'n of United Church of Christ v. FCC, 359 F.2d 994 (D.C. Cir. 1966); Nat'l Welfare Rights Org. v. Finch, 429 F.2d 725, 731–38 (D.C. Cir. 1970). *See also Nichols*, 835 F.2d at 896 (citing numerous cases).

116. Chevron U.S.A. v. NRDC, 467 U.S. 837 (1984) (requiring courts to defer to agency's reasonable interpretation of ambiguous statute).

117. Envirocare, Inc. v. NRC, 194 F.3d 72, 77 (D.C. Cir. 1999) (NRC's rule excluding intervention by competitors of license applicant is reasonable since NRC feared that such intervention would likely serve as a dilatory tactic and an abuse of hearing process).

118. *See* Baros v. Tex. Mex. Ry. Co., 400 F.3d 228, 238 (5th Cir. 2005) ("By failing affirmatively to act to protect their interests by intervening in the agency proceedings, the landowners cannot now advance their claims in a collateral action that necessarily challenges several agency decisions and orders as being issued after the agency's jurisdiction over the line terminated."); Village of Bensenville v. FAA, 457 F.3d 52 61 (D.C. Cir. 2006).

119. A pre-APA case states that intervenors deserved full rights of participation including cross-examination. FCC v. Nat'l Broad. Co., 319 U.S. 239, 244–45 (1943). This decision would probably not be followed under the APA.

120. *See United Church of Christ*, 359 F.2d at 1005–06; *Nichols*, 835 F.2d at 898–99 (emphasizing that trial-type proceedings are not always required for intervenors).

a hearing.[121] However, admission of an intervenor often has exactly this effect, since the agency may have proposed to grant a license to an applicant without any hearing at all.[122] Note also that a party may still be entitled to "appear" and present evidence without being admitted as a party if consistent with the orderly conduct of public business."[123]

4.055 Timeliness of motion to intervene

A petition for intervention must be timely.[124] The timeliness rule in administrative proceedings is similar to Rule 24(a) of the Federal Rules of Civil Procedure.[125] Courts will, however, defer to an agency's discretion in granting a late-filed petition for intervention when there is good cause for the failure to file on time.[126]

4.06 PREJUDICIAL ERROR IN PRE-HEARING AGENCY PROCEEDINGS

APA § 706 requires that, on judicial review, "due account shall be taken of the rule of prejudicial error." This requirement operates most often to excuse minor procedural errors that are not likely to have affected the outcome of the proceeding. Because of this, agency pre-hearing procedural errors are ordinarily grounds for reversal on judicial review only if they actually harm the subject of the agency hearing.[127] Reviewing courts may not presume prejudice.[128] The Supreme Court has held that the

---

121. Vinson v. Wash. Gas Light Co., 321 U.S. 489, 498 (1944).
122. *See, e.g., United Church of Christ*, 359 F.2d at 1008; Dellums v. NRC, 863 F.2d 968 (D.C. Cir. 1988).
123. APA § 555(b).
124. Consolidated Edison Co. v. Breznay, 873 F.2d 301, 307 (Temp. Emer. Ct. App. 1989).
125. *Id.* at 309–10.
126. Citizens for Fair Utility Regulation v. NRC, 898 F.2d 51, 54 (5th Cir. 1990), *cert. denied*, 498 U.S. 896 (1990).
127. *See* Rajah v. Mukasey, 544 F.3d 427, 446 (2d Cir. 2008) ("We hold that pre-hearing regulatory violations are not grounds for termination, absent prejudice that may have affected the outcome of the proceeding, conscience-shocking conduct, or a deprivation of fundamental rights.").
128. Shinseki v. Sanders, 556 U.S. 396, 407–08 (2009). The APA and the statute governing review of veterans' benefits decisions at issue in *Sanders* contain identical requirements that reviewing courts "take due account of the rule of prejudicial error." APA § 706; 38 U.S.C § 7261(b)(2).

standard for establishing prejudice in the administrative law context is the same standard that applies in civil proceedings generally: The party seeking to overturn the agency's decision must establish that, under all the facts and circumstances, the error caused harm in the sense that the error affected the outcome of the proceeding or prevented the party from adequately preparing for the proceeding.[129] The Court has also ruled out the use of other devices that would shift the burden to the agency to show that the error was not prejudicial.[130]

---

129. *Sanders*, 556 U.S. at 407–08.
130. *Id.* at 408–09.

Chapter 5

HEARING REQUIREMENTS

5.01 SUMMARY OF BASIC REQUIREMENTS[1]

Most of the requirements for formal adjudicatory agency hearings[2] are outlined in Section 556 of the APA. These requirements include the following: One or more of the agency heads or an administrative law judge (ALJ) must preside. (§ 5.02) Formal agency adjudicatory hearings are normally required to be open to the public.[3] (§ 5.03) The proponent of a rule or order has the burden of proof, and decisions must be supported by reliable, probative, and substantial evidence. (§ 5.04) Unless specified otherwise by statute or rule, the standard of proof in agency adjudicatory hearings is the familiar preponderance of the evidence standard. (§ 5.04) The Federal Rules of Evidence do not apply in agency hearings, and presiding officers have discretion to admit evidence that would be inadmissible in court, as long as it is probative and its admission is not fundamentally unfair. (§ 5.05) Agencies may take official notice of matters not introduced as evidence.[4] (§ 5.06) Parties to agency hearings and witnesses compelled to appear before an agency have the right to be accompanied by and represented by counsel.[5] (§ 5.07) Parties are generally entitled to present their case by oral or documentary evidence, as well as to submit rebuttal evidence and conduct cross-examination, although absent a contrary rule, the presiding officer has discretion to limit hearings to paper presentations only on a finding that an oral hearing is unnecessary to adequately develop the facts. (§ 5.08)

While Section 556 provides a general outline for the hearing process, it also contemplates that agencies themselves will establish many of the particulars of that process.[6] Consequently, actual agency practices vary considerably.

---

1. *See generally* MORELL E. MULLINS, MANUAL FOR ADMINISTRATIVE LAW JUDGES (Interim Internet ed.), *supra* Chapter 4, note 51 at 70–103, which discusses a large number of issues arising in the conduct of hearings, seen from the perspective of the ALJ and citing numerous agency procedural regulations.
2. *See* Chapter 3, § 3.01 for discussion of when the APA formal adjudication requirements apply. *See* Chapter 7 for discussion of important requirements relating to the integrity of agency hearings including separation of functions within agencies and ex parte contacts in agency hearings.
3. This requirement is not directly stated in the APA but is implied from provisions prohibiting ex parte contacts and constitutional principles.
4. The exclusive record requirement is discussed in Chapter 7, § 7.08.
5. This requirement is contained in APA § 555(b).
6. *See* APA § 556(c) ("Subject to published rules of the agency and within its powers, employees presiding at hearings may. . . ."); APA § 556(c)(11)

5.02 ADJUDICATORY STRUCTURE

One or more of the agency heads or an ALJ must preside over the hearing. APA § 556(b). APA § 556(c) specifies the powers of the presiding officer, including the power to administer oaths, regulate the course of the hearing, issue subpoenas, take depositions, hold settlement conferences, rule on procedural matters, encourage alternate dispute resolution, and take other action authorized by agency rule. The presiding officer is required to conduct the hearing in an impartial manner, and may disqualify himself or herself on a showing of personal bias "or other disqualification" as determined by the agency. APA § 556(b). Absent countervailing constitutional constraints such as the requirements of due process, Congress enjoys the power to prescribe rules of procedure governing hearings before federal agencies.[7]

5.03 OPENNESS

As a general matter, agencies are required to open their hearings to the public. Even in immigration cases, where the government has enormous power, the First Amendment provides the public and the press a right of access to administrative hearings.[8] The public's right of access applies to adversarial administrative cases akin to judicial proceedings, but possibly not to nonadversarial proceedings such as Social Security cases. The right of access also might not apply to cases in which there is no tradition of public access, and such access would play no significant positive role in the functioning of the process in question.[9] In addition to the public's First Amendment right of access, there is authority that a

---

(presiding officers may "take other action authorized by agency rule consistent with this subchapter").

7. *See, e.g.,* Steadman v. SEC, 450 U.S. 91, 95–96 (1981); Vance v. Terrazas, 444 U.S. 252, 265 (1980).

8. This principle was tested by the "Creppy Directive," issued as part of the reaction to the attacks of Sept. 11, 2001, which included a blanket order to close all so-called "special interest" deportation hearings. The Creppy Directive was held to violate the First Amendment right of access in Detroit Free Press v. Ashcroft, 303 F.3d 681 (6th Cir. 2002). However, the Third Circuit disagreed with this conclusion, finding that there was an insufficient tradition of openness in deportation hearings to support a First Amendment right of access. *See* N. Jersey Media Grp., Inc. v. Ashcroft, 308 F.3d 198 (3d Cir. 2002).

9. *See* United States v. Miami Univ., 294 F.3d 797 (6th Cir. 2002) (no public right of access to university disciplinary hearings).

private party has a due process right to compel the agency to open a hearing to the public, but this authority seems somewhat outdated.[10] A related provision is the APA's prohibition on ex parte communications. If such communications are not disclosed, they would obviously undercut the benefits of an open hearing.[11]

Where the right of access applies, an agency is permitted to close a hearing only if it can establish a compelling interest in doing so[12] and if the denial is narrowly tailored to serve that interest. The decision to close the hearing must be supported by findings sufficiently specific that a reviewing court can determine whether the closure order was properly entered.[13]

Notwithstanding the general policy favoring public hearings, courts have held that agencies may close hearings on a case-by-case basis to protect investigative sources and witnesses[14] or to protect witnesses, parties, or spectators.[15] However, the closure order must be narrowly tailored to protect such interests and must be supported by specific findings.[16]

In some cases, a private party (rather than the agency) may wish to close a hearing in order to protect the safety of the party or the witnesses or to safeguard trade secrets. The agency enjoys broad discretion

---

10. *See* Fitzgerald v. Hampton, 467 F.2d 755, 764–66 (D.C. Cir. 1972); Garvey v. Freeman, 397 F.2d 600, 612 (10th Cir. 1968). This authority predates *Mathews v. Eldridge*, discussed in Chapter 2, § 2.04, which calls for contextual balancing to determine the requirements of due process and prevents categorical statements about the requirements of due process. *See also* Morgan v. United States, 304 U.S. 1 (1938) (rudimentary requirements of fair play demand a "fair and open hearing").

11. *See* APA § 557(d); Chapter 7, § 7.04.

12. In *Detroit Free Press*, 303 F.3d at 705–07, the court accepted the government's submission as a compelling interest for secrecy. The government was concerned that open hearings could result in disclosure of investigative information that would jeopardize the struggle against terrorism.

13. In *Detroit Free Press*, 303 F.3d at 710, the court held that the need for secrecy must be established on a case-by-case basis, with specific findings by the immigration judge in each case. Therefore, it rejected the Creppy Directive's blanket closure of all "special interest" proceedings.

14. *Detroit Free Press*, 303 F.3d at 705–07.

15. *See, e.g.,* United States *ex rel.* Lloyd v. Vincent, 520 F.2d 1272, 1274 (2d Cir), *cert. denied*, 423 U.S. 937 (1975).

16. *Detroit Free Press*, 303 F.3d at 707; Pechter v. Lyons, 441 F. Supp. 115, 119–20 (S.D.N.Y. 1977).

in deciding whether to honor this request,[17] but a court can find that such discretion has been abused.[18]

Illustrations:

1. Agency decides federal government contract disputes. It adopts regulations closing all of its hearings to the public in order to protect the government from disclosure of valuable proprietary information. This regulation is invalid because it violates the First Amendment right of the press and public to have access to agency hearings. Particular hearings (or parts thereof) could be closed to the public upon a showing that the government would be harmed by disclosure of particular information involved in the case, but Agency must make specific findings in support of the closure order.

2. Agency holds a hearing concerning allocation of mining rights. A party seeking such rights asks Agency to close the hearing, alleging that an open hearing would allow its competitors to acquire sensitive business information. However, it fails to make a specific showing of precisely how it might be injured by the sort of information that would be disclosed during the hearing. Agency refuses to close the hearing. A court would probably find that this decision was not an abuse of discretion.

---

17. *See, e.g.,* FCC v. Schreiber, 381 U.S. 279 (1965), which upheld the FCC's decision refusing to close an investigatory hearing despite claims by witnesses that confidential business information might be disclosed. The Court referred to the FCC's broad discretion to decide on its own procedures, but it also referred to the general policy favoring disclosure of administrative agency proceedings. *Id.* at 293.
18. *See, e.g., Pechter,* 441 F. Supp. at 117–18, in which an immigration judge wanted to close a hearing in a deportation case to protect the deportee from the public. The court held that this decision would be an abuse of discretion since the agency could take appropriate security protections during the hearing.

5.04 BURDEN OF PROOF

5.041 General rule

APA § 556(d) allocates the burden of proof to the proponent of an order.[19] In operation, this may mean that a private party carries the burden, or instead that the government does, depending on the context. For example, applicants for a government benefit bear the burden of establishing entitlement to the benefit,[20] while an agency seeking to impose sanctions on a private party for violating a regulatory requirement bears the burden of establishing the private party's guilt.[21] In licensing proceedings, the applicant bears the burden of proof.[22] Agencies may, consistent with Section 556(d), establish rebuttable presumptions so long as the ultimate burden of persuasion remains with the proponent of the agency order.[23] Further, while the proponent bears the burden of proof on the final determination of a controversy, the other party might bear the burden with regard to other nondispositive orders or affirmative defenses.[24]

---

19. APA § 556(d) states: "Except as otherwise provided by statute, the proponent of a rule or order has the burden of proof."
20. *See, e.g.,* Dir., Office of Workers' Comp. Programs v. Greenwich Collieries, 512 U.S. 267, 272 (1994); Kerner v. Fleming, 283 F.2d 916, 921–22 (2d Cir. 1960). In *Greenwich Collieries,* the Supreme Court invalidated the agency's "true doubt" rule under which claimant would prevail when there was a "true doubt" as to the claimant's entitlement. When the evidence is weighted toward one side or the other, *Greenwich Collieries* is irrelevant. *See* Grynberg Petroleum Co. v. Salazar, No. 07-CV-02440-MSK-KMT, 2011 WL 940819 at *4 (D. Colo. Mar. 16, 2011) ("the rule becomes unnecessary where one side's evidence is stronger than the other's, even by a small amount").
21. *See, e.g.,* NVE, Inc. v. Dep't of Health & Human Servs., 436 F.3d 182 (3d Cir. 2006); Rice v. NTSB., 745 F.2d 1037, 1039 (6th Cir. 1984); Norris v. FTC, 598 F.2d 1244, 1247 (2d Cir. 1979).
22. Citizens Awareness Network, Inc. v. United States, 391 F.3d 338 (1st Cir. 2004).
23. Cablevision Sys. Corp. v. FCC, 649 F.3d 695 (D.C. Cir. 2011).
24. NLRB v. Transp. Mgmt. Corp., 462 U.S. 393 (1983). *See also Greenwich Collieries,* 512 U.S. at 278 (specifically characterizing *Transp. Mgmt. Corp.* as holding that an agency may, consistent with § 556(d), place the burden on a nonmoving party when that party offers an affirmative defense). *See also* Smithsfork Grazing Ass'n v. Salazar, 564 F.3d 1210 (10th Cir. 2009) (applicant for grazing permit bears burden of proof on petition for stay even assuming agency bears burden on grazing permit order); Barscz v. Dir., Office of Workers' Comp. Programs, 486 F.3d 744, 752–53 (2d Cir.

5.042 Alternative allocation of burden of proof

Section 556 specifically provides that the default rule concerning the burden of proof may be allocated otherwise by statute.[25] The burden may also be altered by agency regulation, *if* an agency possesses statutory authority to so alter it. In such a case, the burden of proof would not be otherwise prescribed "by statute," but the statute would authorize the agency to provide for a different allocation.[26] Moreover, Section 556 itself does not preclude an agency from placing the burden of proof on a party who is not the proponent of an order for the purposes of deciding on that party's affirmative defense.

Illustration:

3. Agency holds eligibility hearing for a public benefit. The burden of persuasion is not specifically allocated by Agency's regulations. The party seeking the benefit has the burden of persuasion.

5.043 Burden of proof: Burden of persuasion versus burden of production

While Section 556 refers to the "burden of proof," the APA fails to define the term. Traditionally, courts distinguish between the burden of persuasion and the burden of production, although the term "burden of proof" is often used loosely to encompass both. In *Director, Office of Workers' Compensation Programs v. Greenwich Collieries,*[27] the Court defined "burden of proof" for the purposes of the APA as the burden of persuasion, distinguishing it from the burden of production. In reaching this conclusion, the Court explicitly departed from the contrary conclusion reached in *NLRB v. Transportation Management Corp.,*[28] as well as lower court cases holding that "burden of proof" in Section 556(d) refers only to

---

2007) (defense has burden to establish set-off for compensation paid in other proceeding).

25. *See supra* note 19. *See, e.g.,* Hazardous Waste Treatment Council v. EPA, 886 F.2d 355, 366 (D.C. Cir. 1989).

26. *See, e.g.,* Amax Coal Co. v. Dir., Office of Workers' Comp. Programs, 312 F.3d 882 (7th Cir. 2002) (because governing statute incorporates APA "except as otherwise provided . . . by regulations of the Secretary" of Labor, agency has authority to reallocate burden of proof).

27. 512 U.S. 267, 276 (1994).

28. 462 U.S. 393 (1983).

the burden of production.[29] It does not violate *Greenwich Collieries* to alter the burden of production as long as the burden of proof (or persuasion) remains with the proponent of the order.[30]

The "burden of persuasion" indicates which party must satisfy the decisionmaker in order to prevail on a given issue. In contrast, the "burden of production," sometimes also called the "burden of going forward with evidence," refers to which party must initially come forward with evidence on an issue. While these distinct burdens are often borne by the same party, at times one party may have the responsibility to come forward with evidence concerning some issue (burden of production) while the other party maintains the responsibility to satisfy the decisionmaker with respect to that issue (burden of persuasion).

Some statutes provide for a burden-shifting procedure under which production of evidence by the proponent of an order shifts the burden to the other party to rebut that evidence. If the second party successfully rebuts the evidence, the ultimate burden of persuasion may shift back to the proponent of the order.[31]

Illustration:

4. Agency issues rule according to which a claimant for workers' compensation will prevail on the claim if the evidence in support of the claim is in equipoise with evidence in opposition to the claim. The rule requires the claimant to introduce evidence in support of the claim, but then effectively shifts the burden of persuasion to Agency by requiring Agency to produce evidence

29. *See, e.g.*, Envtl. Def. Fund v. EPA, 548 F.2d 998 (D.C. Cir. 1976), *cert. denied*, 431 U.S. 925 (1977). The Court chose to ignore fairly explicit legislative history that contradicted its holding. *Greenwich Collieries*, 512 U.S. at 280. For criticism of *Greenwich Collieries*, *see* Peter Strauss, *Changing Times: The APA at Fifty*, 63 U. Chi. L. Rev. 1389, 1413–20 (1996).
30. Nat'l Mining Ass'n v. Dep't of Labor, 292 F.3d 849 (D.C. Cir. 2002).
31. *See, e.g.*, 33 U.S.C. § 920(a), a provision of the Longshore and Harbor Workers' Compensation Act, which requires the employer to produce substantial evidence that a worker's injury was not job-related if the worker produces evidence that he or she was injured in the course of employment. The ultimate burden of persuasion of entitlement to benefits remains with the employee. *See* Albina Engine & Mach. v. Dir., Office of Workers' Comp. Programs, 627 F.3d 1293 (9th Cir. 2010). *See also* Sunbridge Care & Rehab. for Prembroke v. Leavitt, 340 F. App'x 929 (4th Cir. 2009) (Department of Health and Human Services burden-shifting rules apply only when evidence is in equipoise).

against the claim that outweighs claimant's evidence. Under *Greenwich Collieries*, the Agency rule is inconsistent with the APA.

5.044 Standard or degree of proof

Another important distinction is between the "burden of proof," on the one hand, and the "standard of proof" or "degree of proof" on the other, although here again sometimes "burden of proof" is used imprecisely to refer to both.[32] The "standard" or "degree" of proof concerns the quantum of proof that the party who has the burden of persuasion must produce to prevail. Thus in criminal cases the state bears the burden of persuasion, while the standard (or degree) of proof is "beyond a reasonable doubt." Similarly in civil cases the plaintiff normally bears the burden of persuasion and the standard of proof normally is "by a preponderance of the evidence."

In cases of formal adjudication under the APA, the default standard of proof required is "by a preponderance of the evidence."[33] This standard means that the proponent must establish that it is more likely than not that the facts they seek to establish are true. The standard is higher than the "substantial evidence" standard used by a court that is judicially reviewing an agency decision[34] but lower than the "clear and convincing" standard sometimes used in civil cases when a party seeks to prove fraud.[35] Normally, preponderance of the evidence is also the standard of proof in informal adjudication,[36] but, in some situations involving

---

32. *See Greenwich Collieries*, 512 U.S. at 277–78.
33. Steadman v. SEC, 450 U.S. 91 (1981) (violation of antifraud provisions of federal securities law). *Steadman* relies heavily on the legislative history of APA § 556(d). *Id.* at 100–01, citing H. Judiciary Comm., Legislative History of the Administrative Procedure Act 271 (1946). The APA's legislative history is compiled in S. Doc. No. 248, 79th Cong., 2d Sess. (1946). The Court in *Steadman* found no reason to doubt Congress's constitutional power to prescribe the "preponderance" standard even in an area in which a common law court might apply a higher standard.
34. *Steadman*, 450 U.S. at 98–100.
35. *See* Herman & McLean v. Huddleston, 459 U.S. 375, 387–91 (1983) (requiring preponderance standard to be used in district court securities fraud cases even though clear and convincing standard is used in common law fraud cases).
36. Bender v. Clark, 744 F.2d 1424, 1429–30 (10th Cir. 1984).

unusually important rights or serious hardship, courts have mandated a standard more demanding than preponderance.[37]

Illustration:

> 5. Agency brings disciplinary proceeding under APA against Broker for committing securities fraud and seeks to suspend Broker's license for three years. Despite the seriousness of the sanction and the fact that courts have traditionally insisted on a clear and convincing standard of proof in fraud cases, Agency need only establish its case by a preponderance of the evidence.[38]

5.05 RULES OF EVIDENCE

5.051 Inapplicability of Federal Rules of Evidence

APA § 556 contains three specific references to evidence. First, Section 556(c)(3) states that the agency employees presiding over a hearing may "receive relevant evidence." Second, Section 556(d) provides that an agency "shall provide for the exclusion of irrelevant, immaterial, or unduly repetitious evidence." Section 556(d) also requires that an agency hearing decisions be "supported by and in accordance with the reliable, probative, and substantial evidence."

Agencies are not bound by the Federal Rules of Evidence.[39] Agency decisionmakers do not require the same cognitive protections that the

---

37. *See* Woodby v. INS, 385 U.S. 276, 285 (1966) in which the Court requires proof by clear, unequivocal and convincing evidence in a denaturalization proceeding. *Woodby* was distinguished in *Steadman*, 450 U.S. at 102 n.22.

38. *Steadman*, 450 U.S. at 91.

39. *See, e.g.*, R&B Transp., LLC v. U.S. Dept. of Labor, 618 F.3d 37 (1st Cir. 2010) (agencies not bound by Federal Rules of Evidence and have broad discretion over the admission of evidence in agency hearings); FTC v. Cement Inst., 333 U.S. 683, 705 (1948) ("[A]dministrative agencies like the Federal Trade Commission have never been restricted by the rigid rules of evidence"); Villegas-Valenzuela v. INS, 103 F.3d 805, 812 (9th Cir. 1996) (noting "well-settled rule that agencies are not bound by strict rules of evidence" in APA cases); Swift & Co. v. United States, 308 F.2d 849, 851–52 (7th Cir. 1962) (noting examples of circuit precedent that demonstrates rules of evidence do not apply to agency hearings). Regulations may require some agencies to apply the Federal Rules of Evidence to their proceedings. *See, e.g.*, 37 C.F.R. § 41.152 (applying Federal Rules of Evi-

rules of evidence afford to lay jurors. Norms of agency expertise and autonomy thus justify an agency's decision to depart from those rules.[40] Indeed, the turn toward using agency decisionmakers in place of courts may be due partly to a congressional preference to escape from the rigidity of the rules of evidence.[41] In any event,

> the reason these [Federal Rules of Evidence] are not applicable to agencies is that being staffed by specialists the agencies are assumed to be less in need of evidentiary blinders than lay jurors or even professional, though usually unspecialized, judges. Evidence that might merely confuse a lay fact-finder may be essential to the exercise of expert judgment by a specialized professional adjudicator.[42]

Subject to the requirements of due process, an agency has discretion to accept into evidence whatever the agency sees fit, provided that the evidence is "probative" and its admission is consistent with "fundamental fairness."[43] In operation, this means that an agency's decision to accept any evidence the agency deems appropriate is limited only by an "abuse of discretion" standard of judicial review.[44] Agencies are also free to create their own rules of evidence, subject to consistency with the APA, other

---

dence to contested proceedings before the Patent and Trademark Office); Brand v. Miller, 487 F.3d 862 (Fed. Cir. 2007) (discussing same).

40. *See, e.g.,* Donovan v. Sarasota Concrete Co., 693 F.2d 1061, 1066 (11th Cir. 1982).

41. *See* Oceanic Fisheries Co. v. Alaska Indus. Bd., 109 F. Supp. 103, 104–05 (D. Alaska 1953).

42. Peabody Coal Co. v. Dir., Office of Workers' Comp. Program, 165 F.3d 1126, 1129 (7th Cir. 1999). *See also* Gunderson v. U.S. Dep't of Labor, 601 F.3d 1013 (10th Cir. 2010) (agency expertise reduces need for rigid rules of evidence).

43. *See* Martin-Mendoza v. INS, 499 F.2d 918 (9th Cir. 1974), *cert. denied*, 419 U.S. 113 (1975) (hearsay evidence not governed by conventional rules, but rather admissible so long as probative and fundamentally fair).

44. *See, e.g.,* Ala. Ass'n of Ins. Agency v. Bd. of Governors of Fed. Res., 533 F.2d 224 (5th Cir. 1976), *vacated in part on other grounds*, 558 F.2d 729 (1977), *cert. denied*, 435 U.S. 904 (1978) (agency enjoys discretion in determining whether to admit expert evidence, bounded by requirement that exercise of that discretion is not arbitrary). In Steadman v. SEC, 450 U.S. 91, 98 n.17 (1981), the Supreme Court indicated that the words "reliable, probative and substantial" in § 556(d) set minimum quality of evidence standards, but it did not give content to the meaning of those terms.

relevant statutes, and the general requirement that agency action not be arbitrary, capricious, or an abuse of discretion.[45]

Since agencies are not bound by the Federal Rules, they are not required to follow Supreme Court cases that preclude the admissibility of scientific or other expert evidence that fails to meet standards of general acceptability in the scientific community.[46] Nevertheless, agencies are not permitted to follow irrational evidentiary rules.[47]

Illustration:

6. Company challenges the validity of Agency's order on the ground that the evidence supporting it was not substantial. Company argues that while considerable evidence supports the order, that evidence should be heavily discounted because little of it would have been admissible under the rules of evidence in court. Agency order will survive the challenge.

5.052 Hearsay evidence

An agency may allow the admission of evidence that would constitute inadmissible hearsay under the Federal Rules of Evidence, assigning whatever evidentiary weight to that evidence the agency deems appropriate.[48] However, hearsay should not be admitted if it does not satisfy

---

45. *See* Yaman v. U.S. Dep't of State, 634 F.3d 610 (D.C. Cir. 2010) (formal rules of evidence do not apply to agency proceedings, but presiding officer may regulate evidence to ensure relevance, materiality, and competence).

46. *See* Peabody Coal Co. v. McCandless, 255 F.3d 465, 468–69 (7th Cir. 2001), holding that Supreme Court cases relating to expert testimony and based on the Federal Rules of Evidence need not be followed by agencies. The Supreme Court cases are Daubert v. Merrell Dow Pharm., Inc., 509 U.S. 579 (1993) (trial court must determine reliability of scientific evidence); Kumho Tire Co. v. Carmichael, 526 U.S. 137 (1999) (same for nonscientific expert testimony). Nevertheless, expert testimony which would not be admissible in court under the Daubert standard might not meet the test of "reliability" required by APA § 556(d).

47. *Peabody Coal Co.*, 255 F.3d at 469–70 (overturning agency decision that analysis of physician performing autopsy is always preferred over analysis of physicians analyzing tissue slides from autopsy).

48. *See, e.g.,* Richardson v. Perales, 402 U.S. 389, 409–10 (1971) (hearsay under APA is admissible up to the point of relevancy); Bennett v. NTSB, 66 F.3d 1130, 1137 (10th Cir. 1995); Gray v. USDA, 39 F.3d 670 (6th Cir. 1994); Veg-Mix, Inc. v. USDA, 832 F.2d 601 (D.C. Cir. 1987).

the APA's requirement that it be "reliable" or "probative" or if it violates an agency's own evidentiary rule.[49] Among the factors courts consider in deciding whether the agency abused its discretion in admitting a particular item of hearsay evidence are whether the out-of-court declarant was biased, whether the opposing party could have obtained the information before the hearing and could have subpoenaed the declarant, whether the hearsay was in the form of a sworn affidavit (as opposed to anonymous, oral, or unsworn), whether the information was inconsistent on its face or contradicted by direct testimony, whether it was corroborated, whether the declarant or the witness testifying to the hearsay is credible, and whether the information was of the sort that has been recognized by courts as inherently reliable.[50]

Although agencies have broad discretion to admit hearsay evidence, there are instances in which the admission of hearsay might violate due process. The problem is that hearsay evidence, by definition, precludes confrontation and cross-examination of the out-of-court declarant.[51] This result is particularly likely if the evidence does not fall into an established exception to the hearsay rule and credibility issues are critical, if the declarant could have been subpoenaed to appear at the hearing, and if the private party makes a timely request that the declarant be subpoenaed.[52]

Nor are federal agencies bound by the "residuum rule," which in some states precludes agency decisions supported exclusively by

---

49. *See* § 5.051. For cases approving hearsay in agency proceedings, *see* R&B Transp., LLC v. U.S. Dep't of Labor, 618 F.3d 37 (1st Cir. 2010); Robinson v. U.S. Dep't of Labor, 406 F. App'x 69 (7th Cir. 2010).

50. Echostar Commc'ns Corp. v. FCC, 292 F.3d 749 (D.C. Cir. 2002) (agency finding supported by strong affidavit); J.A.M. Builders v. Herman, 233 F.3d 1350, 1354 (11th Cir. 2000); Calhoun v. Bailar, 626 F.2d 145, 149 (9th Cir. 1980), *cert. denied*, 452 U.S. 906 (1981).

51. *See, e.g.*, Lilly v. Virginia, 527 U.S. 116, 124–25 (1999) (hearsay statements admissible in criminal case only if they fall within a firmly rooted hearsay exception or contain particularized guarantees of trustworthiness).

52. *See, e.g.*, Olabanji v. INS, 973 F.2d 1232 (5th Cir. 1992). In this case, the INS ordered Olabanji to be deported because it found that his marriage to Raines (a U.S. citizen) was a sham. It relied on an affidavit by Seeber, who had interviewed Raines. The court held that this procedure violated due process, since the INS could have subpoenaed Raines to testify at the hearing and be subject to cross-examination, but had not done so. The INS could rely on Seeber's affidavit only if it could show that, despite reasonable efforts, it could not have secured Raines's presence.

hearsay evidence.[53] However, courts reviewing agency decisions may find occasionally that decisions supported largely or exclusively by hearsay evidence that the court finds to be of particularly low quality are not supported by "substantial evidence" on the "whole record."[54]

Illustration:

7. Agency revokes employee F's security clearance because it charged that she posted classified information in an area open to persons lacking security clearance. The only evidence that the information was in fact classified came from a statement by employee G that had been taken by Agency's investigator. However, G was unavailable at the time of the hearing and the investigator was not called as a witness. F denied under oath that the information was classified. She also explained that she and G had a strong professional rivalry and disliked each other. Agency is entitled to admit hearsay evidence, but a court could hold that Agency's decision in this case was not supported by substantial evidence.[55]

5.053 What evidentiary rules do apply

Subject to the requirements of APA § 556 and of due process, agencies may prescribe their own rules of evidence.[56] This possibility is contemplated by Section 556(c). When identifying the constraints on agency-prescribed rules of evidence, courts have looked to the language

---

53. *Richardson*, 402 U.S. at 407–08 (Social Security decision based on hearsay evidence was supported by substantial evidence).
54. APA § 706(2)(E). *See, e.g.*, Hoska v. Dep't of Army, 677 F.2d 131, 138–42 (D.C. Cir. 1982). This is a principle of long standing. *See* Consol. Edison Co. v. NLRB, 305 U.S. 197, 230 (1938) ("mere uncorroborated hearsay or rumor does not constitute substantial evidence").
55. *Hoska*, 677 F.2d at 138–42.
56. *See, e.g.*, Elm Grove Coal Co. v. Dir., Office of Workers' Comp. Programs, 480 F.3d 278 (4th Cir. 2007) (upholding agency's evidence-limiting rule as consistent with APA and agency's own statute); *In re* Epstein, 32 F.3d 1559, 1565 (D.C. Cir. 1994).

of Section 556 itself,[57] as well as to the dictates of due process.[58] Beyond these limitations, courts cannot impose additional procedural requirements upon adjudicating agencies.[59] Some agencies, such as the National Labor Relations Board, are required by statute to employ the Federal Rules "so far as practicable,"[60] and other agencies have adopted procedural regulations mandating use of the Federal Rules.[61]

Even though agency adjudications are not governed by the Federal Rules as a general matter, the attorney-client privilege and like privileges may be asserted in connection with agency adjudication.[62]

---

57. *See, e.g.*, U.S. Steel Mining Co. v. Dir., Office of Workers' Comp. Programs, 187 F.3d 384, 388–89 (4th Cir. 1999) (agencies have an affirmative duty to qualify evidence as "reliable, probative, and substantial" before relying upon it); Gallagher v. NTSB, 953 F.2d 1214, 1217 (10th Cir. 1992) (agency may consider any evidence that is not "irrelevant, immaterial, or unduly repetitious").

58. *See, e.g.*, Nat'l Wildlife Fed'n v. Marsh, 568 F. Supp. 985, 992–93 (D.D.C. 1983) (APA allows agencies to fashion rules governing hearing process, but courts will ensure that due process is satisfied); Cunanan v. INS, 856 F.2d 1373, 1374 (9th Cir. 1988) (though not governed by strict rules of evidence, agency proceedings must nevertheless afford due process).

59. Vt. Yankee Nuclear Power Corp. v. NRDC, 435 U.S. 519 (1978) (courts cannot impose procedural requirements above those found in the APA); Pension Benefit Guar. Corp. v. LTV Corp., 496 U.S. 633 (1990) (applying *Vt. Yankee* to adjudications). By the same token, the APA does not excuse procedural requirements found in other statutes. *See, e.g.*, Seacoast Anti-Pollution League v. Costle, 572 F.2d 872, 879 (1st Cir. 1978), *overruled on other grounds by* Dominion Energy Brayton Point v. Johnson, 443 F.3d 12 (1st Cir. 2006) (*see* Chapter 3, § 3.01).

60. *See* 29 U.S.C. § 160(b).

61. *See* 29 C.F.R. § 2200.71 (Occupational Safety and Health Review Comm'n). The Administrative Conference criticized such statutes and regulations. ACUS Recommendation 86-2, 51 Fed. Reg. 25,642 (1986). *See generally* Richard J. Pierce, Jr., *Use of the Federal Rules of Evidence in Federal Agency Adjudications*, 39 Admin. L. Rev. 1 (1987) (surveying agency evidentiary rules and finding that of 280 total regulations governing evidentiary decisionmaking by agencies, 243 make no mention of the Federal Rules of Evidence, while 37 make at least some reference to the Rules).

62. *See, e.g.*, Upjohn Co. v. United States, 449 U.S. 383 (1981) (allowing both attorney-client and work-product privileges in administrative proceedings); SEC v. Lavin, 111 F.3d 921 (D.C. Cir. 1997) (recognizing marital communications privilege).

5.06 OFFICIAL NOTICE

An agency may take "official notice" of both "legislative" and "adjudicative" facts, thus dispensing with the need to introduce testimony to establish such facts.[63] An agency's power to take official notice is considerably broader than a court's power to take judicial notice.[64]

Where an agency's decision rests on a material and disputable fact of which the agency has taken official notice, a party is entitled to an opportunity to demonstrate the contrary.[65] Agencies enjoy discretion concerning the appropriate method of rebuttal in light of all relevant circumstances.[66]

5.07 RIGHT TO COUNSEL[67]

5.071 APA provisions providing right to counsel

Section 555(b) of the APA contains two provisions relating to the right to counsel. These provisions are applicable to both formal and informal

---

63. APA § 556(e) provides, "When an agency decision rests on official notice of a material fact not appearing in the evidence in the record, a party is entitled, on timely request, to an opportunity to show the contrary." *See* Ark. Dairy Co-op Ass'n, Inc. v. USDA, 573 F.3d 815 (D.C. Cir. 2009) (agency properly took official notice of pricing reports issued by USDA). *See generally* RICHARD J. PIERCE JR., ADMINISTRATIVE LAW TREATISE (5th ed. 2012) § 10.6 (providing extended analysis of official notice, its relationship to judicial notice, and the evolution of the distinction between adjudicative facts and legislative facts).

64. *See, e.g.,* Kapcia v. INS, 944 F.2d 702, 705 (10th Cir. 1991) (agency can take official notice of facts within its special technical or scientific competency).

65. APA § 556(e). *See also Kapcia*, 944 F.2d at 709 (fact officially noticed subject to rebuttal evidence); McCoy v. Schweiker, 683 F.2d 1138, 1146 (8th Cir. 1982) (same). *See also* Chapter 2, § 2.054 (Illustration 27 relating to due process and official notice).

66. *See* Rhoa-Zamora v. INS, 971 F.2d 26, 34 (7th Cir. 1992) (opportunity to rebut officially noticed facts can occur in the form of a motion to reopen the proceedings for further evidence). *But see* Castillo-Villagra v. INS, 972 F.2d 1017 (9th Cir. 1992) (agency must provide opportunity to respond at the time of hearing, not in motion to reopen).

67. In some circumstances, due process provides a right to counsel. *See generally* Chapter 2, § 2.05. This section concerns the right to counsel based on the APA.

adjudicatory proceedings. In addition, these provisions are applicable to investigative and pre-hearing stages of the proceeding as well as to the hearing stage.[68] First, a *person compelled to appear* before an agency is entitled to be represented by counsel.[69] This provision covers a witness as well as a party who is compelled to appear.[70] Second, a *party* is entitled to appear in person or by or with counsel.[71] The right to counsel includes the right to have counsel object to questions[72] and also to be accompanied by a nonlawyer technical expert in complex cases.[73] In addition, the person has a right to be represented by an "other qualified" nonlawyer representative, but only if permitted by the agency.[74]

---

68. APA § 555 is applicable to all adjudications; it is not limited to cases brought within the formal adjudication tent by § 554(a). *See* Chapter 3, § 3.01. The right to counsel applies in investigative hearings. FCC v. Schreiber, 329 F.2d 517, 535 (9th Cir. 1964), *modified on other grounds*, 381 U.S. 279 (1965).

69. APA § 555(b) provides: "A person compelled to appear in person before an agency or representative thereof is entitled to be accompanied, represented, and advised by counsel or, if permitted by the agency, by other qualified representative." Persons compelled to appear "are also entitled to have counsel act as their spokesman in argument and where otherwise appropriate." U.S. Dep't of Justice, *Attorney General's Manual on the Administrative Procedure Act* 61. However, the right is waivable. United States v. Weiner, 578 F.2d 757, 773–74 (9th Cir), *cert. denied*, 439 U.S. 981 (1978). *See* Roberts v. Harvey, 441 F. Supp. 2d 111 (D.D.C. 2006) (remand for hearing on claim that waiver of right to counsel was made under duress).

70. *Attorney General's Manual, supra* note 69, at 62; SEC v. Higashi, 359 F.2d 550, 553 (9th Cir. 1966) (holding that witnesses compelled to appear are entitled to counsel).

71. APA § 555(b) provides: "A party is entitled to appear in person or by or with counsel or other duly qualified representative in an agency proceeding." A party to a Social Security hearing must be made aware of his right to counsel and, if he chooses to proceed without counsel, must have knowingly and voluntarily waived counsel. Alvarez v. Bowen, 704 F. Supp. 49, 52 (1989). The terms "person" and "party" are defined in APA §§ 551(2), (3).

72. *Schreiber*, 329 F.2d at 535–38.

73. SEC v. Whitman, 613 F. Supp. 48, 49–50 (D.D.C. 1985) (investigated party has a right for his counsel to be accompanied by a nonlawyer accountant in technically complex SEC investigation).

74. *See* Sperry v. Florida, 373 U.S. 379, 396–97 (1963) (APA did not change prior practice of permitting nonlawyer representatives but permits agencies to decide whether or not to allow them). The Securities and Exchange

5.072 When there is no right to counsel

The right to counsel covers the personal appearance stage but not necessarily subsequent stages at which the private party is not required to be present.[75] Moreover, an agency can exclude an attorney if it has "concrete evidence" that the attorney's presence would obstruct or impede the agency's investigation.[76] An agency may not exclude a particular counsel unless it has good reason, such as contemptuous behavior by the attorney.[77] Agencies may, however, make reasonable rules of practice including rules regarding qualifications for practice before the agency.[78]

5.073 Effective counsel

The right to representation by counsel does not confer a right to "effective assistance" of counsel that is comparable to that arising in criminal cases.[79] However, where due process applies and would guarantee a right to counsel,[80] there may be cases in which ineffective representation by counsel might deny due process.[81] There are numerous immigration cases in which ineffective assistance of counsel is grounds for

---

Commission's rules prohibit nonlawyer representatives, but a nonlawyer expert may accompany counsel. *Whitman*, 613 F. Supp. at 50.

75. In IRS subpoena proceedings, the right to counsel applies to the production of documents, because the taxpayer is required to appear and produce the documents, but it does not extend to the IRS's subsequent examination of documents. United States v. McPhaul, 617 F. Supp. 58, 59–60 (W.D.N.C. 1985), *appeal dismissed*, 786 F.2d 1158 (4th Cir. 1986).

76. *See* Prof'l Reactor Operator Soc'y v. NRC, 939 F.2d 1047, 1051–52 (D.C. Cir. 1991) ("reasonable basis" to believe investigation would be obstructed by attorneys with a conflict of interest insufficient to meet "concrete evidence" standard); SEC v. Csapo, 533 F.2d 7, 11 (D.C. Cir. 1976) (SEC has no basis to sequester counsel solely because of multiple representation).

77. *See* Great Lakes Screw Corp. v. NLRB, 409 F.2d 375, 380–81 (7th Cir. 1969).

78. *See* Goldsmith v. Bd. of Tax Appeals, 270 U.S. 117, 122 (1926).

79. Sartain v. SEC, 601 F.2d 1366, 1375 (9th Cir. 1979) (although due process applied, SEC had no obligation to provide party with counsel or assure reasonably competent and effective counsel); Father & Sons Lumber & Bldg. Supplies, Inc. v. NLRB, 931 F.2d 1093, 1096–97 (6th Cir. 1991).

80. *See generally* Chapter 2, § 2.05.

81. If this proposition is valid, it is probably limited to deportation cases or comparable cases involving a severe deprivation of liberty. Lopez v. INS, 775 F.2d 1015, 1017 (9th Cir. 1985) (dictum—counsel's representation not ineffective); Paul v. INS, 521 F.2d 194, 198 (5th Cir. 1975) (same).

excusing a failure to meet a deadline for filing an appeal from an adverse determination.[82]

5.074 Hearings held without counsel—ALJ's duty to assist

An ALJ must take special care to ensure that a party without counsel is able to receive a fair hearing.[83] A reviewing court must determine whether the ALJ "adequately protect[ed] the rights of [a] pro se litigant by ensuring that all of the relevant facts [were] sufficiently developed and considered."[84] While the ALJ must ensure that the party is able to present its case adequately, a presentation equivalent to what a lawyer might have provided is not required.[85]

---

82. *See, e.g.,* Qamar v. Holder, 339 F. App'x 122 (2d Cir. 2009); Danu v. Ashcroft, 120 F. App'x 910 (3d Cir. 2005). These cases involve the failure of an attorney to notify the client in a timely fashion of an adverse determination and the deadline for filing an appeal.

83. Mullins, *supra* Chapter 4, note 51 at 78–80. For example, in Echevarria v. Sec'y of Health & Human Servs., 685 F.2d 751, 755 (2d Cir. 1982), the court stated that "[w]here, as here, the claimant is unrepresented by counsel, the ALJ is under a heightened duty 'to scrupulously and conscientiously probe into, inquire of, and explore for all the relevant facts.'"

84. Hankerson v. Harris, 636 F.2d 893, 895 (2d Cir. 1980). *See also* Moran v. Astrue, 569 F.3d 108 (2d Cir. 2009) (ALJ failed to adequately develop facts for pro se litigant in Social Security disability benefits case); Rease v. Barnhart, 422 F. Supp. 2d 1334 (N.D. Ga. 2006) (ALJ did not adequately assist pro se litigant in Social Security disability case; due process violated by failure to subpoena medical records); Koschnitzke v. Barnhart, 293 F. Supp. 2d 943 (E.D. Wis. 2003) (disability claimant entitled to fees in part because ALJ did not adequately assist in presenting case). One reason that there are so many cases in which Social Security claimants' rights to ALJ assistance are found to have been violated is that the Social Security Administration's obligations in this regard are spelled out very clearly in 20 C.F.R. § 404.1512(d).

85. *See* Evangelista v. Sec'y of Health & Human Servs., 826 F.2d 136, 143 (1st Cir. 1987). *See also* Lashley v. Sec'y of Health & Human Servs., 708 F.2d 1048 (6th Cir. 1983); Smith v. Harris, 644 F.2d 985, 989 (3d Cir. 1981).

5.08 ORAL VERSUS WRITTEN EVIDENCE

Parties to agency proceedings are generally entitled to present their cases orally with "live" presentation of evidence.[86] Nevertheless, the APA allows an agency to adopt procedures for submission of evidence in written rather than oral form in certain types of cases, provided that the party whose evidence takes written form "will not be prejudiced thereby."[87] The instances in which the agency can dispense with oral proceedings are formal rulemaking, determinations relating to claims for money or benefits, and applications for initial licenses.[88] In those cases, a party seeking to make an oral presentation of evidence must make a convincing detailed showing of why a written presentation would prejudice the party's case.[89]

---

86. "A party is entitled to present his case or defense by oral or documentary evidence, to submit rebuttal evidence, and to conduct such cross-examination as may be required for a full and true disclosure of the facts." APA § 556(d).

87. APA § 556(d), last sentence. According to the Attorney General's Manual, in cases in which oral proceedings can be dispensed with (such as claims for money or benefits, ratemaking, or initial licensing), "veracity and demeanor of witnesses are not important. It is difficult to *see* how any party's interests would be prejudiced by such [written] procedures where sufficient opportunity for rebuttal exists. However, 'to the extent that cross-examination is necessary to bring out the truth the party should have it.'" *Attorney General's Manual, supra* note 69, at 78 (quoting from APA legislative history). In Crestview Parke Care Ctr. v. Thompson, 373 F.3d 743 (6th Cir. 2004), the court approved an agency rule allowing for written submissions in certain circumstances but held that parties in the particular case were entitled to an oral hearing because they had not been notified in advance that their written submissions would be exclusive.

88. *See, e.g.*, Seacoast Anti-Pollution League v. Costle, 572 F.2d 872, 879 (1st Cir. 1978), stating: "The first point is whether the Administrator was empowered to require that the new evidence be submitted in written form. The Administrator may, under [APA §] 556(d), so require in cases of initial licensing. This is an initial licensing."

89. *See* Cunningham v. R.R. Ret. Bd., 392 F.3d 567 (3d Cir. 2004) (written submissions provided adequate opportunity to present case); California *ex rel.* Lockyer v. FERC, 329 F.3d 700 (9th Cir. 2003) (same); Darrell Andrews Trucking, Inc. v. Fed. Motor Carrier Safety Admin., 296 F.3d 1120 (D.C. Cir. 2002) (same).

Furthermore, a party who is otherwise entitled to an oral hearing must request a hearing in order to get one,[90] and in addition may have to make a threshold representation that a hearing is needed to resolve disputed issues of material fact.[91] If a previously adopted rule has foreclosed all factual issues, the party is not entitled to a hearing.[92] Finally, the right to an oral hearing covers the initial hearing of a case but not subsequent appeals within the agency.[93]

Illustration:

8. Broadcaster seeks a permit to acquire a television station. Agency denies the application. A relevant statute provides that a rejected applicant is entitled to an oral hearing on the record. Broadcaster's application is doomed to fail, however, because a valid agency regulation provides that no person can acquire more than five television stations and Broadcaster already owns five. As a hearing on the party's permit application would serve no purpose, the agency need not provide a hearing under Section 556.

5.09 CROSS-EXAMINATION

APA § 556(d) provides that a party is entitled "to conduct such cross-examination as may be required for a full and true disclosure of the facts." As a result, a party may be required to make a threshold showing that the party needs to cross-examine a witness in order to adequately

---

90. *See* Nat'l Indep. Coal Operators' Ass'n v. Kleppe, 423 U.S. 388, 397–98 (1976) (under statute that provided opportunity for public hearing, party had to request hearing to be entitled to it); AJA Assocs. v. Army Corps of Eng'rs., 817 F.2d 1070, 1074 (3d Cir. 1987) (party must request hearing and present reasons why hearing would be useful).

91. Weinberger v. Hynson, Westcott & Dunning, Inc., 412 U.S. 609, 622 (1973) (upholding administrative summary judgment); Costle v. Pac. Legal Found., 445 U.S. 198, 214 (1980) (party seeking hearing has threshold burden to show the need for a hearing; hearing can be dispensed with when there is no disputed issue of material fact).

92. *See, e.g.,* United States v. Storer Broad. Co. 351 U.S. 192, 205 (1956) (agency need not provide formal hearing when party seeking it is disqualified by regulations).

93. *See* Lonzollo v. Weinberger, 534 F.2d 712, 714 (7th Cir. 1976) (oral argument before agency appellate body not a matter of right).

present his case.[94] The APA's legislative history supports the notion that agencies have discretion to limit cross-examination as long as the party can adequately present his or her case.[95] Note that a determination that no oral hearing will be held is, in effect, a determination that cross-examination is not necessary for the party to effectively present his or her case.

A party's right to cross-examination may depend on the party using a subpoena to compel a witness to appear.[96] In *Richardson v. Perales*,[97] the Social Security Administration (SSA) accepted into evidence and relied upon reports by physician-consultants who were not cross-examined by the SSA claimant. The claimant failed to subpoena the writers of the report although he could have done so. Rejecting the claimant's suggestion that his due-process and APA rights were violated, the Court explained:

> The matter comes down to the question of the procedure's integrity and fundamental fairness. We see nothing that works in derogation of that integrity and of that fairness in the admission of consultants' reports, subject as they are . . . to the use of the subpoena and consequent cross-examination. This precisely fits the statutorily prescribed "cross-examination as may be required for a full and true disclosure of the facts."[98]

---

94. *See, e.g.,* Cellular Mobile Sys. of Pa., Inc. v. FCC, 782 F.2d 182, 198 (D.C. Cir. 1985) (cross-examination is not automatic right; party seeking it must establish necessity); Solis v. Schweiker, 719 F.2d 301, 302 (9th Cir. 1983) (ALJ has discretion to decide whether cross-examination is required); Cent. Freight Lines, Inc. v. United States, 669 F.2d 1063, 1068 (5th Cir. 1982) (cross-examination not absolute right).

95. According to the House Judiciary Committee report:

> The provision on its face does not confer a right of so-called 'unlimited' cross-examination. Presiding officers will have to make the necessary initial determination whether the cross-examination is pressed to unreasonable lengths by a party or whether it is required for the 'full and true disclosure of the facts' stated in the provision. Nor is it the intention to eliminate the authority of agencies to confer sound discretion upon presiding officers in the matter of its extent.

APA Legislative History 271, *supra* note 33, at 271.

96. There is authority for the proposition that that pro se parties should be advised of their right to cross-examine adverse witnesses, although an agency's failure to do so will not constitute reversible error absent prejudice. *See* Wasson v. SEC, 558 F.2d 879, 884 (8th Cir. 1977).

97. 402 U.S. 389 (1971).

98. *Id.* at 410. *See also id.* at 402.

Perales has received various interpretations by lower courts. Some have held that due process or fundamental fairness requires a party to have an opportunity for cross-examination in cases where the agency relies on written evidence obtained after the hearing has concluded.[99] Other courts have read *Perales* to mean that a claimant who requested a subpoena has an automatic right to subpoena witnesses who filed written reports and to cross-examine the subpoenaed witnesses.[100] Still others, however, have determined that the right of cross-examination is not absolute; whether a request for cross-examination should be granted or a subpoena allowing for cross-examination should be issued is a matter of agency discretion.[101] Nevertheless, courts tend to conclude that an agency has abused its discretion when it denies a request for cross-examination of the author of written reports or other documents that were important to the agency's decision.[102]

Agencies may make rules limiting cross-examination.[103] However, such agency rules may not reduce cross-examination below the APA

---

99. *See, e.g.,* Wallace v. Bowen, 869 F.2d 187, 191–92 (3d Cir. 1989); Townley v. Heckler, 748 F.2d 109, 114 (2d Cir. 1984); Demenech v. Sec'y of Health & Human Servs., 913 F.2d 882, 884–85 (11th Cir. 1990).

100. *See, e.g.,* Lidy v. Sullivan, 911 F.2d 1075, 1076 (5th Cir. 1990); Coffin v. Sullivan, 895 F.2d 1206, 1212 (8th Cir. 1990); *Wallace,* 869 F.2d at 192; Lonzollo v. Weinberger, 534 F.2d 712, 714 (7th Cir. 1976) ("A written report . . . may be received as evidence in a disability hearing, but the claimant has a right to subpoena the [author] and cross-examine him concerning the report). These cases involve hearings required by section 205(b) of the Social Security Act, 42 U.S.C. § 405(b). According to the *Perales* Court, however, APA § 556(d)'s provisions "conform, and are consistent with, rather than differ from or supersede [section 205 of the Social Security Act]." 402 U.S. at 409. *See also* Solis v. Schweiker, 719 F.2d 301, 302 (9th Cir. 1983) (taking APA § 556(d) to govern scope of SSA disability claimant's right to cross-examination).

101. *See, e.g.,* Souch v. Califano, 599 F.2d 577, 579–80 (4th Cir. 1979) (relying on Richardson v. Perales, 402 U.S. 389 (1971), in reaching conclusion that right to subpoena for purposes of cross-examination is no more than a right to request the issuance of a subpoena).

102. *See, e.g.,* Reilly v. Pinkus, 338 U.S. 269, 276–77 (1949); Dolcin Corp. v. FTC, 219 F.2d 742, 747 (D.C. Cir. 1954); *Solis,* 719 F.2d at 302.

103. Citizens Awareness Network, Inc. v. United States, 391 F.3d 338 (1st Cir. 2004).

minimum, i.e., below what is necessary for a "full and true disclosure of the facts."[104]

Illustration:

9. Following a hearing, Agency issues an order that relies heavily on written reports. Agency did not provide an opportunity for the losing party to subpoena the authors of those reports. Losing Party argues that its right to cross-examination was wrongfully denied. A court may conclude that the error was prejudicial and sustain the challenge to the order.

---

104. APA § 556(d). In *Citizens Awareness Network*, the court approved the agency's regulation governing cross-examination after the agency represented that the regulation allowed for cross-examination whenever it would be required under the APA.

Chapter 6

POST-HEARING REQUIREMENTS

6.01 SUMMARY OF BASIC REQUIREMENTS

APA § 557(c) provides that parties have the right to submit proposed findings and conclusions prior to agency decisions. It also requires decisionmakers at both the preliminary and agency head levels to provide findings, conclusions, and a statement of reasons on all material issues. (§ 6.02) APA § 557(b) allocates responsibility between the administrative law judge (ALJ) or other presiding officer[1] who conducts the hearing and the agency heads or other delegated review body[2] that reviews the ALJ's decision. (§ 6.03)

---

1. In this chapter, the term "ALJ" is used for convenience to refer to the presiding officer at the hearing. In some APA formal adjudication situations, the agency is permitted to designate a presiding officer other than an ALJ. APA § 556(b), discussed in Chapter 10, § 10.03.
2. In this chapter, the term "agency heads" is used for convenience to refer to the administrative body that is empowered to review the decision of a presiding officer. In many cases, the reviewing body is not the agency head or heads, but is a board or individual who serves as the delegate of

6.02 FINDINGS, CONCLUSIONS, AND REASONS[3]

6.021 General requirement

Under the APA formal adjudication provisions, agency decisions must include findings and conclusions, and the reasons or basis therefor, on all material issues of fact, law, or discretion.[4] If necessary to explain the decision, the agency must articulate a rational connection between the basic facts and the ultimate conclusion or the discretionary choice made by the agency.[5] Courts often use this explanation requirement to require agencies to reconsider dubious decisions.[6]

A second APA provision, applicable to both formal and informal adjudication, states that notice of the denial of an application "shall be accompanied by a brief statement of the grounds for denial."[7] In addition to the APA, due process may require an explanation of an agency's

---

the agency head for purposes of reviewing such decisions. *See* Chapter 6, § 6.031.

3. *See* Morell E. Mullins, "Manual for Administrative Law Judges," 23 J. NTL. Ass'N OF ALJs 1, 127–57 (2004). This manual contains discussion of many issues relating to opinion writing from the perspective of the ALJ.

4. APA § 557(c)(A) provides: "All decisions, including initial, recommended, and tentative decisions, are a part of the record and shall include a statement of "(A) findings and conclusions, and the reasons or basis therefor, on all the material issues of fact, law, or discretion presented on the record."

5. Burlington Truck Lines, Inc. v. United States, 371 U.S. 156, 167–68 (1962). In the leading case of Greater Bos. Television Corp. v. FCC, 444 F.2d 841, 851 (D.C. Cir. 1970), *cert. denied*, 403 U.S. 923 (1971), the court said: "The function of the court is to assure that the agency has given reasoned consideration to all the material facts and issues. This calls for insistence that the agency articulate with reasonable clarity its reasons for decision, and identify the significance of the crucial facts, a course that tends to assure that the agency's policies effectuate general standards, applied without unreasonable discrimination." (footnotes omitted)

6. *See, e.g.,* Gunderson v. U.S. Dep't of Labor, 601 F.3d 1013 (10th Cir. 2010). *Gunderson* held that it is insufficient for an ALJ to declare that medical opinions in a black lung benefits case were evenly balanced and that he could not break the tie. Thus the employer won because the employee could not establish his case by a preponderance of the evidence. *See* Chapter 5, § 5.044. The court ruled that a scientific dispute must be resolved on scientific grounds. At the very least, the ALJ must explain why on scientific grounds no conclusion can be reached.

7. APA § 555(e).

decision.[8] Finally, courts often interpret particular statutes to require an explanation.[9]

The requirement that an agency explain its decision serves at least four purposes:

- It informs parties of the resolution of contested issues, thereby providing closure.
- It informs third parties how an agency will likely resolve similar cases in the future.
- It improves the quality of agency decisionmaking.[10]
- It facilitates judicial review.[11]

An agency need not provide a detailed and explicit weighing of each relevant consideration to accomplish these purposes. It is sufficient if the bases of its decision are reasonably discernible and a reviewing court can satisfy itself that the agency took a "hard look" at the relevant issues.[12]

---

8. Goldberg v. Kelly, 397 U.S. 254, 271 (1970) (decisionmaker in welfare case must state reasons for his determination and indicate the evidence he relied on). However, under *Mathews v. Eldridge*, it is difficult to make any categorical statement about the requirements of due process. *See* Chapter 2, §§ 2.04, 2.05. Nevertheless, it would appear that any version of due process would require the decisionmaker to make at least some informal statement of the basis of its decision. *See* Sidney A. Shapiro & Richard E. Levy, *Heightened Scrutiny of the Fourth Branch: Separation of Powers and the Requirement of Adequate Reasons for Agency Decisions*, 1987 DUKE L.J. 387 (requirement of findings and reasons is common law technique to promote rational administrative decisionmaking and facilitate judicial review).

9. *See* Dunlop v. Bachowski, 421 U.S. 560 (1975) (Secretary of Labor must state reasons for his refusal to bring suit to set aside an election).

10. *See Bachowski*, 421 U.S. at 572 (stating, *inter alia*, "a reasons requirement promotes thought by the Secretary and compels him to cover the relevant points and eschew irrelevancies") (citing Bachowski v. Brennan, 502 F.2d 79, 88–89 n.14 (3d Cir. 1974)).

11. *See* Armstrong v. Commodity Futures Trading Comm'n, 12 F.3d 401, 403 (3d Cir. 1993).

12. *See, e.g.*, Benmar Transp. & Leasing Corp. v. ICC, 623 F.2d 740, 745 (2d Cir. 1980). The "hard look" embellishment mentioned in *Benmar* has become a standard gloss on the APA requirements. The source of the "hard look" doctrine is Greater Bos. Television Corp. v. FCC, 444 F.2d 841, 851 (D.C. Cir. 1970): "[The court's supervisory function calls on it to intervene] if the court becomes aware, especially from a combination of danger signals, that the agency has not really taken a 'hard look' at the

6.022 Post hoc rationalizations

The duty to state findings, conclusions, and reasons is that of the agency decisionmakers (ALJs or agency heads). Explanations by agency counsel in the course of litigation do not satisfy this obligation and are normally disregarded by reviewing courts.[13] According to one decision, however, the court will uphold a decision based on a post hoc explanation furnished by the agency official who was responsible for the decision.[14] If an agency fails to explain its decision, the normal remedy is a remand to the agency to furnish the necessary explanation, not a trial in court to determine why the agency took the action it did.[15]

6.023 Justifying departure from precedent

An agency is not required to follow its own prior decisions. However, an agency's deviation from its prior decisions creates a presumption that it has failed to engage in reasoned decisionmaking.[16] The agency rebuts this presumption by furnishing an explanation of why it changed course.[17] An agency can meet this burden of explanation by identifying

---

salient problems, and has not genuinely engaged in reasoned decision-making. . . . If satisfied that the agency has taken a hard look at the issues with the use of reasons and standards, the court will uphold its findings, though of less than ideal clarity, if the agency's path may be reasonably discerned, though of course the court must not be left to guess as to the agency's findings or reasons." (footnotes omitted).

13. *See, e.g.*, SEC v. Chenery Corp. 318 U.S. 80, 92–94 (1943).
14. Bagdonas v. Dep't of Treasury, 93 F.3d 422, 426–27 (7th Cir. 1996). *Bagdonas* upheld an unexplained agency decision after the agency official having decisional authority furnished the necessary explanation. The court noted that this was hardly the preferred approach to judicial review of even informal agency action.
15. Camp v. Pitts, 411 U.S. 138, 142–43 (1973).
16. This is true with respect to rulemaking as well as for adjudication. *See, e.g.*, Motor Vehicle Mfrs. Ass'n v. State Farm Mut. Auto. Ins. Co., 463 U.S. 29, 42 (1983).
17. *See, e.g.*, JSG Trading Corp. v. USDA, 176 F.3d 536, 544–46 (D.C. Cir. 1999) (obligation to state principled rationale for departure from precedent); Henry v. INS, 74 F.3d 1, 6 (1st Cir. 1996) (agency may not maintain conflicting lines of precedent governing identical situation). As the court put it in *Greater Bos. Television Corp.*, 444 F.2d at 852: "But an agency changing its course must supply a reasoned analysis indicating that prior policies and standards are being deliberately changed, not casually ignored, and

factual differences between prior cases and the immediate case or emphasizing the importance of considerations not previously contemplated.[18] The existence of one inconsistent prior case or even several marginally inconsistent cases is not necessarily sufficient to establish that an agency is ignoring its own precedent. Rather, the issue is whether the agency has acted consistently, viewing its prior decisions as a whole.[19] When an agency acknowledges that it has changed its policy in an adjudicatory decision, it is not required to demonstrate that the reasons supporting the new policy are better than the reasons supporting the old one, provided that the new policy meets the tests of legality and reasonableness.[20]

In the case of agencies with a very high volume of adjudication, such as the Social Security Administration (SSA), there is no practicable way to explain variations in outcomes. In such settings, an agency can achieve consistency only through adopting legislative or interpretive rules or through management techniques.[21]

Illustration:

1. Agency revokes Company's license because of Company's payments to employees of companies with whom Company was dealing. There was no evidence of guilty intent, and the employers had knowledge of the payments. Agency finds that such payments above a minimal amount automatically constitute

---

if an agency glosses over or swerves from prior precedents without discussion it may cross the line from the tolerably terse to the intolerably mute." (footnotes omitted)

18. *See, e.g.,* Envtl. Action v. FERC, 996 F.2d 401, 411–12 (D.C. Cir. 1993); W. Coast Media, Inc. v. FCC, 695 F.2d 617, 621 (D.C. Cir. 1982). On the other hand, courts sometimes require agencies not only to enumerate factual differences, but also to explain the relevance of those factual differences. *See, e.g.,* Pub. Media Ctr. v. FCC, 587 F.2d 1322, 1331–32 (1978); Melody Music, Inc. v. FCC, 345 F.2d 730, 733 (D.C. Cir. 1965).

19. *See, e.g.,* NLRB v. Sunnyland Packing Co. 557 F.2d 1157, 1160 (5th Cir. 1977) (agency decision upheld despite a single conflicting precedent where its action was founded on frequently reaffirmed precedent)

20. FCC v. Fox Television Stations, Inc., 556 U.S. 502 (2009).

21. *See* ACUS Recommendations 87-7, 52 Fed. Reg. 49,143 (Dec. 30, 1987) and 89-8, 54 Fed. Reg. 53,495 (Dec. 29, 1988) (recommending SSA publication, for precedential value, of some agency opinions that treat recurring issues). *But see* Chapter 10, § 10.09 (management of ALJs) and Chapter 7, § 7.07 (risks of management violating ex parte communication and separation of functions requirements, and violating the exclusive record rule).

"commercial bribery" regardless of other factors, which invariably requires license revocation. In two earlier decisions Agency had not applied a per se rule. The departure from prior agency precedent requires explanation and justification, the absence of which is reversible error.[22]

6.03 ADMINISTRATIVE REVIEW OF ALJ DECISIONS

The final adjudicatory authority of the agency resides with the head of the agency unless it has been delegated by statute or agency regulation to a subordinate decisionmaker. Courts review the decision of the agency heads (or other delegated reviewing authority), not the decision of the ALJ or other presiding officer.[23]

6.031 Structures of internal review

Most agencies have at least one level of internal administrative review. Such review, however, is not a constitutional right,[24] nor is it required by the APA.

The appellate structure generally follows one of several models.[25] The traditional structure places responsibility on the agency head or heads to review initial decisions. Some agencies utilize an intermediate reviewing authority between the hearing officer and the agency head. In those agencies, review at the agency head level may be a matter of right or it may be discretionary. In some agencies, such as the Department of Agriculture, a judicial officer, rather than the agency head, has final reviewing authority. In agencies with larger caseloads, administrative review is conducted by a specially constituted appellate body (such as the Appeals

---

22. *JSG Trading Corp.*, 176 F.3d at 544–46.
23. *See* Welch v. Heckler, 808 F.2d 264, 266–68 (3d Cir. 1986) (Social Security Appeals Council is final arbiter of disability claims, so court reviews its decision rather than ALJs); Iran Air v. Kugelman, 996 F.2d 1253, 1259–61 (D.C. Cir. 1993) (undersecretary to whom review authority delegated can overturn ALJ decision); White v. Sullivan, 965 F.2d 133, 136 (7th Cir. 1992) (court reviews decision of Social Security Appeals Council, not ALJ decision); Castillo-Rodriguez v. INS, 929 F.2d 181, 183 (5th Cir. 1991) (party erroneously sought review of ALJ decision rather than that of Board of Immigration Appeals, but court elected to proceed with the appeal).
24. Guentchev v. INS, 77 F.3d 1036, 1037 (7th Cir. 1996).
25. See Russell L. Weaver, *Appellate Review in Executive Department and Agencies*, 48 ADMIN. L. REV. 251 (1996) (examining appellate structures used in various federal agencies).

Council in the SSA or Board of Immigration Appeals in the Immigration and Naturalization Service). Some administrative schemes call for one agency to make and enforce policy and prosecute cases and another separate agency to adjudicate these cases.[26]

6.032 Initial and other preliminary decisions

The agency heads may themselves conduct administrative hearings,[27] but seldom do so. Normally, a presiding officer (usually an ALJ) conducts the hearing and renders an "initial decision." That initial decision becomes the final decision of the agency unless either the private party or the agency staff lodges a timely appeal to the reviewing authority or that authority reviews the initial decision sua sponte.[28]

In rare situations, either by general rule or in specific cases, the agency heads may make the initial decision in a case already heard by a presiding officer such as an ALJ. In such cases, the presiding officer certifies the record to the agency heads for decision and also renders a recommended decision for consideration by the agency heads.[29]

---

26. George Johnson, *The Split Enforcement Model: Some Conclusions From the OSHA and MSHA Experience*, 39 ADMIN. L. REV. 315 (1987). This is also the pattern in tax cases; the Internal Revenue Service (IRS) prosecutes the cases; the cases are heard by the Tax Court, which is independent of the IRS.

27. U.S. Dep't of Justice, *Attorney General's Manual on the Administrative Procedure Act* 81.

28. APA § 557(b).

29. APA § 557(b). A recommended decision does not become final even if nobody protests it but must be followed by an agency head decision. *Attorney General's Manual, supra* note 27, at 82. In cases of formal rulemaking or initial licenses, the agency heads may issue a tentative decision or any of its responsible employees can recommend a decision. *Id.* at 82–83. Even these procedures may be omitted in a case in which the agency finds on the record that due and timely execution of its functions imperatively and unavoidably so requires. APA § 557(b)(1), (2). See White Eagle Coop. Ass'n v. Conner, 553 F.3d 462, 481–82 (7th Cir. 2009), which concerned an amendment to a milk marketing order adopted after a formal rulemaking process. The agency head issued an interim rule without having first issued a recommended decision, but the agency's statement explained that emergency conditions were present. The court thought the agency's rather conclusory statement that serious milk price deterioration was occurring was "marginally sufficient" to meet the APA's finding requirement.

Illustration:

2. Contractor applies to Agency for a permit to build a dam on a navigable body of water. The formal adjudication provisions of the APA apply to this determination. Although Agency normally uses ALJs to conduct hearings, it refers Contractor's permit application to Staff Member who has not previously been involved in the decision. Staff Member conducts a hearing and recommends that the application be denied. After considering Contractor's exceptions to this decision, the heads of Agency issue a decision denying the application. Because the case involved initial licensing,[30] the procedure followed by Agency complies with the APA.

6.033 Opportunity for party submissions

Before a preliminary agency decision, the parties are entitled to a reasonable opportunity to submit proposed findings and conclusions and supporting reasons for the findings and conclusions.[31] They are also entitled to submit exceptions to preliminary decisions and reasons for the exceptions.[32] The agency's ruling on each finding, conclusion, or exception presented is part of the record of the case.[33]

The opportunity to submit proposed findings or conclusions or exceptions contemplated by Section 557(c) does not apply to recommendations made to the agency heads by staff advisors at the time the heads are reviewing a preliminary decision.[34]

---

30. *See* APA § 551(8) for a definition of "license."
31. APA § 557(c)(1), (3).
32. APA § 557(c)(2), (3).
33. APA § 557(c).
34. T.S.C. Motor Freight Lines, Inc. v. United States, 186 F. Supp. 777, 789–90 (S.D. Tex. 1960), *aff'd per curiam sub nom.* Herrin Transp. Co. v. United States, 366 U.S. 419 (1961). The *T.S.C.* case held that parties have no right to submit exceptions to staff recommendations to the agency heads. The court emphasized that the ultimate responsibility for decision lies with the agency heads, but agency members must be allowed to seek the assistance of staff advisors to perform that responsibility. The fact that the assistance is off the record is inherent in the institutional character of administrative decisions. As discussed in Chapter 7, § 7.0633, so long as the staff members have not assumed an adversary role in the case, they can engage in off-the-record discussions with the decisionmakers.

Illustration:

3. Agency allows its members to call on staff attorney/advisors who have had no prior contact with a particular case to review the record of proceedings previously conducted before an ALJ and to advise the agency heads about their final decision. The recommendations of the attorney/advisors need not be served on the parties, and parties are not entitled to submit proposed findings or exceptions to the recommendations of the attorney/advisors.[35]

6.034 Administrative review procedures

An agency's enabling act or its procedural rules furnish details of the administrative review process.[36] The person claiming that the administrative review authority has jurisdiction bears the burden of demonstrating that jurisdiction.[37] Nevertheless, the agency has a duty to inform disappointed parties of the means for seeking administrative review of an initial decision.[38] Obviously, a multi-member agency head or other reviewing authority must have a quorum of its members in order to conduct review of an initial decision.[39]

Generally parties seeking administrative review must satisfy conditions similar to those that apply to judicial review. They must adhere to filing deadlines and must exhaust remedies by raising issues before the

---

35. *See T.S.C.*, 186 F. Supp. 777 (involving a somewhat more formalized process of agency staff review and recommendations for agency disposition of initial decisions).
36. *E.g.*, Bethesda Hosp. Ass'n v. Bowen, 485 U.S. 399 (1988) (interpreting requirements for jurisdiction of Provider Reimbursement Review Board).
37. Clark v. USPS, 989 F.2d 1164, 1167 (Fed. Cir. 1993); Van Werry v. Merit Sys. Prot. Bd., 995 F.2d 1048, 1050–52 (Fed. Cir. 1993).
38. Gonzalez v. Sullivan, 914 F.2d 1197, 1203 (9th Cir. 1990) (due process requires notice reasonably calculated to afford parties their right to present objections). Frequently, agency regulations require such notice. Shiflett v. USPS, 839 F.2d 669, 673 (Fed. Cir. 1988) (enforcing procedural regulation that requires agency to give notice of appeal rights).
39. *See* New Process Steel L.P. v. NLRB, 130 S. Ct. 2635 (2010), holding that the NLRB lacked a three-member quorum when vacancies left only two of the five members of the Board in office. Construing statutory provisions unique to the NLRB, the Court held that the problem could not be solved through a resolution (passed by four members before two of their terms expired) that delegated the Board's powers to review ALJ decisions to a three-member subcommittee (whose membership quickly fell to two).

presiding officer before such issues can be considered by the reviewing body.[40] However, unless prohibited by agency regulations from doing so, the review authority may consider an issue sua sponte even though the issue had not been raised before the ALJ or even reopen the proceeding and take additional evidence.[41]

6.035 Agency treatment of initial decisions

6.0351 Disclosure of initial decision

The initial decision is part of the record and must be disclosed to the parties prior to the agency review stage as well as for purposes of judicial review. The APA provides that the parties are entitled to a reasonable opportunity to submit for the consideration of the agency reviewers "(1) proposed findings and conclusions; or (2) exceptions to the decisions or recommended decisions of subordinate employees or to tentative agency decisions; and (3) supporting reasons for the exceptions or proposed findings and conclusions."[42] This provision means that the parties are entitled to disclosure of an initial decision prior to the decision by the agency reviewers.[43]

---

40. *Clark*, 989 F.2d at 1167 (failure to meet deadlines for seeking review); NLRB v. George Koch Sons, Inc., 950 F.2d 1324, 1337 (7th Cir. 1991) (failure to present issue to ALJ is waiver of party's ability to present it to agency heads).
41. APA § 557(b) (reviewing body has all powers which it would have in making initial decision except as it may limit the issues on notice or by rule).
42. APA § 557(c).
43. In Ballard v. Comm'r, 544 U.S. 40 (2005), the Supreme Court considered a Tax Court practice in which certain cases were heard by "special trial judges" whose initial decisions were considered by a Tax Court judge who issued the final Tax Court decision. The special trial judge and the Tax Court judge worked collaboratively on the final opinion. The opinion of the special trial judge was not disclosed to the parties at any time and was withheld from appellate courts. The Supreme Court held that the Tax Court rule at issue did not authorize nondisclosure of the initial decision to the parties or to reviewing courts. The opinion states that "it is routine in federal judicial and administrative decisionmaking both to disclose the initial report of a hearing officer, and to make that report part of the record available to an appellate forum. A departure of the bold character practiced by the Tax Court . . . demands, at the very least, full and fair statement in the Tax Court's own Rules." *Id.* at 46–47. As part

6.0352 *Agency adoption of initial decision*

The agency heads or other reviewing authority may adopt the presiding officer's initial decision without providing independent findings or reasons. Such adoption does not violate the agency's obligation to consider the issues in the case[44] or to make findings or give reasons for its decisions.[45] In cases of summary adoption, the reviewing court takes the initial decision as that of the agency and accords it the normal degree of deference.[46] However, if the agency heads' approval of the ALJ decision is ambiguous or incomplete, a reviewing court may insist that the heads elaborate on their decision.[47]

---

of a survey of judicial and administrative practice, *id.* at 62, the Court quoted the APA provision that "All decisions, including initial, recommended, and tentative decisions, are a part of the record" on appeal and called attention to the provision that the reviewing court shall evaluate the "whole record." APA §§ 557(c), 706.

44. *But see* Tukhowinich v. INS, 64 F.3d 460, 464 (9th Cir. 1995) (finding that reviewing authority failed to provide independent consideration since it assumed that the judge's decision considered certain relevant factors that the judge had failed to consider).

45. *See* Chen v. INS, 87 F.3d 5, 7–8 (1st Cir. 1996) (citing many cases); Guentchev v. INS, 77 F.3d 1036, 1038 (7th Cir. 1996).

46. *See* Alaelua v. INS, 45 F.3d 1379, 1382 (9th Cir. 1995) (where Board of Immigration Appeals summarily adopted immigration judge's decision, court reviews judge's decision for abuse of discretion). In *Guentchev,* 77 F.3d at 1038, in rejecting a challenge to a summary affirmance of an initial decision, the court noted:

> Perhaps some summary dispositions obscure the Board's reasons, or hide the lack of reasons. What the Board's order says, however, is that the Board agrees with the immigration judge's reasons, and we have no greater reason to doubt that statement than we have to doubt that the explanation in an elaborate opinion is an honest recapitulation of the reasons for decision. To adopt someone else's reasoned explanation is to give reasons. . . . Writing imposes mental discipline, but we lack any principled ground to declare that members of the Board must use words different from those the immigration judge selected.

47. Armstrong v. Commodity Futures Trading Comm'n, 12 F.3d 401, 404 (3d Cir. 1993) (agency head decision that the ALJ reached a "substantially correct result" is not a summary affirmance and violates the agency heads' obligation to give reasons for decision); *Tukhowinich,* 64 F.3d at 465 (hold-

Illustration:

4. ALJ finds Dealer liable for violating agency regulations. The agency head affirms, stating: "The ALJ reached a substantially correct result. Because the parties have not raised important questions of law or policy concerning the ALJ's findings of fact and conclusions, we affirm without opinion. The ALJ's decision shall not be cited as agency precedent." The agency head's decision should be reversed since it leaves the court to guess as to what portions of the ALJ's findings or conclusions were incorrect.[48]

6.0353 *Agency rejection of initial decision*

Agency heads or other reviewing authorities owe no obligation to pay deference to initial decisions. The APA provides that "on appeal from or review of the initial decision, the agency has all the powers which it would have in making the initial decision except as it may limit the issues on notice or by rule."[49] Where the agency and the ALJ disagree on issues of law, facts, discretion, or policy, a court reviews the decision of the reviewing authority, not the ALJ's decision.[50]

At the same time, however, the initial decision is part of the record for purposes of judicial review.[51] The reviewing authority must therefore explain its rejection of the initial decision.[52] Most important, with respect

---

ing that reviewing authority's statement "finding no error in the decision of the immigration judge, we, accordingly, affirm his decision" does not make it clear that it adopted the immigration judge's reasoning).

48. *Armstrong*, 12 F.3d at 404.

49. APA § 557(b). One case interpreted an agency's rules so as to allow the agency head full powers to review an ALJ decision (even the rule seemed to limit the issues that a petitioner could raise before the agency heads). The petitioner claimed that the rules limited the head to the arbitrary and capricious standard of review. Vineland Fireworks Co. v. Bureau of Alcohol, Tobacco, Firearms & Explosives, 544 F.3d 509 (3d Cir. 2008).

50. *See, e.g.*, Deere & Co. v. Int'l Trade Comm'n, 605 F.3d 1350, 1358 (Fed. Cir. 2010) (agency has power to go beyond ALJ's findings); Ryan v. Commodities Futures Trading Comm'n, 145 F.3d 910, 918 (7th Cir. 1998) (agency free to discount weight that ALJ places on testimony).

51. All preliminary decisions are part of the record. APA § 557(c).

52. *See, e.g.*, Simon v. Simmons Foods, Inc., 49 F.3d 386, 389–90 (8th Cir. 1995), stating that an agency departing from the findings of the ALJ must show that it gave attentive consideration to the ALJ's conclusions. Generally, the

to issues of credibility (particularly credibility judgments based on the demeanor of witnesses), if the reviewing authority disagrees with the initial decision, this disagreement detracts from the substantiality of the evidence supporting the agency's decision.[53] Nevertheless, the agency heads or other reviewing authority are empowered to reverse an initial decision, even on a matter of witness credibility, if it finds the testimony implausible and if it justifies its departure from the initial decision.[54]

Illustration:

5.   Agency orders Employer to reinstate Employee because Employer fired Employee for trying to organize a union. Employer states that he fired Employee for stealing. The ALJ believed Employer's testimony, but the agency heads write a detailed opinion explaining that they do not believe Employer's testimony. A reviewing court might overturn Agency's decision on the basis that it does not meet the substantial evidence test.[55]

---

agency gives such consideration if its decision reflects an awareness of the ALJ's findings and gives reasons for reaching a different conclusion. *See also* Dart v. United States, 848 F.2d 217, 230 (D.C. Cir. 1988) (peremptory reversal of fact finding violates requirement of reasoned decisions); Harberson & Talley v. NLRB, 810 F.2d 977, 984 (10th Cir. 1987) (agency must give ALJ decision due weight and articulate reasons for rejecting it); Local 441, IBEW v. NLRB, 510 F.2d 1274, 1276 (D.C. Cir. 1975) (agency must make clear it is aware of its disagreement with ALJ and must set forth bases for the disagreement).

53. The leading case is Universal Camera Corp. v. NLRB, 340 U.S. 474, 496 (1951), which states: "We intend only to recognize that evidence supporting a conclusion may be less substantial when an impartial, experienced examiner who has observed the witnesses and lived with the case has drawn conclusions different from the Board's than when he has reached the same conclusion. The findings of the examiner are to be considered along with the consistency and inherent probability of testimony. The significance of his report, of course, depends largely on the importance of credibility in the particular case."

54. *See Universal Camera*, 340 U.S. at 492 (rejecting contention that Board can reverse ALJ findings only when they are clearly erroneous); FCC v. Allentown Broad. Corp., 349 U.S. 358, 364 (1955) (rejecting view that Board cannot reverse ALJ without very substantial preponderance in testimony).

55. *Universal Camera Corp.*, 340 U.S. at 496.

Some agency statutes or regulations depart from the general rule and require reviewing courts to defer to decisions of presiding officers rather than to the decisions of the reviewing authority. In such cases, the court applies the substantial evidence test to the findings contained in the initial decision, not those made by the reviewing authority.[56]

---

56. *See, e.g.,* Dantran, Inc. v. U.S. Dep't of Labor, 171 F.3d 58, 71–75 (1st Cir. 1999) (interpreting statute and regulations to allow administrative review only for clear error of ALJ decisions on disbarment under Service Contract Act); *Dart,* 848 F.2d at 229–31 (interpreting Export Administration Act to limit agency review of ALJ decisions); Chen v. GAO, 821 F.2d 732, 735–38 (D.C. Cir. 1987) (regulations of General Accounting Office Personnel Appeals Board limited its review of ALJ to substantial evidence test); Old Ben Coal Co. v. Prewitt, 755 F.2d 588 (7th Cir. 1985) (under Black Lung Benefits Act, court must sustain ALJ findings that are supported by substantial evidence regardless of the convincing power of Benefits Review Board's opinion).

Chapter 7

INTEGRITY OF THE DECISIONMAKING PROCESS

7.01 OVERVIEW

This chapter covers a number of related doctrines that concern integrity of the decisionmaking process. Adjudicatory decisionmakers must not be biased (§ 7.02) and must take personal responsibility for their decisions (§ 7.03). The APA prohibits ex parte communications with decisionmakers (§ 7.04) and legislative interference with their function (§ 7.05). It requires internal separation of functions between adversarial personnel and decisionmakers (§ 7.06) and imposes additional separation of function requirements on initial decisionmakers (§ 7.07). The exclusive record requirement limits the decisionmaker to consideration of evidentiary material presented at trial plus that which is officially noticed. (§ 7.08). Finally, the rule of necessity in some cases trumps the normal rules relating to decisionmaker integrity. (§ 7.09).

Readers should approach this chapter critically. The statements of current law in this chapter are responsive to past claims and complaints, and notions of fairness and integrity evolve over time; as a result, courts may reach different conclusions in newer cases. Additionally, in 2007, the ABA amended the Model Code of Judicial Conduct, making it applicable to the Administrative Law Judiciary;[1] applying the Model Code to some of the cases and illustrations in this chapter might result in different decisions. Finally, and most importantly, it is only the rarest situation in which an administrative law judge (ALJ) or administrative judge does not hold himself or herself to the highest standards of conduct, which far exceed some of the conduct that courts have held minimally acceptable in some of the authorities and illustrations in this chapter.

7.02 BIAS OF ADJUDICATORY DECISIONMAKERS

7.021 General rule

Agency heads should disqualify a presiding officer if the officer is biased and refuses to disqualify himself or herself. Agency heads should disqualify themselves if they are biased.[2]

A decision by a biased decisionmaker may violate due process as well as the APA. The constitutional and statutory standards for ascertaining the presence of bias are probably the same. Note that the rule of necessity discussed in § 7.09 may trump the bias rule. Bias is never presumed; it must be proved.[3]

---

1. MODEL CODE OF JUD. CONDUCT, Application sec. I.B (2007). The Reporters' Explanation of Changes to the 2007 Model Code at 4–5 state that the rationale for applying the Rules to ALJs "derives from the fact that they perform essentially the same function as a trial judge hearing a case without a jury." See also the Housekeeping Revisions to the Code, which state that the "Application Section's definition of a judge as 'anyone who is authorized to perform judicial functions' is meant to apply to the broadest possible range of individuals, and would not, therefore, permit the exclusion of a judicial officer whose official title does not make reference to administrative 'law.'" The Model Code, Reporters' Explanation of Changes, and Housekeeping Revisions are available at http://www .americanbar.org/groups/professional_responsibility/publications/ model_code_of_judicial_conduct.html (last visited Jan. 14, 2012). Application of the 2007 Model Code does not displace the 1989 Model Code of Judicial Conduct for Federal Administrative Law Judges.
2. The APA is not clear on the subject of whether agency heads are authorized to disqualify colleagues whom they believe are biased, and the issue is disputed.
3. *See* Withrow v. Larkin, 421 U.S. 35, 47 (1975). Similarly, in United States v. Morgan, 313 U.S. 409, 421 (1941) (*Morgan IV*), the Court declared that administrative judges are generally presumed to be people of "conscience and intellectual discipline, capable of judging a particular controversy fairly on the basis of its own circumstances."

Because agency adjudicators, particularly agency heads, have responsibilities that are broader than simply adjudicating, the rules relating to disqualification of judges for bias do not entirely parallel the rules relating to administrative adjudicators.[4]

Some statutes and agency regulations may contain standards for what constitutes bias.[5]

7.022 Timing

A party should move to disqualify an adjudicator by reason of bias as soon as the party is aware of the grounds for such motion. The grounds for disqualification should be asserted by a "timely and sufficient affidavit of personal bias or other disqualification of a presiding or participating employee."[6] A party who fails to make a timely motion for disqualification

---

4. A federal judge must be disqualified if "his impartiality might reasonably be questioned." 28 U.S.C. § 455(a). In addition, a judge must be disqualified if the judge possesses "personal knowledge of disputed evidentiary facts concerning the proceeding" or if the judge was a former government employee and has "expressed an opinion concerning the merits of the particular case in controversy." *Id.* § 455(b)(1), (b)(3). These standards do not directly apply to administrative adjudicators. *See generally* Peter L. Strauss, *Disqualifications of Decisional Officials in Rulemaking*, 80 COLUM. L. REV. 990, 1010–27 (1980). However, the Federal Circuit applied section 455 as interpreted by Liteky v. United States, 510 U.S. 540, 555 (1994) (recusal required when a federal judge displays "a deep-seated favoritism or antagonism that would make fair judgment impossible"). Bieber v. Dep't of the Army, 287 F.3d 1358, 1362–63 (Fed. Cir. 2002). The most recent Supreme Court case on the subject of judicial bias, Caperton v. A.T. Massey Coal Co., 129 S. Ct. 2252 (2009), held there was a violation of due process when Massey's chairman gave extraordinarily high campaign contributions to a candidate for the West Virginia Supreme Court, that candidate won, and that candidate refused to recuse himself when reviewing a $50 million jury award against Massey. The Court also suggested that the candidate may have violated Canon 2 of the Model Code of Judicial Conduct. *Id.* at 2266.
5. *See, e.g.*, I.R.C. § 6330(b)(3) (stating that an impartial appeals officer is "an officer or employee who has had no prior involvement with respect to the unpaid tax specified in [the collection due process notice] before the first hearing under this section"). See Cox v. Comm'r, 514 F.3d 1119 (10th Cir. 2008) (appeals officer who had prior involvement with the taxpayers' other years' liabilities had "prior involvement" pursuant to section 6330(3)(b)).
6. APA § 556(b). The affidavit requirement applies to a motion to disqualify an agency head as well as an ALJ. Keating v. Office of Thrift Supervision,

has waived the right to do so.[7] The D.C. Circuit has explained that claims of bias must be timely to protect the efficiency and integrity of the administrative process, as well as the reputations of the parties involved.[8]

When a party makes a complaint alleging bias, the agency should investigate in a timely manner.[9]

7.023 Definition of bias

The APA does not identify the sorts of mindsets that would constitute bias, but numerous cases supply the contours of both prohibited and

---

45 F.3d 322, 327 (9th Cir. 1995) (request for recusal unaccompanied by affidavit insufficient).

7. Marcus v. Dir., Office of Workers' Comp. Programs, 548 F.2d 1044, 1050–51 (D.C. Cir. 1976); Duffield v. Charleston Area Med. Ctr., Inc., 503 F.2d 512, 515–17 (4th Cir. 1974). One questionable decision states that if there is no prescribed procedure for disqualification of a biased adjudicator in a state agency, a party is not required to attempt to disqualify a biased adjudicator in order to subsequently raise the issue on appeal. Stivers v. Pierce, 71 F.3d 732, 748 (9th Cir. 1995).

8. *See Marcus*, 548 F.2d at 1050 ("If the issue of bias is raised in a timely fashion, permitting more prompt attention to the matter, each party's rights to a fair and impartial tribunal are better protected. On the other hand, when a party voices its misgivings in tardy or dilatory fashion, not only may time and effort be wasted in the event that disqualification is ultimately required, but the good faith of the claimant will quite naturally be placed in some doubt."). *See also* White Eagle Coop. Ass'n v. Conner, 553 F.3d 467, 476 (7th Cir. 2009) (the rule that claims of bias must be timely protects the efficiency and integrity of the administrative process, as well as the reputations of the parties involved) (citing *Marcus*, 548 F.2d at 1050); Power v. Fed. Labor Relations Auth., 146 F.3d 995, 1002 (D.C. Cir. 1998) (employee's embarrassment over the workplace incident that led to the hearing was not an extraordinary circumstance justifying a late claim of bias).

9. *See, e.g.*, Lowry v. Barnhart, 329 F.3d 1019 (9th Cir. 2003) (noting with sarcasm the "blinding speed" (review not completed after nearly 2-1/2 years) at which the Social Security Administration (SSA) acted on a one-page complaint of bias in only two hearings pursuant to SSA interim rules stating that "every complaint will be reviewed or investigated in a timely manner. The SSA completed its review with a one-page letter and filed that concurrent with its answering brief to the Ninth Circuit. The Ninth Circuit noted, "Sadly this is not the first time a party has graced us with so-called 'excerpts of record' that have never seen the light of courtroom day," *id.* at 1025, and imposed sanctions against the agency).

permissible forms of bias.[10] The Comment to the Model Code of Judicial Conduct also lists examples of manifestations of bias.[11]

7.0231 *Pecuniary or other personal bias*

Bias consists of a pecuniary[12] or other personal interest[13] in the case to be decided. Bias may also be established by an institutional pecuniary interest such that the deciding agency benefits from a decision.[14]

---

10. Whether a plaintiff has overcome the presumption of regularity and established a bias claim is a highly fact-specific inquiry. *See Stivers,* 71 F.3d at 741–48 (combining elements of several types of bias).
11. Comment [2] to the Model Code of Judicial Conduct Rule 2.3 states:

    > Examples of manifestations of bias or prejudice include but are not limited to epithets; slurs; demeaning nicknames; negative stereotyping; attempted humor based upon stereotypes; threatening, intimidating, or hostile acts; suggestions of connections between race, ethnicity, or nationality and crime; and irrelevant references to personal characteristics. Even facial expressions and body language can convey to parties and lawyers in the proceeding, jurors, the media, and others an appearance of bias or prejudice. A judge must avoid conduct that may reasonably be perceived as prejudiced or biased.

12. The presence of a personal or pecuniary interest in the case creates an appearance of bias that is sufficient to disqualify an adjudicator regardless of the presence of actual bias. See Aetna Life Ins. Co. v. Lavoie, 475 U.S. 813 (1986) (state supreme court justice disqualified because he was conducting personal lawsuits that raised the same question as the case before the court); Tumey v. Ohio, 273 U.S. 510 (1927) (traffic court judge disqualified because he retained portion of fines). At some point, however, a pecuniary interest becomes so attenuated that it is disregarded. *See, e.g.,* N.Y. State Dairy Foods, Inc. v. Ne. Dairy Compact Comm'n, 198 F.3d 1, 14–15 (1st Cir. 1999). The pecuniary interest rule does not apply to agency prosecutors as opposed to decisionmakers. Marshall v. Jerrico, Inc., 446 U.S. 238 (1980) (prosecutors not disqualified even though civil penalties assessed by prosecuting agency are returned to the agency).
13. *See, e.g.,* Dresser v. Ohio Hempery, Inc., No. 98-2425, 2004 WL 464895 (Mar. 8, 2004) (noting National Transportation Safety Board (NTSB) reversal of ALJ decision for "unacceptable appearance of impartiality" after the ALJ learned that his son was counsel for defendants in a related civil case).
14. Ward v. Village of Monroeville, 409 U.S. 57 (1972) (traffic court judge disqualified because he was also mayor and fines went into the city budget).

Illustrations:

1. K is a licensed broker-dealer. Agency charges K with violations of its regulations and proposes to revoke his license. H is one of three members of Agency. H's responsibilities with Agency are part-time, and he continues to operate his own brokerage business while heading Agency. H and K have the only brokerage firms in town. A court could find that H was biased against K.[15]

2. Chairman of the Securities Exchange Commission (SEC) recuses himself from participating in a review of MFS Security Corporation's termination as a member organization of the New York Stock Exchange. One member's conflict of interest is not imputed to other members of the commission. Also, the structure of the SEC (appointment by the president with only for-cause removal, and allowing only three commissioners from one political party) suggests it is free from imputed conflicts.[16]

However, the incentive must be a "strong" one. *See* Alpha Epsilon Phi Tau Chapter Hous. Ass'n v. City of Berkeley, 114 F.3d 840, 845–47 (9th Cir. 1997) (agency not disqualified even though about 5 percent of its budget depends on registration fees it collects from landlords found to be subject to rent control law); Esso Standard Oil Co. v. Cotto, 389 F.3d 212, 219 (1st Cir. 2004) (structural bias established when adjudicative body stood to benefit financially from the proceeding because any fine imposed would flow directly to the agency's budget, amount of fine was unprecedented, hearing examiners were biased, and there was evidence of procedural unfairness). The rule of necessity described in § 7.09 might trump cases in which an entire agency might be disqualified by an institutional pecuniary interest; however, in Esso Standard Oil Co. v. López-Freytes, 522 F.3d 136, 148–50 (1st Cir. 2008), the court enjoined the agency from taking action until it cured the constitutional infirmities.

15. Wilkerson v. Johnson, 699 F.2d 325, 328 (6th Cir. 1983); *Stivers*, 71 F.3d at 743 (dictum) (only lawyer in town would have pecuniary interest against granting license to second lawyer).

16. MFS Sec. Corp. v. SEC, 380 F.3d 611 (2d Cir. 2004). The court also noted that mere potential for embarrassment to the former chairman and threat of controversy to the entire commission was not sufficient to constitute a conflict of interest requiring recusal of all commissioners.

7.0232 *Personal animus*

Bias consists of a personal animus against a party, witness, or counsel,[17] or a group to which they belong.[18] Bias may also be established in cases in which the adjudicator has been the target of personal abuse or criticism from a party arising outside of the hearing.[19]

Illustration:

3. Assume the same facts as Illustration 1, except that there are many stock brokerage firms in town. H is a long-time enemy of K, dating back to college days. They had exchanged harsh words on several occasions. A court could find that H was biased against K.

7.0233 *Prejudgment*

Bias consists of prejudgment of the facts concerning a particular party.[20] Extrajudicial statements often reveal such prejudgment by a decisionmaker.[21]

---

17. *Stivers*, 71 F.3d at 744–46. In order to justify disqualification of an administrative judge based on animus because of comments made during the hearing that are based on testimony at the hearing, the comments must display a deep-seated favoritism or antagonism that would make fair judgment impossible. Bieber v. Dep't of Army, 287 F.3d 1358, 1361–63 (Fed. Cir. 2002) (relying on Liteky v. United States, 510 U.S. 540, 555 (1994) (involving recusal of federal judges)).

18. Berger v. United States, 255 U.S. 22 (1921) (judge's statements evidence bias against Germans).

19. Withrow v. Larkin, 421 U.S. 35, 47 (1975); Mayberry v. Pennsylvania, 400 U.S. 455, 465 (1971) ("No one so cruelly slandered is likely to maintain that calm detachment necessary for fair adjudication").

20. *See, e.g.*, Khouzam v. Attorney Gen., 549 F.3d 235, 257 (3d Cir. 2008) (no neutral and impartial decisionmaker when claimant's only opportunity to make arguments on his own behalf to the agency was to send a letter explaining why that agency's already issued decision was wrong).

21. *See* McClure v. Indep. Sch. Dist. No. 16, 228 F.3d 1205, 1215–16 (10th Cir. 2000) (bias where decisionmakers publicly stated their intent to terminate plaintiff's employment prior to the hearing at which the matter of the termination was to be decided); Bakalis v. Golembeski, 35 F.3d 318, 324 (7th Cir. 1994) (public statements that college president should be dis-

Illustration:

4. Assume the same facts as Illustration 1, except that there are many stock brokerage firms in town. H is interviewed on a radio talk show while the proceeding against K is pending. In response to a question, H declared that K had committed very serious regulatory violations and that his license should be revoked. A court could hold that H was biased against K.

7.0234 Campaign contributions

Bias may be established by large campaign contributions in a contested election. The Supreme Court's 2009 *Caperton v. A.T. Massey Coal Co.* decision involved one individual who had a case that would likely be heard by the West Virginia Supreme Court, who contributed $1,000 directly to one candidate's campaign, $2.5 million to a political organization that supported that candidate, and more than $500,000 on independent expenditures supporting that candidate. The candidate won the election and was the tiebreaker in a split decision ruling in favor of the contributor. The U.S. Supreme Court applied *Withrow v. Larkin* and concluded that this "exceptional case" created a serious risk of actual bias.[22]

---

missed combined with history of personal criticism of board by president); Cinderella Career & Finishing Schools, Inc. v. FTC, 425 F.2d 583, 590 (D.C. Cir. 1970) (speech relating specific facts of pending case and announcing that deception had occurred indicated prejudgment); Texaco, Inc. v. FTC, 336 F.2d 754, 760 (D.C. Cir. 1964) (speech named particular case that was still pending and suggested prejudgment of the merits); Am. Cyanamid Co. v. FTC, 363 F.2d 757 (6th Cir. 1966) (adjudicator was author of congressional committee report expressing views on facts to be adjudicated). This requirement may be more a matter of etiquette and appearances rather than substance, however. It can be avoided by the use of guarded language. *See* Kennecott Copper Corp. v. FTC, 467 F.2d 67, 80 (10th Cir. 1972) (using complaint in a case as example does not indicate prejudgment).

22. Caperton v. A.T. Massey Coal Co., 129 S. Ct. 2252 (2009); *Withrow*, 421 U.S. at 35.

7.024 What does not constitute bias

Bias is not established by the fact that the decisionmaker rejected claims or testimony by or on behalf of a particular party.[23]

Illustration:

> 5. Agency charges K, a licensed broker-dealer, with violations of Agency's regulation and proposes to revoke K's license. F, an ALJ employed by Agency, hears the case. F believes all of the witnesses against K and none of the witnesses called by K. F makes numerous rulings on matters of evidence, all of which are against K, and some of which are legally incorrect. F specifically declares that he thinks K was lying. Agency adopts F's decision. A court would not hold that F was biased against K (but might reverse Agency's decision on account of the erroneous evidence rulings).

Bias is not established by the fact that a decisionmaker has fixed views about law or policy or about factual propositions not related to specific parties.[24]

---

23. NLRB v. Pittsburgh S.S. Co., 337 U.S. 656 (1949). "Bias cannot be inferred from a mere pattern of rulings by a judicial officer, but requires evidence that the officer had it 'in' for the party for reasons unrelated to the officer's view of the law, erroneous as that view might be." McLaughlin v. Union Oil Co. of Cal., 869 F.2d 1039, 1047 (7th Cir. 1989). However, irregularities in the hearing process can suggest bias when combined with other evidence of either personal animosity or prejudgment. Stivers v. Pierce, 71 F.3d 732, 745–46 (9th Cir. 1995) (harshness, harassment, and delays in hearing process combined with other evidence of pecuniary interest and personal animus).

24. FTC v. Cement Inst., 333 U.S. 683, 702–03 (1948), holding that the FTC's conclusion based on a prior investigation that the multiple basing point pricing system was illegal does not disqualify the agency heads from deciding a case based on the same legal theory. The *Cement Inst.* case thus indicates that fixed views about legislative facts are probably not disqualifying. The case also illustrates the principle discussed in the text of § 7.024 that a decisionmaker who has previously come into contact with the facts of a case while "in role" is not treated as having prejudged the facts. To some extent, the *Cement Inst.* case may also be based on the principle of necessity discussed in Chapter 7, § 7.09.

Illustration:

6. Assume the same facts as Illustration 3 (the radio interview), except that H stated that the type of regulatory violations with which K was charged were extremely serious. A court would not hold that H was biased against K.

Bias is not established by the fact that a decisionmaker has been exposed to the facts of a particular dispute while carrying out an assigned task for the agency (i.e., while "in role"). For example, an ALJ is not disqualified simply because he has already heard and decided an earlier phase of the same case,[25] and agency heads are not disqualified from deciding a case in which they previously heard evidence from agency prosecutors and decided to issue a complaint.[26] Similarly, agency heads are not disqualified from conducting hearings concerning the discharge of employees who engaged in an illegal strike simply because the agency heads previously had negotiated with the strikers.[27]

Illustration:

7. Assume the same facts as Illustration 1, except that there are many stock brokerage firms in town. H receives complaints that K has violated regulations. H personally investigates these complaints, speaking to numerous witnesses and subpoenaing documents. H then tells Agency's enforcement personnel to issue a complaint against K. Later, H votes to revoke K's license. A court would not hold that H was biased against K.

Bias is not established because a decisionmaker is a member of a profession, the interests of which might be served by a decision in the case.[28]

---

25. NLRB v. Donnelly Garment Co., 330 U.S. 219, 227–28 (1947).
26. *Withrow*, 421 U.S. at 58.
27. Hortonville Joint Sch. Dist. v. Hortonville Educ. Ass'n, 426 U.S. 482 (1976).
28. Friedman v. Rogers, 440 U.S. 1, 18–19 (1979) (by statute a majority of agency heads must be independent optometrists; case involves discipline of optometrists employed by corporations); *Stivers*, 71 F.3d at 742–44 (board member's interest as member of regulated occupation in rejecting license application is insufficient in itself but plaintiff might still be able to establish pecuniary bias because of the substantiality of the board member's personal interest). However, *Friedman* is inconsistent with an earlier case that held that if all of the agency heads must by statute be

Illustration:

> 8. Assume the same facts as Illustration 1, except that there are
> many stock brokerage firms in town. H's firm is located several
> blocks away from K's firm. A court would not hold that H is
> biased against K.

Bias is not established by a hearing officer's attempt to clarify questions and answers, and to obtain all of the applicable evidence.[29] "Expressions of impatience, dissatisfaction, annoyance, and even anger, that are within the bounds of what imperfect men and women sometimes display[,] do not establish bias."[30] Bias is not established by an ALJ that cuts and pastes proposed findings into a decision if the decision reflects an independent review of the record.[31]

---

independent optometrists, a court could find that the agency is biased against corporate optometrists. Gibson v. Berryhill, 411 U.S. 564 (1973).

29. Holly Hill Farms v. United States, 447 F.3d 258, 270 (4th Cir. 2006) (no bias when hearing transcript makes clear that the hearing officer did not act as counsel for the agency, but rather was simply attempting to ensure that the proceeding remained on track and that relevant information was addressed. The hearing officer explained that he was "not trying lead them, but 'trying to maintain . . . focus and stick to the relevant facts."

30. Rollins v. Massanari, 261 F.3d 853, 857–58 (9th Cir. 2001). *But see* MODEL CODE OF JUDICIAL CONDUCT R. 2.3 (suggesting some actions that could establish bias).

31. Casino Ready Mix v. NLRB, 321 F.3d 1190, 1202 (D.C. Cir. 2003), (affirming the NLRB's decision because it "adopted the ALJ's findings only to the extent that they were consistent with the Board's Decision and Order. The Decision and Order reflects the Board's own independent review of the record, which the Board affirmatively states that it conducted."); Waterbury Hotel Mgmt. v. NLRB, 314 F.3d 645, 651 (D.C. Cir. 2003) ("wholesale cutting and pasting from proposed findings and conclusions warrants particularly close scrutiny, [but noted] we have never held . . . this practice alone demonstrates impermissible bias"). The D.C. Circuit has not established a process for the NLRB to review an ALJ's decision that includes copied materials, but the court affirmed one case where the NLRB conducted a review of the entire record, remanded the offending decision for rehearing with a different ALJ, and conducted a review of the entire record of the subsequent decision. J.J. Cassone Bakery v. NLRB, 554 F.3d 1041, 1045 (D.C. Cir. 2009).

7.025 Bias of single member

If a single member of a multimember agency is biased and is not disqualified from deciding the case, the agency's decision should be reversed, even though the biased member's vote was not necessary to the decision.[32]

Illustration:

> 9. Assume the same facts as Illustration 1, 2, or 3. H is one member of Agency, which is a multimember agency. H is biased and has not been disqualified. The court should reverse Agency's decision and require Agency to conduct a new hearing at which H would not participate.

Bias by a single member of a multimember body is not imputed to other members of the body,[33] nor is bias by agency staff who advise and create a record for the agency members to review imputed to the agency members themselves.[34]

7.03 PERSONAL RESPONSIBILITY OF DECISIONMAKERS

An agency decisionmaker who did not hear the presentation of evidence must be personally familiar with the issues in the case.[35] An agency

---

32. *Stivers*, 71 F.3d at 746–48; Cinderella Career & Finishing Schools, Inc. v. FTC, 425 F.2d 583, 592 (D.C. Cir. 1970); Hicks v. City of Watonga, 942 F.2d 737, 748 (10th Cir. 1991).
33. *See, e.g.*, Blinder, Robinson & Co. v. SEC, 837 F.2d 1099, 1106–7 (D.C. Cir. 1988) (stating, "It would be a strange rule indeed that inferred bias on such a tenuous basis, and then presumed that the bias spread contagionlike to infect [the other] Commissioners. . . . To do so would manifest profound disrespect for Congress' deliberately structuring agencies as (typically) multi-member bodies, with staggered terms and with requirements that the President appoint a certain number of members from the political party other than his own [and] would flout what Justice White, in writing for the Court in *Withrow*, called 'a presumption of honesty and integrity' on the part of those who serve in office.").
34. United States v. Oregon, 44 F.3d 758, 772 (9th Cir. 1994).
35. Morgan v. United States, 298 U.S. 468 (1936) (Morgan I). *Morgan I* was the source of the famous dictum "The one who decides must hear." *Id.* at 481. However, the Court clearly did not mean that the decisionmaker (in that case the Secretary of Agriculture) had to physically hear testimony.

decisionmaker can comply with the personal responsibility requirement in the following ways:

- by acquiring a cursory knowledge of the facts and arguments by reading portions of the transcript and briefs[36]
- by hearing oral argument
- by reading reports of lower-level decisionmakers[37]
- by reading summaries prepared by staff members or receiving a briefing by staff members[38]
- by delegating the power to make the adjudicatory decision to a lower-level decisionmaker (if such delegation is authorized by law)

Courts presume that an agency decisionmaker complied with the personal responsibility rule. Absent evidence suggesting that a violation has occurred, it is improper to conduct discovery on the extent to which a decisionmaker familiarized himself or herself with the issues or the manner in which this occurred. Doing so would intrude too far on the decisional process of judges.[39]

Instead, the case requires only that the decisionmaker "consider and appraise the evidence." *Id.* at 482. It is unclear whether the rule stated in *Morgan I* arises out of due process or out of a statutory requirement that a "full hearing" be provided.

36. Morgan v. United States, 304 U.S. 1, 17–18 (1938) (Morgan II).
37. *See* Yaretsky v. Blum, 629 F.2d 817, 823–25 (2d Cir. 1980) (upper-level decisionmaker supplied with hearing officer's summary and recommendation need not review transcript); Bates v. Sponberg, 547 F.2d 325, 333 (6th Cir. 1976) (due process satisfied when upper-level decisionmakers are supplied with report of hearing panel without transcripts of testimony). This is true even when the final decisionmaker imposes a more severe sanction than the fact-finder recommends. Tigrett v. Rector & Visitors of the Univ. of Virginia, 290 F.3d 620, 629 (4th Cir. 2002).
38. *Morgan I*, 298 U.S. at 481 (evidence "may be sifted and analyzed by competent subordinates").
39. United States v. Morgan, 313 U.S. 409, 422 (1941) (Morgan IV); San Luis Obispo Mothers for Peace v. NRC, 789 F.2d 26, 44–45 (D.C. Cir. 1986) (plaintiffs must make required showing of misconduct before court would examine transcripts of closed meeting). In Nat'l Nutritional Foods Ass'n v. FDA, 491 F.2d 1141, 1144–46 (2d Cir. 1974), a newly appointed secretary signed 27 regulations and 6 notices during the first 13 days he was in office, thus suggesting he could not possibly have become personally familiar with most of them. Noting that *Morgan IV* had taken back most or all of *Morgan I*, the court declined to order discovery. It stated that the

7.04 PROHIBITION ON EX PARTE COMMUNICATIONS

7.041 General rule

The APA's ex parte communications provision[40] applies to both formal adjudication and formal rulemaking.[41] It prohibits off-the-record communications that are relevant to the merits of the proceeding between agency decisionmakers and interested persons outside the agency.[42] Agencies may not create exceptions to this prohibition.[43] If prohibited communications occur, they must be disclosed.

---

secretary had time to read the summaries and confer with his staff about each set of regulations, and it would presume that he had done so.

40. APA § 557(d)(1)(A) provides that "no interested person outside the agency shall make or knowingly cause to be made to any member of the body comprising the agency, administrative law judge, or other employee who is or may reasonably be expected to be involved in the decisional process of the proceeding, an ex parte communication relevant to the merits of the proceeding." This provision was added to the APA by the Government in the Sunshine Act, Pub. L. No. 94-409, § 4(a), 90 Stat. 1241 (1976). Prior to enactment of § 557(d), a series of decisions prohibited ex parte contact with agency decisionmakers. The cases apparently drew on a combination of due process, arbitrary and capricious review, and the supervisory powers of the federal courts. *See, e.g.,* Sangamon Valley Television Corp. v. United States, 269 F.2d 221 (D.C. Cir. 1959); Mass. Bay Telecasters, Inc. v. FCC, 261 F.2d 55, 66 (D.C. Cir. 1958).

41. APA § 557(a) applies to hearings required to be conducted in accordance with § 556; § 556, in turn, covers hearings required by both §§ 553 and 554 to be conducted in accordance with § 556. Under § 553(c), "when rules are required by statute to be made on the record after opportunity for an agency hearing, sections 556 and 557 apply instead of [the informal notice and comment provisions of § 553(c)]."

42. APA § 557(d)(1)(B) prohibits ex parte communications *to* decisionmakers and also prohibits communications *by* decisionmakers to interested persons outside the agency.

43. Elec. Power Supply Ass'n v. FERC, 391 F.3d 1255 (D.C. Cir. 2004) (Federal Energy Regulatory Commission (FERC) regulations could not allow contact between staff decisionmakers and market monitors, who work for regional transmission organizations and whose purpose is to report "objective information about RTO [Regional Transmission Organization] markets, evaluate the behavior of market participants, and recommend how markets can operate more competitively and efficiently").

Different rules apply to communications between agency staff members and agency decisionmakers, and are discussed under the topic of separation of functions.[44] Agency procedural regulations or ALJ codes of conduct frequently impose restrictions on ex parte communications that are more stringent than those contained in the APA.[45] The subject of ex parte communications is closely related to the nonconsultation rule (§ 7.072) and the exclusive record rule (§ 7.08).

7.042 Purposes of the rule

The APA's prohibition on ex parte contacts serves several distinct purposes. First, prohibition and disclosure of ex parte communications avoids the appearance of impropriety. Second, prohibition and disclosure are necessary for fair decisionmaking; only if a party knows the

---

44. *See* Chapter 7, § 7.06. For example, under separation of functions, non-adversary staff members can conduct off-the-record communications with agency heads, whereas the ex parte communications ban prohibits nearly all off-the-record contacts. *See* § 7.0633. Separation of functions applies to "adversaries," but the ex parte contact rule applies to a much broader class of "interested persons." Separation of functions does not apply to formal rulemaking; the ex parte contact rule does apply to formal rulemaking. There are important exceptions to separation of functions (including initial licensing and ratemaking, and an agency head exception); no such exceptions apply to the prohibition on ex parte communications.

45. *See* Model Code of Judicial Conduct for Federal Administrative Law Judges (1989); Model Code of Judicial Conduct (2007). For example, Rule 2.9 of the 2007 Model Code contains restrictions on ex parte communications. These restrictions do not limit prohibited communications to those only from interested parties, but prohibit initiation or consideration of any ex parte communications "outside the presence of the parties or their lawyers." Rule 2.9(A). Also, the code does not limit the prohibition to information "relevant to the merits" of a proceeding, *see infra* § 7.0432, but spells out how to handle administrative and emergency matters. Rule 2.9(A)(1). Further, the code does not allow a judge to receive advice on the law without allowing the parties an opportunity to object or to receive factual information outside of the record. Rules 2.9(A)(2); (3). To date there are no court decisions addressing differing obligations between the 2007 Model Code and the APA or other agency statutes.

arguments presented to a decisionmaker can the party respond effective-ly.[46] Third, disclosure is necessary for meaningful judicial review.[47]

Agencies may adopt regulations that implement APA § 557(d) but may not adopt regulations that modify, abrogate, or violate the statutory ban on ex parte communications.[48]

7.043 Definitions

7.0431 Interested person

The term "interested person" is intended to have a broad and inclusive meaning. It means any person whose interest in the matter is greater than the general interest that a member of the public as a whole may have.[49] The term covers the staff of other agencies as well as members of the legislative and executive branches.[50] Regulated entities that an agency requires to perform a market monitoring function are interested persons.[51]

---

46. Prof'l Air Traffic Controllers Org. (PATCO) v. Fed. Labor Relations Auth. (FLRA), 685 F.2d 547, 563 (D.C. Cir. 1982).

47. *Id.* at 564 n.32.

48. *Elec. Power Supply Ass'n*, 391 F.3d 1255 (finding unlawful FERC orders creating a market monitor exemption to the proscription against ex parte communications). *See also supra* note 45.

49. The interest need not be monetary and is not limited to persons who are parties or intervenors in the agency proceeding. "The term includes, but is not limited to, parties, competitors, public officials, and nonprofit or public interest organizations with a special interest in the matter regulated. The term does not include a member of the public at large who makes a casual or general expression of opinion about a pending proceeding." *See* H. R. Rep. No. 94-880, pt. 1, at 19–20 (1976), *reprinted in* 1976 U.S.C.C.A.N. 2183.

50. As discussed in Chapter 7, § 7.05, the ex parte provision should not be applied in a way that would frustrate legitimate executive or legislative oversight of agencies. Thus a communication from Congress or the White House staff of a general character, not intended to influence the result of a specific adjudication, should not be considered "relevant to the merits" and thus not in violation of § 557(d).

51. Market monitors, who are charged with "ensuring that markets within [their assigned Regional Transmission Organizations (RTOs)] do not result in wholesale transactions or operations that are unduly discriminatory or preferential or provide opportunity for the exercise of market power," have an interest in contested proceedings concerning their RTOs

Illustrations:

10. A pending proceeding concerns sanctions against a union of air traffic controllers that conducted an illegal strike against the federal government. The president of a teacher's union engages in an ex parte communication with the head of the agency conducting the proceeding. The teacher's union president is an interested person because of his involvement in public sector labor relations.[52]

11. A pending proceeding concerns whether to grant an exemption from the Endangered Species Act. Members of the White House staff engage in ex parte contact with decisionmakers. The president and his staff are interested parties with respect to every agency proceeding.[53]

7.0432 *Relevant to the merits*

The term "relevant to the merits of the proceeding" means that the communication concerns a specific issue in a pending case (and is intended to influence the decision on that issue). It concerns matters of law and discretion and, thus, is broader than the term "fact in issue" under APA § 554(d)(1).[54] According to the legislative history, procedural

---

that is "greater than the general interest the public as a whole may have." *Elec. Power Supply Ass'n*, 391 F.3d at 1265.

52. *PATCO*, 685 F.2d at 569–70. In a questionable dictum, the court in *PATCO* stated that the communication would have been improper even if the teachers' union president were not an interested person. "*It is simply unacceptable behavior for any person directly to attempt to influence the decision of a judicial officer in a pending case outside of the formal public proceedings.* This is true for the general public, for 'interested persons'; and for the formal parties to the case." *Id.* at 570 (emphasis in original). This dictum seems contrary to the legislative history of § 557(d) quoted *supra* note 49.

53. Portland Audubon Soc'y v. Endangered Species Comm., 984 F.2d 1534, 1545 (9th Cir. 1993). The court stated that presidential intervention is more likely to influence the result than a communication from any other person; hence the president and his staff must be treated as interested persons in every case in which they take an interest.

54. H. R. Rep. No. 94-880, *supra* note 49, at 20. For discussion of this phrase, *see* § 7.072. *See also supra* note 45 (noting that the Model Code of Judicial Conduct does not limit the prohibition on ex parte communications to contacts that are "relevant to the merits").

inquiries are not relevant to the merits,[55] nor are settlement discussions.[56] However, it would be improper if agency decisionmakers relied on information learned during a settlement negotiation without having it placed on the record.

7.0433 *Ex parte communications*

The APA defines the term "ex parte communication" as an oral or written communication not on the public record with respect to which reasonable prior notice to all parties is not given.[57] The term does not include a request for a status report on any matter or proceeding covered by the adjudication sections of the APA.[58] However, a request for a status report may in effect amount to an indirect or subtle effort to influence

---

55. H. R. REP. No. 94-880, *supra* note 49, at 20. Similarly, the term excludes "general background discussions about an entire industry which do not directly relate to specific agency adjudication involving a member of that industry. . . . It is not the intent of this provision to cut an agency off from access to general information about an industry that an agency needs to exercise its regulatory responsibilities. . . ." *Id.*

56. *See* La. Ass'n of Indep. Producers v. FERC, 958 F.2d 1101, 1112 (D.C. Cir. 1992). The court observed that involvement of agency decisionmakers in settlement negotiations does not involve the evils of most ex parte communications. During settlement negotiations, the adjudicators are not resolving issues on the merits, there is no surreptitious attempt to influence the adjudicators, and there is no judicial review. Moreover, the agency placed summaries of the settlement meetings into the record. *See also* N.Y. State Dep't of Law v. FCC, 984 F.2d 1209, 1217–18 (D.C. Cir. 1993) (same result under FCC ex parte regulations).

57. APA § 551(14). Under the legislative history, a communication would not be ex parte if it were placed on the public record when made or if all parties had reasonable advance notice of the communication. The public record means the docket or other public file containing all materials relevant to the proceeding. H. R. REP. No. 94-880, *supra* note 49, at 22.

58. APA § 551(14). The term "status reports" can mean an inquiry by a party to a decisionmaker about the status of the case or it can refer to a congressional inquiry. See Massman Constr. Co. v. Tenn. Valley Auth., 769 F.2d 1114, 1127 (6th Cir. 1985) (request by TVA to find out when a decision would be issued was a request for a status report that did not deprive opposing party of due process). The legislative history also states that the APA section is not intended to prohibit routine inquiries by members of Congress or referrals of constituent correspondence. H. Rep. No. 94-880, *supra* note 49, at 21–22.

the substantive outcome of the proceeding, which would be a prohibited communication.[59]

"An improper attempt to influence an adjudication is not a concern if it does not reach the ultimate decision maker. Judicial evaluation of [ex parte] pressure must focus on the nexus between the pressure and the actual decision maker."[60]

The APA section on ex parte communications does not constitute authority to withhold information from Congress,[61] nor does it extend to "disposition of ex parte matters authorized by law."[62]

7.044 Coverage of ex parte contact prohibition

7.0441 *Agency personnel prohibited from receiving or making ex parte communications*

The prohibition on ex parte communication covers members of the body that make up the agency (so-called agency heads), ALJs, or any "other employee who is or may reasonably be expected to be involved in the decisional process of the proceeding."[63] Thus, it covers communications by or to agency employees other than ALJs who serve as initial decisionmakers, as well as employees who may reasonably be expected to serve as advisers to decisionmakers.[64]

---

59. H. R. REP. No. 94-880, *supra* note 49, at 20–21. "In doubtful cases the agency official should treat the communication as ex parte so as to protect the integrity of the decisionmaking process." *Id.* at 21. *See also supra* note 45.

60. Press Broad. Co. v. FCC, 59 F.3d 1365, 1369 (D.C. Cir. 1995), citing ATX, Inc. v. U.S. Dep't of Transp., 41 F.3d 1522, 1527 (D.C. Cir. 1994).

61. APA § 557(d)(2). Presumably, Congress was concerned that if a decisionmaking official responded to a request for information from a congressional committee, this might be construed as an unlawful ex parte communication. For discussion of congressional interference in ongoing adjudicatory matters, *see* Chapter 7, § 7.05.

62. APA § 557(d)(1). "This exemption might include, for example, requests by one party to a proceeding for subpoenas, adjournments, and continuances." H. R. REP. No. 94-880, *supra* note 49, at 19.

63. APA § 557(d)(1)(A), (B).

64. *See* Chapter 7, § 7.0633, explaining that separation of functions under the APA does not prohibit nonadversarial agency employees from serving as decisional advisers to agency heads or furnishing ex parte advice to the agency heads. For this purpose, such advisers may be full-time agency employees or those working part-time for the agency such as consul-

Illustration:

12. The FCC must decide whether to grant a television license to applicant X or applicant Y. X contacts AA, the attorney adviser to an FCC commissioner. X discusses the reasons why X's application is superior to Y's application. Because AA may reasonably be expected to be involved in the decisional process, X's communication violated APA § 557(d).

7.0442 *Indirect contacts*

Because the ex parte provision covers communications that an interested person may "cause to be made," it covers indirect contacts. For example, if A (an interested person) asks B (not an interested person) to communicate with an agency head on A's behalf, A would violate the section.[65]

Illustration:

13. Assume the same facts as Illustration 12, except that X asks Z to make the contact with AA. Z is a lifelong friend of AA. X has caused an ex parte communication to be made and has violated the APA. If Z had made the communication with AA on his own behalf, and Z had no interest in the proceeding except that as a television viewer he liked X's program proposals, Z would not be considered an "interested person" and his communication would probably not violate APA § 557(d).[66]

---

tants. H. R. REP. No. 94-880, *supra* note 49, at 19. One decision indicated that § 557(d) prohibits communications to agency employees who were formerly involved in the decisional process but are no longer with the agency or who have recused themselves. North Carolina v. EPA, 881 F.2d 1250, 1257 (4th Cir. 1989) (single-judge opinion on stay request).

65. H. R. REP. No. 94-880, *supra* note, 49 at 20. However, if B contacted the agency official without A's knowledge, approval, or encouragement, A would not be guilty of causing an ex parte communication.

66. *But see* note 52, citing dictum in *PATCO* that any communication designed to influence an adjudicator is illegal regardless of whether the outside person is an interested party.

7.0443 Outside the agency

APA § 557(d) applies only to communications from persons "outside the agency." Communications to decisionmakers from staff members inside the agency are covered by the provision on separation of functions.[67] The president is considered to be "outside the agency" even though the agency is in the executive branch.[68] An organization in which an agency requires regulated entities to participate is not "outside the agency."[69]

7.045 Time when prohibition goes into effect

The prohibition on ex parte communication goes into effect at such time as the agency shall designate, but not later than the time at which a proceeding is noticed for hearing. However, if the person responsible for the communication has knowledge that it will be noticed, the prohibition begins at the time of his or her acquisition of such knowledge.[70]

7.046 Placing communications on the record

If an adjudicatory decisionmaker makes or receives prohibited communications, the decisionmaker shall place on the record all such written communications, and memoranda stating the substance of all such oral communications. In addition, the decisionmaker shall place on the record all written responses, and memoranda stating the substance of all oral responses, to such communications.[71] Section 557(d) does not provide any exceptions to this requirement.

---

67. *See* Chapter 7, § 7.06.
68. Portland Audubon Soc'y v. Endangered Species Comm., 984 F.2d 1534, 1545–46 (9th Cir. 1993).
69. Elec. Power Supply Ass'n v. FERC, 391 F.3d 1255, 1265 (D.C. Cir. 2004).
70. APA § 557(d)(1)(E). *Cf.* MODEL CODE OF JUD. CONDUCT R. (2007) Rule 2.9(A) (2007), which applies not only to "pending" but also to "impending" matters.
71. APA § 557(d)(1)(C). According to the legislative history, "in some cases, placing the communication on the record will not provide sufficient notice to all parties. Each agency should consider requiring by regulation that in certain cases actual notice of the ex parte communication to be provided to all parties." H. R. REP. No. 94-880, *supra* note 49, at 21.

7.047 Sanctions for prohibited communications

Adjudicatory decisionmakers may, consistent with the interests of justice and the policy of underlying statutes, require a party who makes or causes to be made a prohibited communication to show cause why his or her claim or interest in the proceeding should not be dismissed, denied, disregarded, or otherwise adversely affected on account of such violation.[72] Moreover, the agency may, to the extent consistent with the interests of justice and the policy of the underlying statutes, consider a violation of the section sufficient grounds for a decision adverse to a party who knowingly violates it.[73]

7.048 Role of the courts

The APA does not spell out the role of reviewing courts in enforcing the prohibition on ex parte communications. Courts have frequently required an agency to hold an evidentiary hearing to ascertain whether ex parte communications had occurred and the circumstances of such communications.[74] Decisions blemished by ex parte communication are voidable rather than void. The court must decide whether the agency's decisionmaking process was irrevocably tainted so as to make the ultimate judgment of the agency unfair, either to an innocent party or to the public interest.[75]

---

72. APA § 557(d)(1)(D). However, such a show-cause hearing is not required in every case; it lies within the discretion of the presiding officer. H. R. REP. No. 94-880, *supra* note 49, at 21. A showing should not be required where the violation was clearly inadvertent. *Id.*

73. APA § 556(d). *See* Press Broad. Co. v. FCC, 59 F.3d 1365, 1370–71 (D.C. Cir. 1995) (FCC should consider adverse consequences to applicant because party making contacts could not have reasonably believed the proceeding was unrestricted). According to the legislative history, the interests of justice might dictate that a claimant for an old age benefit not lose his claim even if he violates the rules. On the other hand, where two parties have applied for a license and the applications are of relatively equal merit, an agency may rule against a party who committed a prohibited contact. H. R. REP. No. 94-880, *supra* note 49, at 22. In addition, an agency might censure or dismiss an official who engaged in a prohibited contact or prohibit an attorney who violates the section from appearing before the agency. *Id.* at 21.

74. *PATCO*, 685 F.2d at 547; *Portland Audubon*, 984 F.2d at 1549.

75. *PATCO*, 685 F.2d at 564; *Press Broad.*, 59 F.3d at 1369–70 (D.C. Cir. 1995). In making this determination, a court must exercise equitable discretion. A

7.049 Ex parte communications in informal adjudication

The APA adjudication provisions do not apply to informal adjudication.[76] Whether a court would reverse an informal adjudication decision because ex parte communications had occurred is unclear. Older and current authorities support the argument that ex parte communication can deprive a party of procedural due process (assuming that due process is applicable to the case).[77] In addition, some cases suggest that courts will reverse decisions tainted by ex parte communication because such deci-

---

number of considerations may be relevant: the gravity of the communications, whether they influenced the agency's ultimate decision, whether the party making the improper contact benefited from the ultimate decision, whether the contents of the communication were unknown to opposing parties, and whether vacation of the agency's decision and remand for a new proceeding would serve a useful purpose. *PATCO*, 685 F.2d at 564–65. *See id.* at 567 (inadvertent contact does not call for sanction); *id.* at 568 (contact did not prejudice opposing party or affect ultimate result); *id.* at 571–73 (contact was brief, nonthreatening, had no effect on ultimate decision, did not prejudice opposing party); *Press Broad.*, 59 F.3d at 1365 (decisionmakers who were subject of ex parte communication recused themselves and decision was made after de novo consideration by full commission); Freeman Eng'g Assocs., Inc. v. FCC, 103 F.3d 169, 184 (D.C. Cir. 1997) (no taint because decision rejected arguments made in ex parte written communication).

76. *But see* Chapter 3, note 11 (explaining Citizens Awareness Network, Inc. v. NRC, 391 F.3d 338 (1st Cir. 2004), which held that NRC rules met the requirements of the APA even though they were designated as "informal" and provided for only limited discovery and opportunity for cross-examination).

77. Sangamon Valley Television Corp. v. FCC, 269 F.2d 221, 224 (D.C. Cir. 1959) ("basic fairness" requires disclosure of ex parte contacts); Home Box Office, Inc. v. FCC, 567 F.2d 9, 56 (D.C. Cir. 1977) (reading *Sangamon* as due process case); an example of more recent authority is Stone v. FDIC, 179 F.3d 1368, 1374–75 (Fed. Cir. 1999) (stating, "Not every ex parte communication is a procedural defect so substantial and so likely to cause prejudice that it undermines the due process guarantee and entitles the claimant to an entirely new administrative proceeding. Only ex parte communications that introduce new and material information to the deciding official will violate the due process guarantee of notice.") *See also* Ward v. United States, 634 F.3d 1274 (Fed. Cir. 2011) (finding error by Merit Systems Protection Board for failing to consider due process issues). *Ward* applied Blank v. Dep't of the Army, 247 F.3d 1225, 1228 (Fed. Cir. 2001) (stating that the court "must reverse a decision of the Board

sions are inconsistent with the statutory requirement that a "hearing" be provided,[78] or under the courts' supervisory powers, or because the record in the case is incomplete.[79]

However, there are several lines of reason that courts might follow to affirm an informal adjudication decision when there has been an ex parte communication. First, courts might conclude that under the three-factor balancing test in *Mathews v. Eldridge*,[80] there was no substantial or prejudicial defect. Second, the Supreme Court has held that lower courts are not permitted to impose procedural requirements on informal adjudication;[81] however, it is unlikely that a court would refuse to enforce an agency regulation that prohibits ex parte communications.[82] Third, the word "hearing" does not necessarily entail trial-type procedures.[83] Fourth, the Supreme Court generally requires judicial review to take place on the written record before the agency.[84]

7.05 LEGISLATIVE INTERFERENCE WITH ADJUDICATION

7.051 General rule

The APA contains no provisions relating to legislative pressure on adjudicators.[85] It seems well established that such legislative pressure can

---

if it . . . is not in accordance with the requirements of the Due Process Clause of the Fifth Amendment or any other constitutional provision").

78. Nat'l Small Shipments Traffic Conference v. ICC, 590 F.2d 345, 350–51 (D.C. Cir. 1978); U.S. Lines v. Fed. Mar. Comm'n, 584 F.2d 519, 539–41 (D.C. Cir. 1978).

79. *U.S. Lines*, 584 F.2d at 533–35, 541–42; *Home Box Office*, 567 F.2d at 54–55.

80. Mathews v. Eldridge, 424 U.S. 319 (1976), discussed in Chapter 2, §§ 2.04, 2.05.

81. Pension Benefit Guar. Corp. v. LTV Corp., 496 U.S. 633, 655–56 (1990).

82. *See, e.g.*, Drake v. Comm'r, 125 T.C. 201 (2005) (enforcing Revenue Procedure prohibiting ex parte communications "between any Appeals employees . . . and employees of other Internal Revenue Service officers . . . to the extent that such communications appear to compromise the independence of Appeals").

83. United States v. Fla. E. Coast Ry., 410 U.S. 224, 234–35 (1973).

84. Camp v. Pitts, 411 U.S. 138 (1973).

85. However, congressional pressure could be a prohibited ex parte communication; members of Congress with a political interest in the matter could be interested parties. *See* Chapter 7, § 7.0431. However, many congressional communications to an agency would be status inquiries, which are not prohibited by § 557(d). However, a request for a status

violate the due process rights of aggrieved parties.[86] Where due process is inapplicable, however, it is less clear whether legislative pressure requires a reviewing court to reverse agency action. Moreover, courts must tread lightly in this area because congressional interference may be a form of legislative oversight.

7.052 *Mathews* balancing

In deciding whether to reverse, remand, or enjoin a decision because of legislative pressure, courts generally consider whether due process was denied in the circumstances of the particular case.[87] An agency may

---

report could be an indirect or subtle attempt to influence the substantive outcome of the proceeding and thus could be a prohibited ex parte communication. *See* § 7.0433.

86. Pillsbury Co. v. FTC, 354 F.2d 952, 964 (5th Cir. 1966) (The FTC ordered Pillsbury to divest itself of acquired assets. After an interlocutory FTC decision applying the rule of reason rather than a per se rule, the FTC chair was called before a congressional committee and grilled about the interlocutory decision. Other FTC members were present at the hearing. The FTC later upheld an ALJ decision requiring divestiture. The court held that legislative pressure denied Pillsbury due process and reversed.); Koniag, Inc. v. Andrus, 580 F.2d 601, 610–11 (D.C. Cir. 1978) (Congressman's letter to secretary two days before decision compromised appearance of impartiality; the court remanded because "we cannot say that 3 1/2 years later, a new Secretary in a new administration is thereby rendered incapable of giving these cases a fair and dispassionate treatment.").

87. *See* Esso Standard Oil Co. v. Lopez-Feytes, 522 F.3d 136, 148 (1st Cir. 2009); ATX, Inc. v. U.S. Dep't of Transp., 41 F.3d 1522, 1529–30 (D.C. Cir. 1994); Monieson v. Commodities Futures Trading Comm'n, 996 F.2d 852, 865 (7th Cir. 1993); Power Auth. of N.Y. v. FERC, 743 F.2d 93, 109–10 (2d Cir. 1984); Am. Pub. Gas Ass'n v. Fed. Power Comm'n, 567 F.2d 1016, 1067–71 (D.C. Cir. 1977); Gulf Oil Corp. v. FPC, 563 (3d Cir. 1977) F.2d 588, 610–12; *Koniag*, 580 F.2d at 610. In *Esso Standard Oil*, the court enjoined the Puerto Rico Environmental Quality Board from imposing a $76 million penalty on company that had spilled fuel in part because a Puerto Rico Senate report threatened criminal prosecution against agency officials for acting slowly in response to the spill; the hearings examiner selection process created an appearance and incentive for bias, and the penalty would go directly to the agency's budget). In *ATX*, which involved an application for a license, a congressman testified at the hearing that the license should be denied. The court thought that congressional opinion testimony creates a strong

cure political bias in an early stage of a proceeding through subsequent intra-agency review proceedings.[88]

Courts considering whether to vacate a decision tainted by legislative pressure might apply the three-factor balancing test normally employed in due process cases.[89] Among the factors that courts might consider are whether or not congressional pressure probably influenced the decision of the adjudicators, whether the communication concerned disputed facts as opposed to issues of law or policy, and whether the particular application of pressure served a legitimate purpose such as congressional oversight of legislation or administration.[90]

Illustrations:

14. The FTC issued a complaint against B alleging that the advertising for B's charm school would mislead potential students. An

---

potential for appearance of impropriety, but the court upheld the agency decision denying the license. The congressman's testimony contained no threats, was made on the record, was based on information already available to the ALJ, and was not relied on in any of the decisions. The court explained that "judicial evaluation of pressure must focus on the nexus between the pressure and the actual decision maker." *ATX*, 41 F.3d at 1527–30. In *Gulf Oil*, the congressional pressure related to the FPC's decision to hold lengthy show-cause hearings rather than seek an injunction, not to the merits of the case. The court thought that pressure on a question of law was less objectionable than pressure relating to factual issues. In addition, the agency had ignored the suggestion. *Gulf Oil*, 563 F.2d at 610–12. In *Koniag*, the interim decisions in several pending cases were criticized in a congressional hearing, but only an agency adviser was called to testify, not the adjudicators themselves. The court was unsure whether *Pillsbury* applied to advisers; but at worst, the adviser was not asked to prejudge any of the claims. *Koniag*, 580 F.2d at 609–11.

88. *See, e.g.,* Aera Energy, LLC v. Salazar, 642 F.3d 212 (D.C. Cir. 2011). The Interior Board of Land Appeals removed whatever undue influence had tainted the agency official's decision, citing *ATX*, 41 F.3d at 1528 and D.C. Fed'n of Civic Ass'ns v. Volpe, 459 F.2d 1231, 1247 n.84 (D.C. Cir. 1971).

89. Mathews v. Eldridge, 424 U.S. 319 (1976), discussed in Chapter 2, §§ 2.04, 2.05.

90. The court might decide whether to set aside an agency decision tainted by legislative pressure in accordance with the standards developed in ex parte communication cases. *See* § 7.048; Power Auth. of N.Y. v. FERC, 743 F.2d at 110.

ALJ issued a proposed decision that the advertising was not misleading. While the matter was pending before the FTC commissioners, C, the FTC chair, testified at a Senate oversight hearing. D, the chair of the Senate Committee, strongly criticized the ALJ decision in the B case, stating that the advertising was obviously misleading and that the decision ignored important consumer protection issues. Subsequently, the FTC unanimously reversed the ALJ decision and issued a cease and desist order against B. A court could hold that the legislative pressure denied B due process.

15. Assume the same facts as Illustration 14, except that rather than discussing the B case, D asked C for C's recommendations concerning whether the statute should be amended to insert specific language concerning educational advertising. D indicated concern that misleading advertising by vocational schools was rampant. A court would probably hold that the legislative pressure did not deny B due process. A court would also probably hold that the congressional hearing was not a prohibited ex parte communication since it occurred at a public committee hearing.

7.053 Commencement of the proceeding

Congressional interference in a pending case prior to the time the case enters the hearing phase is less likely to require reversal than interference in a case after it reaches the hearing phase.[91]

---

91. DCP Farms v. Yeutter, 957 F.2d 1183, 1187–88 (5th Cir. 1992). In the *DCP Farms* case, a county committee recommended approval of crop subsidy payments to a group of related trusts. A chair of the relevant congressional subcommittee met with U.S. Department of Agriculture (USDA) officials and later wrote to the USDA secretary objecting to this decision. The secretary responded that the USDA would take a "very aggressive position in dealing with this case." The case was then set for a hearing at the national level. The court held that *Pillsbury* was inapplicable because the case had not yet reached the hearing phase. The communication involved a larger policy debate, and applying *Pillsbury* would "erect no small barrier to congressional oversight." *Id.* at 1187. Actual bias, not appearance of bias, should be the standard, the court indicated.

Illustration:

16. Assume the same facts as Illustration 14, except that the Senate Committee hearing occurred after the FTC issued its complaint, but six months before the ALJ hearing. D strongly criticized B and praised C for issuing the complaint. A court would probably hold that the legislative pressure did not deprive B of due process.

7.054 Irrelevant factors

Congressional pressure, which caused the agency to consider an irrelevant factor in making a discretionary decision, would render the agency decision arbitrary and capricious.[92] Courts appear quite cautious in applying this standard to invalidate agency decisions. They are concerned that a rigid application of the standard would interfere with legitimate congressional oversight as well as impair agency flexibility in dealing with Congress.[93]

Illustrations:

17. Indian tribe T applies to Agency to take certain land into trust so that T can operate a gambling casino on the property. The statute prescribes no procedure for such requests and provides no

---

92. D.C. Fed'n of Civic Ass'ns v. Volpe, 459 F.2d 1231, 1245–49 (D.C. Cir. 1971). In the *D.C. Fed'n* case, an agency approved construction of a bridge after a member of Congress threatened to deny funding for the D.C. subway unless the bridge was approved. The court held that the decision was arbitrary and capricious because congressional pressure caused an unlawful decisional factor to be introduced in the decision to build the bridge.

93. *ATX, Inc.*, 41 F.3d at 1528 (introduction of bills in Congress to prevent licensee from entering airline business was not pressure against decisionmakers; pressure on agency head to set matter for hearing did not shape decision on the merits); *DCP Farms*, 957 F.2d at 1188 (finding that congressional pressure concerned a relevant rather than an extraneous factor); Chemung Cnty. v. Dole, 804 F.2d 216, 222 (2d Cir. 1986) (finding no improper political influence on FAA); Peter Kiewit Sons' Co. v. U.S. Army Corps of Eng'rs., 714 F.2d 163 (D.C. Cir. 1983) (no clear showing that agency decisionmaker was aware of congressional pressure); Sokaogon Chippewa Cmty. v. Babbitt, 929 F. Supp. 1165, 1173–81 (W.D. Wis. 1996) (political pressures related to relevant factors and did not influence decisionmaker, discovery denied).

standards for the decision. Agency conducts an informal public hearing on T's request. Following the hearing, H, the head of Agency, announces that he will probably grant T's application. Congressman C contacts H and threatens to cut Agency's budget in half if the application is granted. C is well positioned to carry out this threat. H rejects T's application, stating reasons that are not arbitrary and capricious. A court would probably set aside H's decision and remand for reconsideration because the pressure by C apparently caused H to consider an irrelevant factor.

18. Assume the same facts as Illustration 17, except that C tells H that T's application should be rejected because there are already too many Indian gambling casinos nearby and T's would not be economically viable. A court would probably refuse to set aside H's decision because of pressure by C since economic viability is an appropriate factor for H to consider.

7.06 SEPARATION OF FUNCTIONS

7.061 General rule

The APA provides that an agency staff member who has engaged in an adversary function[94] in a case may not participate or advise in an adjudicatory decision in that case or a factually related case.[95]

---

94. The terms "adversary" and "adversary function" are not used by the APA; this book uses those terms to refer to the "performance of investigative or prosecuting functions," the terms used in the statute.
95. APA § 554(d) provides:

> An employee or agent engaged in the performance of investigative or prosecuting functions for an agency in a case may not, in that or a factually related case, participate or advise in the decision, recommended decision, or agency review pursuant to section 557 of this title, except as witness or counsel in public proceedings. This subsection does not apply—
>
> (A) in determining applications for initial licenses;
> (B) to proceedings involving the validity or application of rates, facilities, or practices of public utilities or carriers; or
> (C) to the agency or a member or members of the body comprising the agency.

7.062 Rationale for separation of functions

The APA's separation of functions requirement assumes that Congress will create agencies that are responsible for exercising the functions of investigation, prosecution, and adjudication. If the same individual is both an adversary and an adjudicator, the adjudication process may seem unfair and may truly be unfair. Consequently, the APA requires that agencies separate these functions internally.[96] The APA provision applies only to agency formal adjudication, not to formal rulemaking. It probably applies to all formal adjudications (other than those explicitly excepted), regardless of whether the case is prosecutorial or nonprosecutorial in nature, although this proposition is not yet settled.[97] Due

---

A party wishing to assert rights under § 554(d) must assert them through a disqualification motion as soon as he becomes aware of the facts. Gibson v. FTC, 682 F.2d 554, 560–67 (5th Cir. 1982).

96. Congress was concerned that prosecutors or investigators, if allowed to serve as adjudicators, might rely on nonrecord information and might have acquired a will-to-win incompatible with fair adjudication. U.S. Attorney General's Committee on Administrative Procedure, *Final Report* 56, S. Doc. No. 8, 77th Cong., 1st Sess. (1941); Administrative Procedure Act Legislative History 24–25, S. Doc. 248, 79th Cong. 1st Sess. (1946). The precise degree to which agencies should and must separate functions has long been a subject of dispute. See generally RICHARD J. PIERCE, JR., ADMINISTRATIVE LAW TREATISE § 9.9 (4th ed. 2002); Michael Asimow, *When the Curtain Falls: Separation of Functions in the Federal Administrative Agencies*, 81 COLUM. L. REV. 759 (1981); Antonin Scalia, *Chairman's Message—Separation of Functions: Obscurity Preserved*, 34 ADMIN. L. REV. v (Win. 1982); Willis B. Snell, Chairman's Message, 33 ADMIN. L. REV. vii (Spr. 1981). *But see* CHARLES H. KOCH, JR., ADMINISTRATIVE LAW AND PRACTICE § 5.25 (2d ed. 1997) (noting that "the presiding official is pivotal to the factfinding function of an evidentiary hearing and hence, unlike the trial judge, an administrative judge has a well established affirmative duty to develop the record").

97. There is an unresolved issue about whether APA separation of functions applies to nonprosecutorial cases, meaning cases in which no wrongdoing is alleged. On the one hand, the reference to "investigative or prosecuting functions" suggests a limitation to prosecutorial cases. However, if that were true, why would the section make explicit exceptions for initial licensing and rate disputes that would be nonprosecutorial in nature? *See* PIERCE, *supra* note 96, at 682–84; Asimow, *supra* note 96, at 772–73. For example, In Richardson v. Perales, 402 U.S. 389 (1971), the Court upheld the system of Social Security adjudication in which a single ALJ has both investigatory and adjudicatory responsibilities, which might indicate that § 554(d) is

process may require separation of functions even in cases to which the APA's separation of functions provision does not apply.[98] The APA sets forth some additional rules of separation of functions applicable only to ALJs,[99] and the Model Code of Judicial Conduct treats such issues under ex parte rules.[100]

---

inapplicable to nonprosecutorial cases. However, the Court did not address § 554(d) directly; as a result, it is unclear whether the *Perales* case is authority for this proposition. Similarly, in Yang v. McElroy, 277 F.3d 158, 162 (2d Cir. 2002), the court observed that under 8 U.S.C. § 1229(b)(1), an immigration judge, unlike an Article III judge, is not merely the fact-finder and adjudicator, but also has an obligation to establish the record. As in the *Perales* case, the court made no mention of § 554(d).

98. For discussion of due process and the ingredients of formal hearings, *see* Chapter 2, § 2.04. A combination of adversary and adjudicatory roles at the agency head level does not automatically violate due process. Withrow v. Larkin, 421 U.S. 35, 58 (1975) (agency heads both investigated and adjudicated licensing case). However, particular combinations may well add up to due process violations, especially if occurring below the agency head level. *See, e.g.,* Humphries v. County of Los Angeles, 554 F.3d 1170, 1197 (9th Cir. 2009) (a single person, charged with investigating serious allegations of child abuse, may not adjudicate those allegations for placement on the Child Abuse Central Index (CACI) and serve as appellate commissioner in review of his own decision); Karpova v. Snow, 497 F.3d 262, 271 (2d Cir. 2007) (it is a troublesome question to determine when a single individual could serve as prosecutor and judge in the same case without violating due process); White v. Ind. Parole Bd., 266 F.3d 759, 766–68 (7th Cir. 2001) (2–1 decision) (in prison discipline case, investigating officer could advise board ex parte but could not serve as member of the board); Utica Packing Co. v. Block, 781 F.2d 71 (6th Cir. 1986) (agency head dismissed the judicial officer because the head disagreed with the decision, replaced him with a new judicial officer, then moved that the new officer reconsider the case); Walker v. City of Berkeley, 951 F.2d 182 (9th Cir. 1991) (attorney played adversary and adjudicatory roles in same case). Of course, whether a particular combination of functions violated due process would be evaluated under the usual three-factor analysis. Mathews v. Eldridge, 424 U.S. 319 (1976).

99. *See* Chapter 7, § 7.07.

100. *See, e.g.,* MODEL CODE OF JUDICIAL CONDUCT R. 29 (2007), Rule 2.9. *See supra* note 45.

7.063 Operation of separation of functions

7.0631 Definition of adversary staff member

The APA's separation of functions provision prohibits staff members who have carried out "adversary functions"[101] in a case from taking part in adjudicatory decisionmaking of that case. For this purpose, the phrase "adversary function" means significant and personal participation in the functions of prosecution, investigation, or advocacy.[102] Adversary functions typically involve participation in developing or presenting evidence or argument for or against a party to an adjudicative proceeding. This book refers to an agency employee who has personally engaged in an adversary function in a case (or a factually related case) as an "adversary."[103]

A staff member who has supervised, or has been supervised by, an adversary does not for that reason become an adversary unless the staff member has become significantly and personally involved in adversary functions.[104]

---

101. As explained *supra* note 94, the terms "adversary" and "adversary function" are not used in the statute but are shorthand for the phrase "performance of investigative or prosecuting functions" used in APA § 554(d).

102. Insignificant participation, such as might occur if a staff member answered a technical question asked by an adversary, should not turn the staff member into an adversary. Similarly, insignificant involvement by an adversary in the adjudicatory function does not violate the APA. *See* Greenberg v. Bd. of Governors of the Fed. Reserve Sys., 968 F.2d 164, 167 (2d Cir. 1992) (ALJ's law clerk had previously engaged in adversary functions but did only "some administrative things" for the ALJ; adversary's ministerial participation in decisionmaking does not violate APA).

103. In a questionable decision, one court held that an agency staff member must be disqualified as an adjudicator under § 554(d) if he had access to nonrecord information even though he did not serve an adversary role. Grolier, Inc. v. FTC, 615 F.2d 1215 (9th Cir. 1980) (FTC member's attorney adviser disqualified to serve as ALJ if exposed to any ex parte information about case). For due process purposes, the Court has made clear that "mere exposure to evidence presented in nonadversary investigative proceedings is insufficient in itself to impugn the fairness of the board members at a later adversary hearing." Withrow v. Larkin, 421 U.S. 35, 55 (1975). The same should be true for statutory separation of functions.

104. U.S. Department of Justice, *Attorney General's Manual on the Administrative Procedure Act* 58 (a supervisor who is consulted extensively by subordinates becomes an adversary in the case); Utica Packing Co. v. Block, 781 F.2d 71,

7.0632 *Separation of adversaries from decisionmaking*

An adversary cannot serve as a decisionmaker at the level of initial hearing, intermediate review, or agency head review. Similarly, an adversary cannot furnish off-the-record advice to a decisionmaker concerning an issue in the case, regardless of whether that issue involves fact, law, or policy.[105] The prohibition on off-the-record advice by an adversary to a decisionmaker applies regardless of whether the decisionmaker is rendering an initial decision, intermediate decision, or final agency-head level decision.

Decisionmakers can engage in off-the-record communications with adversary staff members if the communications concern a subject other than the adjudicatory matter in which the staff member was an adversary, such as a pending rulemaking or judicial review.[106]

7.0633 *Nonadversary staff advisers*

The separation of functions provision does not preclude agency decisionmakers from receiving off-the-record advice from nonadversary agency staff members such as legal advisers or technical experts.[107]

Illustrations:

19. M is a staff member of Agency who investigated alleged violations by X Co. of its water pollution permit. An ALJ issues a proposed decision that X Co. violated its permit. H is one of the heads of Agency. Later, when the heads are reviewing the proposed decision, H asks M whether X Co.'s violation was serious

---

76 (6th Cir. 1986) (dictum) (adviser to the decisionmaker not disqualified under § 554(d) merely because his supervisor was an adversary). The issue about whether APA separation of functions applies to supervisors or subordinates of adversaries solely by virtue of their institutional link is not completely resolved. Asimow, *supra* note 96, at 774–76 (1981).

105. Greene v. Babbitt, 943 F. Supp. 1278, 1285–86 (W.D. Wash. 1996) (policy and legal advice by adversary to agency head violated § 554(d)).

106. *Attorney General's Manual supra* note 104, at 58 n.8.

107. Such advice, however, must not violate the exclusive record requirement by furnishing evidentiary material that is not in the record. *Id.* at 55, 57. In contrast, under APA § 554(d)(1), it appears that an ALJ (as opposed to other agency decisionmakers) cannot receive off-the-record advice concerning a "fact in issue" from anyone, including nonadversary agency staff members. *See* Chapter 7, § 7.062; Butz v. Economou, 438 U.S. 478, 513–14 (1978).

enough to justify revoking X Co.'s permit. M cannot give this advice off the record.[108]

20. Assume the same facts as Illustration 19, except that H seeks off-the-record technical advice from S, an agency employee who specializes in water pollution issues, but who was not previously involved in the X Co. case. S can give this advice.

21. Assume the same facts as Illustration 19, except that at the same time that H is reviewing the ALJ decision in the X Co. case, H seeks off-the-record advice from M about an issue arising out of a rulemaking proceeding concerning water pollution or arising out of judicial review of another water pollution case. M can give this advice.

22. Assume the same facts as Illustration 19. B is M's supervisor. B took no significant role in the investigation of X Co.'s permit violations, although B did read M's report. H asks B for off-the-record advice. B can give this advice.

23. Assume the same facts as Illustration 20, except that S had participated as an adversary in an earlier, unrelated water pollution case against X Co., which involved similar facts to the present dispute. S can advise H in the current case since the two cases against X Co. are not considered "factually related."[109]

7.0634 Initial determinations

The separation of functions requirement does not preclude agency decisionmakers from taking part in a determination to launch an investigation or issue a complaint or similar preliminary decision, and later

---

108. *Attorney General's Manual supra* note 104, at 56–57.
109. Marshall v. Cuomo, 192 F.3d 473, 484 (4th Cir. 1999) (staff member is not disqualified as adviser even though involved as adversary in unrelated previous case against same respondent involving similar facts). See *Attorney General's Manual supra* note 104, at 54 n.6 (factually related cases are ones brought against the same respondent, not ones with similar factual patterns against different respondents). *But see* Chapter 7, § 7.08; such communication might conflict with the exclusive record rule; hence agencies may decide that the better practice when asking potentially outcome-determinative questions is to do this on the record, so the parties can respond to any such advice.

serving as a decisionmaker in the same case, even though this determination exposes the decisionmaker to communications by adversary staff members. Similarly, separation of functions does not preclude a staff member from taking part in this sort of preliminary decision and then acting as an off-the-record adviser to decisionmakers.[110]

Illustration:

24. Assume the same facts as Illustration 19. C is the general counsel of Agency. After considering M's report concerning X Co.'s discharges, C decides that Agency should issue a complaint that would start the adjudicatory process. Whether to issue a complaint is a decision reserved to the heads of Agency. C and M take part in a meeting with H that is not open to outsiders. C discusses M's report and urges the heads to issue a complaint. The heads, including H, issue the complaint. Later, when the heads are reviewing the ALJ's proposed decision, H asks C for off-the-record advice. H is not disqualified from hearing the case and C can furnish the advice.

7.064 Exceptions to separation of functions requirement

The requirement of separation of functions is inapplicable in initial license proceedings or to proceedings involving the validity or application of rates, facilities, or practices of public utilities or carriers.[111] The initial licensing exception covers any form of permission sought from an agency, including a modification of an existing license sought by the licensee, but does not cover proceedings in which the agency denies renewal of a license.[112]

An agency may choose to separate functions in connection with initial licensing or ratemaking (or similar determinations concerning the validity or application of rates, facilities, or practices of public utilities or carriers), but the agency is not required to do so.

---

110. Withrow v. Larkin, 421 U.S. 35, 56; RSR Corp. v. FTC, 656 F.2d 718, 723 (D.C. Cir. 1981); Envt'l Def. Fund v. EPA, 510 F.2d 1292, 1304–06 (D.C. Cir. 1975) (predecisional conference approved even though related proceeding was ongoing).
111. APA § 554(d)(A), (B). The rationale for these exemptions is that initial licensing and the various determinations relating to rates, facilities, or practices are more like rulemaking than adjudication because they are dominated by policymaking concerns. *Attorney General's Manual supra* note 104, at 51.
112. *Id*. at 51–53.

Illustration:

25. Assume the same facts as Illustration 19, except that the issue involves an amendment to Z Co.'s permit to allow it to discharge a larger volume of wastewater into the stream. M investigates Z Co.'s application and concludes that it should be denied because Z Co. violated the terms of its existing permit. H asks M to furnish off-the-record advice with respect to Agency's decision on Z Co.'s application. M can give the advice.

7.065 Agency head exception

Under the "agency head" exception, the requirement of separation of functions does not prohibit an agency head from personally engaging in an adversary function and later participating in an adjudicatory decision in the same or a factually related case.[113] However, the individual must be an agency head at the time of both the investigation and the decision.[114]

The agency head exception does not permit agency heads to receive off-the-record advice from an adversary staff member.[115]

Illustrations:

26. Assume the same facts as Illustration 19, except that H personally conducts the investigation of X Co.'s alleged violation. H may choose to recuse herself from taking part in Agency's review of the proposed decision in the X Co. case, but if H chooses to participate in the agency review, she is permitted to do so, assuming that she is not disqualified by reason of having prejudged the facts.[116]

27. Assume the same facts as Illustration 19, except that M becomes an agency head after completing his investigation. M must recuse

---

113. APA § 554(d)(C); *Attorney General's Manual supra* note 104, at 58.
114. Amos Treat & Co. v. SEC, 306 F.2d 260, 266–67 (D.C. Cir. 1962). Cf. Grolier, Inc. v. FTC, 615 F.2d 1215, 1220 (9th Cir. 1980) (agency head's adviser cannot serve as ALJ if he had been exposed to nonrecord information in his former position, but could have continued to serve as adviser).
115. *Attorney General's Manual supra* note 104, at 56–57; Greene v. Babbitt, 943 F. Supp. 1278 (W.D. Wash. 1996). *But see* White v. Ind. Parole Bd., 266 F.3d 759, 766 (7th Cir. 2001) (dictum) (agency heads can discuss case privately with experts who gave testimony at the hearing).
116. *See* Chapter 7, § 7.023.

himself from taking part in Agency's review of the proposed decision in the X Co. case.

7.07 SEPARATION OF FUNCTIONS AND PRESIDING OFFICERS

7.071 Scope

The APA contains several provisions concerning separation of functions that apply only to presiding officers at hearings. These provisions state a special rule concerning off-the-record communications about factual matters and provide for the organizational independence of ALJs. These special provisions are subject to the same exceptions as the general separation of functions rule.[117]

For convenience, presiding officers will sometimes be referred to as ALJs, although in some circumstances non-ALJs can serve as presiding officers.[118] Of course, the general separation of functions rule (§ 7.06) and the general ex parte contacts rule (§ 7.04) apply to ALJs as well. Like the general separation of functions rule, the provisions relating to ALJs apply only in cases of formal adjudication.

7.072 ALJ nonconsultation rule

Among the APA's provisions protecting the independence of ALJs,[119] the act provides that an ALJ is not permitted to consult off-the-record with any person, inside or outside of the agency, concerning a fact in issue.[120] This nonconsultation rule is closely related to the prohibition against ex parte communications (§ 7.04) and the exclusive record rule (§ 7.08).

The Supreme Court stated that this provision means that ALJs cannot consult *any* agency staff member, even one who has not been involved in the case in any way, concerning a fact in issue.[121] Note that this provision prohibits only consultations concerning "facts in issue." It would not, therefore, preclude off-the-record consultations between an ALJ and

---

117. *See* Chapter 7, § 7.064.
118. *See* Chapter 10, § 10.03.
119. *See* Chapter 10, §§ 10.04–10.10.
120. The employee who presides at the reception of evidence "may not consult a person or party on a fact in issue, unless on notice and opportunity for all parties to participate." APA § 554(d)(1).
121. Butz v. Economou, 438 U.S. 478, 513–14 (1978) (dictum).

another person concerning a question of law, policy, undisputed facts, or discretion so long as the consultation did not concern a disputed factual question.[122] The term "facts in issue" is narrower than the term "relevant to the merits," which is used in the ex parte contacts provision.[123]

As a matter of policy, agencies may wish to preclude ALJs from holding off-the-record discussions with agency staff members concerning any matter "relevant to the merits," especially in an accusatory case, to avoid any risk of violating the exclusive record rule and any appearance that the proceeding is not fair. For example, an ALJ could present legal questions to the parties and allow briefing or oral argument. Nonlawyer adjudicators could ask a nonadversary attorney for legal advice in writing with copies to the parties and provide an opportunity for response.

Illustrations:

28. A, an ALJ for Agency, is engaged in deciding a technically complex case concerning alleged illegal discharges into a river by X Co. of the chemical QQ in violation of X Co.'s permit. The facts in issue include whether X Co. actually discharged QQ into the water and whether QQ is harmful to fish populations. S is an Agency staff member who is an expert on fish biology and has not been involved in the X Co. case in any way. S cannot communicate off-the-record with A regarding either issue.

29. Assume the same facts as Illustration 28, except that A wishes to consult off-the-record with GC, Agency's general counsel, concerning the legal question of whether it is permissible to revoke a permit because of an accidental and de minimis discharge of a pollutant in violation of a water pollution permit. GC has not been involved in the X Co. case in any way. Under the APA, A is permitted to hold an off-the-record consultation with GC on this issue. However, H may wish, as a matter of policy, to preclude

---

122. Many ALJs consider such consultation improper and not a model of integrity and independence. More importantly, in some situations, (e.g., when an ALJ must work through a mixed question of law and fact where resolution of one is not independent of the other), such consultation might violate the exclusive record rule (*see* Chapter 7, § 7.08), APA (*see* Chapter 7, § 7.04), and Model Code prohibitions on ex parte communications (*see supra* note 45). The 2010 Model State Administrative Procedure Act addressed such consultation in section 408(2)(e)(C). *See* Chapter 12, § 12.052, especially note 148.

123. *See* Chapter 7, § 7.0432 for discussion of "relevant to the merits."

such consultations in accusatory cases such as the X Co. matter. Nothwithstanding the absence of an express prohibition against such an off-the-record conversation, many ALJs would choose to avoid such conversations based on codes of judicial conduct.[124]

7.073 Command influence

The APA provides that an ALJ may not be responsible to or be subject to the supervision or direction of an agency staff member who engages in the performance of investigative or prosecuting functions.[125] This provision requires that the agency be structured in such a way that no staff member who supervises or directs an agency's ALJs, other than the agency heads,[126] can engage at any time in adversary functions.[127] Unlike the general separation of function rule, which bars consultations with persons who have performed adversary functions in a particular case, the command influence rule precludes staff members who play such functions in *any case* from directing or supervising ALJs.

A staff member who formerly engaged in adversary functions, but whose present position precludes him or her from engaging in such functions, is permitted to supervise or direct ALJs. However, any supervision or direction must not violate the nonconsultation rule, the exclusive record rule, and principles addressed in codes of judicial conduct.[128]

---

124. *See supra* note 45.
125. APA § 554(d)(2) provides that an employee who presides at the reception of evidence "may not be responsible to or subject to the supervision or direction of an employee or agent engaged in the performance of investigating or prosecuting functions for an agency."
126. APA § 554(d)(1) would seem to prohibit an ALJ from receiving direct comment on a "fact in issue" from a supervising agency head. Although there is no direct authority to date, it is possible that a court could find an agency head who supervises staff members involved in investigative or prosecuting functions, and ALJs might indirectly or inadvertently exert improper command influence over an ALJ. Such a case would seem to be fact-specific, and an ALJ would almost certainly recognize such influence and take steps to avoid it. At a minimum, Rules 2.4 and 2.9 of the Model Code of Judicial Conduct (2007) prohibiting external influences and ex parte communications would seem to apply.
127. *See* Chapter 7, § 7.0631 for explanation of the term "adversary function."
128. *See* Chapter 7, § 7.072 (nonconsultation rule); § 7.08 (exclusive record rule); supra note 45 (addressing model codes of judicial conduct).

This command influence issue is separate from the indirect influence that might result from management initiatives designed to improve ALJ performance, which is thoroughly discussed in Chapter 10, § 10.092.

Illustrations:

30. General Counsel of Agency supervises Agency's staff of advocates. General Counsel cannot be in the chain of persons supervising or directing Agency's ALJs.[129]

31. M, one of the heads of Agency, frequently engages personally in the investigation of alleged permit violations. M can supervise or direct Agency's ALJs.

7.08 EXCLUSIVE RECORD RULE

The APA provides that the transcript constitutes the exclusive record for decision.[130] Due process also mandates the exclusive record principle.[131] The exclusive record rule is closely related to the prohibition against ex parte communications (§ 7.04) and the nonconsultation rule (§ 7.072). Thus, in finding the facts, it is improper for a decisionmaker to rely on evidence that the decisionmaker happens to know or learns outside the hearing.[132]

Of course, a decisionmaker is entitled to rely on facts that are officially noticed, subject to an opportunity for rebuttal.[133] The proper use of official notice does not violate the exclusive record rule. However, it is

---

129. *Attorney General's Manual supra* note 104, at 56.
130. APA § 556(e) provides: "The transcript of testimony and exhibits, together with all papers and requests filed in the proceeding, constitutes the exclusive record for decision in accordance with section 557 of this title."
131. Goldberg v. Kelly, 397 U.S. 254, 271 (1970) ("the decisionmaker's conclusion as to a recipient's eligibility must rest solely on the legal rules and evidence adduced at the hearing"). *See also* Ohio Bell Tel. Co. v. Pub. Utils. Comm'n of Ohio, 301 U.S. 292 (1937) (commission decided rate question on evidence outside the record and never disclosed).
132. *See, e.g.*, Seacoast Anti-Pollution League v. Costle, 572 F.2d 872, 881–82 (1st Cir.), *cert. denied*, 439 U.S. 824 (1978) (administrator relies on scientific panel whose report referred generally to scientific literature); Air Prods. & Chems., Inc. v. FERC, 650 F.2d 687, 692–700 (5th Cir. 1981) (use of "various reports" in files to decide key issue is improper).
133. *See* APA § 556(e) and Chapter 5, § 5.05.

necessary to draw a distinction[134] between taking official notice of facts and evaluating evidence in the record. In the case of official notice, the agency must allow an opportunity for rebuttal, but an agency decision-maker who uses his or her experience and expertise to evaluate the evidence offered at the hearing (for example, by rejecting the opinion of an expert witness) need not furnish an opportunity for rebuttal.[135] Similarly, a decisionmaker is entitled to utilize its expertise in making predictions and forecasts without violating the exclusive record principle.[136]

7.09 THE RULE OF NECESSITY

The rule of necessity provides that if the result of disqualifying one or more decisionmakers is that the agency is prevented from acting, the decisionmakers should not be disqualified.[137]

An agency might be prevented from acting either because the only person or persons authorized to decide the case are all disqualified, or because so many members of a multihead agency are disqualified that the agency cannot assemble a quorum.

A court confronted with application of the rule of necessity might consider several steps short of allowing an otherwise disqualified adjudicator to decide the case. In some cases, a statute or regulation allows a decisionmaker to delegate the decision to other agency employees.

---

134. The distinction is not always easily drawn. *See* Ernest Gellhorn, *Rules of Evidence and Official Notice in Formal Administrative Hearings,* 1971 Duke L.J. 1, 43–44.

135. *But see* Davis & Randall, Inc. v. United States, 219 F. Supp. 673, 679–82 (W.D.N.Y. 1963), which suggested that an agency could not simply reject the testimony of an expert witness without the agency developing its objections at the hearing. This approach tends to merge the rules about official notice and evaluation of evidence.

136. *See, e.g.,* Fed. Power Comm'n v. Transcon. Gas Corp., 365 U.S. 1, 29 (1961) (expert regulator can estimate economic effects without taking evidence).

137. United States v. Will, 449 U.S. 200, 211–17 (1980) (Supreme Court should not disqualify itself in a case in which all federal judges had pecuniary interest); MFS Sec. Corp. v. SEC, 380 F.3d 611, 620 (2d Cir. 2004) (concluding that the entire commission was not conflicted when only past and current chairmen had personal conflicts of interest, thus avoiding a rule of necessity issue); Valley v. Rapides Parish Sch. Bd., 118 F.3d 1047, 1052 (5th Cir. 1997) (party avoids rule of necessity by challenging only some but not all biased school board members); Brinkley v. Hassig, 83 F.2d 351, 357 (10th Cir. 1936) (state medical board should not disqualify itself even though all members might be biased).

In such case, the rule of necessity is not applicable, and a court should require the delegation to take place. Similarly, a statute or regulation may permit the appointing authority to replace a decisionmaker for purposes of a particular case. A court should require such replacement to occur if it is legally possible to do so. Finally, a court should consider exercising more intense scrutiny than it normally would exercise in cases in which a decisionmaker could not be disqualified because of the rule of necessity. Thus, the court should consider subjecting fact-findings and discretionary decisions to more rigorous examination than would be required or permitted by the substantial evidence or arbitrary and capricious tests.

Chapter 8

ALTERNATIVE DISPUTE RESOLUTION

8.01 ALTERNATIVE DISPUTE RESOLUTION
UNDER THE APA

Alternative dispute resolution (ADR) refers to various techniques for the resolution of disputes other than through litigation. For a time ADR in the public sector had lagged behind the private sector, with the long-standing exception of negotiation, mediation, and arbitration as the core processes for adjudication of labor relations cases. However, when ADR became institutionalized as a routine process in federal civil litigation, ADR gradually gained acceptance in administrative law.

In 1990, Congress amended the APA by enacting the Administrative Dispute Resolution Act (ADRA).[1] The act was amended in

---

1. Alternative Means of Dispute Resolution in the Administrative Process, 5 U.S.C. §§ 571–584 et seq. (1990). *See generally* WILLIAM F. FUNK ET AL., FEDERAL ADMINISTRATIVE PROCEDURE SOURCEBOOK 289–319 (4th ed. 2008). The Sourcebook contains a helpful bibliography on the subject of ADR, including numerous reports and recommendations of the Administrative Conference of the United States.

important respects and made permanent in 1996.[2] In passing ADRA, Congress intended to recognize and to encourage the use of various techniques of ADR in administrative adjudication and all other administrative functions. Ultimately, the direction by President Bill Clinton for the Department of Justice to create the Interagency Alternative Dispute Resolution Working Group (IADRWG) proved key to achieving that goal.

The 1990 act had relied upon the Administrative Conference of the United States (ACUS) to provide ongoing consultation and training in ADR activities, and to coordinate the growth of ADR in federal agencies. After Congress terminated funding for ACUS in 1995, the IADRWG, also known as the Federal ADR Council, assumed that role and continues that role now, even though Congress has refunded ACUS. The IADRWG has become the central, official forum for development of federal agency ADR policies, guidelines, and best practices, often working in collaboration with sections of the American Bar Association.[3]

8.011 Authority to use ADR

ADRA provides: "An agency may use a dispute resolution proceeding for the resolution of an issue in controversy that relates to an administrative program,[4] if the parties agree to such proceeding."[5] This provi-

---

2. Administrative Dispute Resolution Act (ADRA), Pub. L. No. 104-320, § 2, 110 Stat. 3870 (Oct. 19, 1996). The 1996 ADRA authorized agencies to use ADR, mandated that each agency appoint a dispute resolution specialist, and required agencies to develop ADR policies.

3. *See* the IADRWG website at http://www.adr.gov (last visited January 15, 2012); IADRWG, *Report for the President on the Use and Results of Alternative Dispute Resolution in the Executive Branch of the Federal Government* (April 2007); and publications developed through the American Bar Association, *e.g.*, MARSHALL BREGER, ET AL., ADMINISTRATIVE DISPUTE RESOLUTION DESKBOOK (2001), JEFFREY M. SENGER, FEDERAL DISPUTE RESOLUTION: USING ADR WITH THE FEDERAL GOVERNMENT (2004).

4. "Administrative program" is broadly defined to include any function that "involves protection of the public interest and the determination of rights, privileges, and obligations of private persons through rule making, adjudication, licensing, or investigation." ADRA § 571(2). Section 3(a) of Pub. L. No. 101-552 (the 1990 ADRA) mandated agencies to consider ADR in connection with formal and informal adjudication, rulemakings, enforcement actions, issuing and revoking licenses, contract administration, litigation brought by or against the agency, and other agency actions. Section 3(d) urged agencies to review their contracts and grants to authorize ADR.

5. ADRA § 572(a).

sion makes the foundational point that an agency is authorized to use the modalities of ADR only if the parties consent.[6]

The term "dispute resolution proceeding" in this sentence means "any process in which an alternative means of dispute resolution is used to resolve an issue in controversy in which a neutral is appointed and specified parties participate."[7] And the key term "alternative means of dispute resolution" means "any procedure that is used to resolve issues in controversy, including but not limited to, conciliation, facilitation, mediation, factfinding, minitrials, arbitration, and use of ombuds, or any combination thereof."[8]

The latter definition makes two more foundational points: An agency is authorized to use all of the modalities of ADR, and the provision covers all administrative adjudication, both formal and informal.[9]

ADRA also made clear that an agency is encouraged to employ ADR techniques.[10] It required each agency to adopt a policy addressing the use of ADR in its entire range of activity (including adjudication, rulemaking, contracting, and all other agency action) and required the agency head to designate a senior official as the dispute resolution specialist to be responsible for implementing agency policy.[11]

---

6. ADRA § 572(c) provides: "Alternative means of dispute resolution authorized under this subchapter are voluntary procedures which supplement rather than limit other available agency dispute resolution techniques."
7. ADRA § 571(6) (emphasis added).
8. ADRA § 571(3).
9. *See* Chapter 3, § 3.01 for the distinction between formal and informal adjudication.
10. ADRA § 573(c).
11. ADRA, Pub. L. No. 101-552, § 3. Cabinet level agencies have adopted regulations to implement ADRA in programs throughout their divisions. For example, 7 C.F.R. § 2.24(a)(4)(xx): (A) authorizes the Secretary of Agriculture to designate a "senior official to serve as the Department Dispute Resolution Specialist" under ADRA to "provide leadership, direction and coordination for the Department's conflict prevention and resolution activities"; (B) authorizes the issuance of regulations to achieve these goals; (C) to provide ADR services; (D) to develop and issue standards; and (E) to monitor agency programs and report at least annually to the Secretary. The Agriculture Department, like other federal agencies, uses ADRA to address a wide range of issues, from contracting and procurement, to workplace disputes, to civil rights actions against the department.

8.012 When ADR should not be used

ADR is not appropriate in every case.[12] ADRA lists a number of situations in which the agency should consider not using it:[13]

- An authoritative resolution is required for precedential value and ADR would not produce an authoritative precedent.
- The matter involves significant policy issues and ADR would not likely serve to develop policy.
- Consistency of result is especially important and ADR proceedings might not produce consistent results.
- The matter significantly affects persons or organizations who are not parties to the proceeding.
- A full public record of the proceedings is important and ADR would not provide one.
- The agency must maintain continuing jurisdiction over the matter and ADR would interfere with fulfilling that requirement.[14]

8.013 Neutrals

The ADR techniques referred to in ADRA all involve "neutrals." A neutral is "an individual who, with respect to the issue in controversy, functions specifically to aid the parties in resolving the controversy."[15] A

---

12. *See* IADRWG, *Federal ADR Program Manager's Resource Manual* (2008) ("The Program Manager's Manual" available at http://www.adr.gov/manual (last visited Jan. 15, 2012)), Part II: Chapter 5 "Supporting Uses of ADR," providing additional guidance about the willingness of the parties to participate and issues concerning adequate documentation of claims. Debate continues about when and what type of ADR process should be used, if at all, depending upon the nature of the dispute, the disputants, and the policies at issue, since ADR with the federal government as the real party in interest inevitably involves a serious imbalance of power. See Phyllis E. Bernard, *Mediating with an 800-Pound Gorilla: Medicare and ADR*, 60 Wash. & Lee L. Rev. 1417 (Fall 2003).
13. ADRA § 572(b).
14. For a comprehensive study of federal agency ADR and its appropriateness, see Lisa Blomgren Bingham et al., *Dispute Resolution and the Vanishing Trial: Comparing Federal Government Litigation and ADR Outcomes*, 24 Ohio St. J. on Disp. Resol. 225 (2009).
15. ADRA § 571(9). The IADRWG has promoted the concept of sharing neutrals among agencies to assure fairness and objectivity. *The Program Manager's Manual, supra* note 12, Part II, Chapter 3, explains different models

neutral may be a federal employee or any other individual acceptable to the parties to an ADR proceeding.[16] The neutral serves at the will of the parties.[17]

8.014 Modalities of ADR

Although the ADRA refers to a large number of different ADR modalities, these can be grouped into two categories: mediation and arbitration.[18]

8.0141 Mediation

Mediation refers to the use of a neutral (referred to as a mediator) to help the parties reconcile their differences, but the neutral has no power to impose a solution if the parties cannot reach one with the mediator's aid.

Illustration:

1. M, an employee of Agency, filed with the Equal Employment Opportunity Commission (EEOC) a sexual harassment complaint against a fellow, nonsupervisory employee. M's claim meets the prima facie requirements but is factually weak and is unlikely to be the basis of a class action. Instead of denying the complaint or undertaking an enforcement action, EEOC refers M and Agency to mediation. The goal is to work out a settlement, which might include nonmonetary relief.[19]

---

for developing and maintaining a roster of internal or external neutrals, and sharing and evaluating neutrals, in addition to benefits and costs of each option.

16. ADRA § 573(a). The neutral cannot have any conflict of interest unless it is disclosed and all parties consent. *Id.*

17. ADRA § 573(b).

18. The IADRWG has identified an ADR "spectrum" that includes variations on the basic themes of negotiation, mediation, or arbitration to include, e.g., convening, confidential listener, cooperative problem-solving, dispute panels, early neutral case evaluation, multioption ADR, partnering, peer review, and a two-track approach that uses ADR concurrently with litigation. *The Program Manager's Manual, supra* note 12, Part III, Chapter 1 "Glossary of Terms and Techniques."

19. The EEOC has moved toward using mediation as a primary means to resolve cases filed with the agency. Although not without controversy

ADRA refers to a number of techniques that can all be grouped under mediation. Thus the term "factfinding" refers to a presentation of the issues to a neutral who then makes "findings"; these findings may assist the parties to settle the case.[20] "Conciliation" may be synonymous with "mediation," but may also refer to techniques for reducing tensions and improving communications in situations of volatile conflict.[21] "Facilitation" sometimes refers to neutrals who intervene procedurally (to conduct meetings and coordinate discussions) but avoid becoming involved in resolving disputed substantive issues.[22] "Minitrials" are abbreviated

---

(see, e.g., Suzy Fox & Lamont E. Stallworth, *Employee Perceptions of Internal Conflict Management Programs and ADR Processes for Preventing and Resolving Incidents of Workplace Bullying: Ethical Challenges for Decision-Makers in Organizations*, 8 EMPL. RTS. & EMPLOY. POL'Y J. 375 (2004), including a discussion of the U.S. Postal Service REDRESS program), mediation has become standard practice both in employment discrimination matters (*see, e.g.*, GAO Report to Congressional Committees, *Equal Employment Opportunity: Pilot Projects Could Help Test Solutions to Long-Standing Concerns with the EEO Process*, GAO-09-712 (August 2009)) and as an emerging best practice in workforce management (*see, e.g.*, David M. Walker, Comptroller General of the U.S. Government Accountability Office, Testimony Before the Subcommittee on the Federal Workforce and Agency Organization, Committee on Government Reform, House of Representatives, *Human Capital Observations on Final DHS Human Capital Regulations*, GAO-05-391T (March 2, 2005)).

20. Fact-finding can use a neutral third party or a private expert (usually for technical or scientific matters). The parties agree in advance whether the results of the fact-finding will be conclusive or only advisory. Federal Rule of Evidence 706 gives courts the option of appointing neutral expert fact-finders who could be called as a witness subject to cross-examination. The IADRWG also identifies the practice of "joint fact-finding" in which party representatives "work together to develop responses to factual questions." *The Program Manager's Manual, supra* note 12, Part III, Chapter 1 "Glossary of Terms and Techniques" at 7.

21. Under guidance provided by the IADRWG, one of the chief objectives of conciliation is to build trust among the parties, even if they are not able to meet face-to-face but instead use the conciliator to carry messages. *Id.* at 4.

22. The facilitator's role under ADRA can be distinguished from the typical agency mediator in that the facilitator focuses almost solely on the process for reaching a solution, not on the substantive issues contributing to the solution. *See id.* at 6–7. Significant attention has been given to both process and outcome in handling environmental conflicts, on the principle that effective solicitation of input from stakeholders can reduce legal

mock trial presentations to the senior officials of the parties, usually assisted by a neutral; these officials then attempt to settle the dispute.[23]

Illustration:

2. Consumer has a long-running dispute with a federally chartered savings and loan (S&L) concerning the payoff amount on Consumer's auto loan. Consumer believes that the S&L has engaged in unethical and illegal practices. The ombudsman of the Office of Thrift Supervision serves as an intermediary between the S&L's headquarters and Consumer, conciliating the dispute by setting up a series of telephone conversations between the disputants, which may enable them to resolve the dispute.[24]

8.0142 Arbitration

Arbitration refers to a process in which a neutral is empowered to impose a solution. In the case of binding arbitration, both parties are bound by the arbitrator's decision.[25] In the case of nonbinding arbitration,

---

challenges. Further, federal action must coordinate with multiple governmental jurisdictions regarding natural resources. *See, e.g.,* GAO, Report to the Chairman, Subcommittee on Public Land and Forests, Committee on Energy and Natural Resources, U.S. Senate, *Natural Resources: Opportunity Exists to Enhance Federal Participation in Collaborative Efforts to Reduce Conflicts and Improve Natural Resource Conditions,* GAO-08-262 (February 2008).

23. *The Program Manager's Manual, supra* note 12, Part III, Chapter 1 "Glossary of Terms and Techniques" at 9.

24. The American Bar Association has worked with the IADRWG Task Force to develop guidance for ombuds working in agencies throughout the federal government. *See* ABA Coalition of Federal Ombudsmen and Federal Interagency ADR Working Group Steering Committee, *A Guide for Federal Employee Ombuds: A Supplement to and Annotation of the Standards for the Establishment and Operations of Ombuds Offices* (May 9, 2006), including the February 2004 Standards.

25. In the original ADRA, the agency head could reject the arbitral decision within 30 days. Under this approach, arbitration was binding on the private party but not the agency. Under the 1996 amendments to ADRA, however, this provision was repealed; an agency that agrees to binding arbitration is bound by the result. ADRA § 580(c). However, the arbitration agreement must set forth a maximum award that can be issued by the arbitrator and may limit the range of possible outcomes. ADRA

the arbitrator's decision is advisory; either party can reject the decision and proceed with the agency adjudicatory process.[26]

ADRA empowers arbitrators to regulate the proceedings, administer oaths, and issue subpoenas in the same manner as the agency could.[27] It provides for a relatively formal arbitral proceeding, including examination and cross-examination of witnesses; it requires the arbitrator to follow statutory and regulatory requirements, precedents, and policy directives; and it prohibits ex parte communications to the arbitrator.[28] The arbitrator's award must include a brief, informal discussion of the factual and legal basis for the award.[29] ADRA limits judicial review of administrative arbitral awards in the same way that federal law limits those of other arbitrators.[30] An agency's decision to use or not use any method of dispute resolution is not reviewable because it is committed to agency discretion.[31]

The IADRWG has issued guidance on structuring agency arbitrations pursuant to ADRA. In addition to the principles explained above, agencies are encouraged to place a cap on the monetary relief that can

---

§ 575(a)(2). The arbitration award may not serve as an estoppel in any other proceeding for any issue resolved in the arbitration. This provision seems odd; it would appear to make more sense if it referred to any issue not resolved in the arbitration. Apparently the provision is related to the 1990 provision that allowed the agency to opt out of a binding arbitral award. In any event, the award cannot be used as a precedent or otherwise be considered in any factually unrelated proceeding. ADRA § 580(d).

26. The Federal ADR Council (IADRWG) developed a detailed set of principles for both nonbinding and binding arbitration within federal agencies, which has been elaborated upon by various agencies. *Core Principles for Federal Non-Binding Workplace ADR Programs; Developing Guidance for Binding Arbitration—A Handbook for Federal Agencies*, 65 Fed Reg. 50,005 (Aug. 16, 2000).

27. ADRA § 578.

28. ADRA § 579.

29. ADRA § 580(a)(1).

30. ADRA § 581(a), referring to 9 U.S.C. §§ 9–13.

31. ADRA § 581(b). There is one exception: A nonparty adversely affected by an arbitral award can seek review of the agency's decision to arbitrate under the Act. In such cases, a district court would decide whether the agency's decision to use arbitration was clearly inconsistent with the criteria set forth in § 572(b) for appropriate use of ADR. ADRA § 581(b)(1), referring to 9 U.S.C. § 10(b).

be awarded, and the arbitral award must be in writing.[32] The Federal Aviation Administration, the Federal Motor Carrier Safety Administration, the Department of the Navy, the Department of the Treasury, and the Internal Revenue Service number among the agencies that have, in consultation with the attorney general, issued guidance on the use of binding arbitrations under ADRA.

Illustration:

3. Company has bid on a contract to supply the Department of Energy. The contracting officer has indicated that he will deny Company's bid on the basis of past performance. Company would prefer a speedy, consensual resolution of the dispute, but is apprehensive about engaging in mediation due to the level of tension. The case is not yet docketed. The Board of Contract Appeals refers the case to arbitration, with a board-supplied neutral to determine the facts and make an award.[33]

8.015 Confidentiality[34]

Confidentiality is obviously important in ADR proceedings. The parties must be able to speak candidly to the neutral without concern that their statements can be used against them in subsequent litigation.[35]

---

32. Phyllis Hanfling and Martha McClellan, *Developing Guidance for Binding Arbitration—A Handbook for Federal Agencies*, published at 65 Fed. Reg. 50006-50014 (Aug. 16, 2000).

33. *See* 62 Fed. Reg. 24,804, 24,808 (May 7, 1997). ADR, especially arbitration, plays a major role in resolving federal contract disputes arising within many agencies. The Government Accountability Office reports annually to the Office of the General Counsel concerning bid protests, including ADR and informal conferencing to resolve disputes. *E.g.,* U.S. Gov't Accountability Office, GAO-09-471SP, *Bid Protests at GAO: A Descriptive Guide*, 9th ed. (2009); For an analysis of conflicts over authority between ADRA and the Court of Federal Claims, see Robert S. Metzger & Daniel A. Lyons, *A Critical Assessment of the GAO Bid-Protest Mechanism*, 2007 Wis. L. Rev. 1225 (2007).

34. *See* ABA Ad Hoc Committee on Federal ADR Confidentiality, *Guide to Confidentiality Under the Federal Administrative Dispute Resolution Act,* (March 2005).

35. The Electronic Guide to Federal Procurement includes a standard ADR confidentiality clause noting the interplay with Federal Rule of Evidence 408 and Federal Acquisition Regulation 33.214. The Departmental

ADRA generally makes any "dispute resolution communication"[36] confidential. It provides that the neutral "shall not voluntarily disclose or through discovery or compulsory process be required to disclose any dispute resolution communication or any communication provided in confidence to the neutral."[37] Any dispute resolution communication that is disclosed in violation of these provisions is not admissible in any proceeding relating to the issues in controversy with respect to which the communication was made.[38]

Illustration:

4. In a mediation to resolve a dispute between Agency and Contractor, both sides separately give the mediator a number of documents prepared in advance. They contain highly sensitive information. Counsel for Contractor expressly requests that the mediator keep Contractor's document confidential. Counsel for Agency does not make a specific request. Nevertheless, both sets of documents will be considered "communications provided in confidence." For Contractor, the request was express. But for Agency, the understanding was implied, since the documents were provided under circumstances in which nondisclosure is usually expected.[39]

Appeals Board of the U.S. Department of Health and Human Services uses a standard mediation form that provides additional clarifications about confidentiality given the sensitivity of issues before it: http://www.hhs.gov/dab/divisions/adr/mediation/confident.html (last visited Jan. 15, 2012)

36. This term means "any oral or written communication prepared for the purposes of a dispute resolution proceeding, including any memoranda, notes or work product of the neutral, parties, or nonparty participant; except that a written agreement to enter into a dispute resolution proceeding, or final written agreement or arbitral award reached as a result of a dispute resolution proceeding, is not a dispute resolution communication." ADRA § 571(5).
37. ADRA § 574(a). Similar constraints prevent any party from disclosing any information concerning any dispute resolution communication. ADRA § 574(b). The exceptions to this provision are similar to the exceptions relating to neutral confidentiality. ADRA § 574(b)(1)–(5).
38. ADRA § 574(c). The term "issue in controversy" is defined in § 571(8). Such communications are also exempt from disclosure under the Freedom of Information Act. ADRA § 574(j).
39. Confidentiality in Federal Alternative Dispute Resolution Programs, 65 Fed. Reg. 83,085, 83,090 (2000).

There are some exceptions to the confidentiality rule. The communication can be disclosed if all parties and the neutral consent or if it has already been made public.[40] In addition, the communication can be made public if a court determines that such disclosure is necessary to prevent a manifest injustice, establish a violation of law, or prevent harm to the public health and safety.[41] In each of these cases, the situation must be one of sufficient magnitude to outweigh the integrity of ADR proceedings in general by reducing the confidence of parties in future cases that their communications will remain confidential.[42]

Illustration:

5. During a mediation regarding the dismissal of a federal employee, the employee divulges to the mediator that he charged personal goods to his government credit card. In a later action against the employee for misuse of government funds, the neutral is asked to testify about what he learned in the mediation. The court may require the neutral to testify if it is determined that the neutral's testimony is necessary to help establish a violation of law and that the need for the information is of sufficient magnitude as to outweigh the integrity of dispute resolution proceedings in general by reducing the confidence of parties in future cases that their communications will remain confidential.[43]

---

40. ADRA § 574(a)(1)–(2). If the communication was provided by a nonparty participant, that person must also consent. The communication can be made public if required by statute, but in such cases the neutral should make the communication public only if no other person is reasonably available to disclose it. ADRA § 574(a)(3).
41. ADRA §§ 574(a)(4)–(b)(5). The neutral shall make reasonable efforts to notify the parties and affected nonparties of a threatened disclosure through the legal process. Any party or nonparty who receives such notice and within 15 calendar days does not offer to defend a refusal by the neutral to disclose the information shall have waived any objection to disclosure. ADRA § 574(e).
42. ADRA § 574(a)(4).
43. The Federal IADRWG Steering Committee, working with the American Bar Association and the Association for Conflict Resolution, developed *A Guide for Federal Employee Mediators: A Supplement to and Annotation of the Model Standards for Conduct for Mediators* (May 9, 2006), which reminds the mediator and participants that although communications with mediators are ostensibly confidential, they remain subject to the laws and rules pertaining to the relevant administrative agencies and courts. More detailed

8.02 ADRA AND ALJS

ADRA also added several provisions to § 556 of the APA to encourage administrative law judges (ALJs) to attempt to settle cases. Helping to settle cases without full-fledged litigation is now an essential part of the work of federal ALJs.[44]

Presiding officers in APA formal adjudication may:

- Hold conferences for the settlement or simplification of issues by consent of the parties or by the use of the ADR methods set forth in ADRA;[45]
- Inform the parties as to the availability of one or more ADR methods and encourage their use;[46] and
- Require the attendance at any settlement conference of at least one representative of each party who has authority to negotiate concerning resolution of issues in controversy.[47]

While ALJs commonly preside over settlement conferences and assist the parties to achieve a negotiated solution, it is inadvisable for an ALJ to function as a full-fledged mediator and then adjudicate the case if the parties fail to settle. As a result, many agencies assign a different ALJ to mediate a case.[48]

---

guidance concerning workplace mediations is found in another IADRWG Steering Committee manual prepared in consultation with the American Bar Association: *Protecting the Confidentiality of Dispute Resolution Proceedings: A Guide for Federal Workplace ADR Program Administrators* (April 2006). These materials incorporate the best practices discussions begun by the Department of Justice and ADR Council, and are continually updated on the IADRWG website. http://www.adr.gov (last visited Jan. 15, 2012).

44. Individual agencies and the IADRWG have developed best practices, training, and written guidance both for ALJs and for the public concerning ADR in adjudication. *See, e.g.,* U.S. Environmental Protection Agency, Office of Administrative Law Judges, *Practice Manual* (May 2009) under "Answers to Some Common Questions": "What procedures apply to ADR?" (explaining EPA Procedural Rule 22.18(d)) and "What if I want to settle or do not want to go to hearing?" (explaining Rule 22.18(d) and Rule 22.22).

45. APA § 556(c)(6).

46. APA § 556(c)(7).

47. APA § 556(c)(8).

48. *See supra* note 15 (mentioning discussion of shared neutrals in the Program Manager's Manual).

Chapter 9

INFORMAL ADJUDICATION

9.01 SUMMARY OF INFORMAL ADJUDICATION PROCEDURES

The term "informal adjudication" describes the process for issuing orders[1] when the formal adjudication provisions of the APA are not applicable.[2] (§ 9.02) Informal adjudication comprises a wide variety of agency procedures, some resembling what is traditionally thought of as adjudication and others not resembling adjudication at all.[3] Perhaps 90 percent of federal agency adjudication is informal rather than formal.[4] (§ 9.03) With the exception of a few provisions set forth in APA §§ 555 and 558 (§§ 9.04–9.06), the APA does not spell out the procedures that an agency must follow when engaging in informal adjudication.[5]

9.02 INFORMAL ADJUDICATION CONTEXTS

Informal adjudication is used in a wide variety of contexts.[6] Some of the types of cases subject to informal adjudication include the following:

- grants, benefits, loans, and subsidies
- licensing and accrediting[7]

---

1. *See* Chapter 1, § 1.04 for discussion of the definitions of "order" and "adjudication" under the APA.
2. *See* Chapter 3, § 3.01 for discussion of when the APA's formal adjudication provisions are applicable.
3. *See* Izaak Walton League of Am. v. Marsh, 655 F.2d 346, 361 n.37 (D.C. Cir.), *cert. denied*, 454 U.S. 1092 (1981) ("informal adjudication is a residual category including all agency actions that are not rulemaking and that need not be conducted through on the record hearings").
4. Paul R. Verkuil, *A Study of Informal Adjudication Procedures*, 43 U. CHI. L. REV. 739, 741 (1976).
5. *Izaak Walton League*, 655 F.2d at 361 n.37 ("[t]he APA fails to specify the procedures that must be followed" when an agency issues an order but formal adjudication is not required).
6. *See* Verkuil, *supra* note 4, at 757–79.
7. APA § 558(c) contains procedural requirements applicable to many licensing disputes regardless of whether the agency must use formal adjudication. *See* § 9.06. Many license disputes are resolved through informal adjudication. *See, e.g.,* Everett v. United States, 158 F.3d 1364, 1368 (D.C. Cir. 1998), *cert. denied*, 526 U.S. 1132 (1999) (informal adjudication properly used to determine grant of helicopter landing permit); City of West Chicago v. U.S. Nuclear Regulatory Comm'n, 701 F.2d 632 (7th Cir. 1983) (informal adjudication used in determining modification of thorium ore processing license).

- inspections, grading, and auditing
- planning, policymaking, economic development, and public works[8]
- orders penalizing a nontenured government employee, a prison inmate, or other regulated party[9]
- orders occurring in connection with the regulation of labor relations[10]
- orders requiring a regulated party to remedy a statutory or rule violation[11]
- internal agency interpretation of statutory provisions[12]

---

8. This category includes matters such as highway route and design approval. *See, e.g.,* Citizens to Preserve Overton Park v. Volpe, 401 U.S. 402 (1971); *Izaak Walton League,* 655 F.2d at 361 (decisions relating to Corps of Engineers construction project appropriately taken through informal adjudication).
9. *See, e.g.,* Pension Benefit Guar. Corp. v. LTV Corp., 496 U.S. 633 (1990) (administrative action against pension plan costing employer millions of dollars); Cont'l Seafoods, Inc. v. Schweiker, 674 F.2d 38, 41 n.8 (D.C. Cir. 1982) (determination whether importation of food product should be banned because of salmonella contamination).
10. *See, e.g.,* NLRB v. Del. Armaments, Inc., 431 F.2d 494 (3d Cir.), *cert. denied,* 400 U.S. 957 (1970) (approving informal process for setting aside union representation election and ordering employer to produce a list of employees eligible to vote in election).
11. *See, e.g.,* Chem. Waste Mgmt., Inc. v. EPA, 873 F.2d 1477, 1479 (D.C. Cir. 1989) (orders requiring corrective action for hazardous waste facility); United States v. Iron Mountain Mines, Inc., 987 F. Supp. 1250, 1259 (E.D. Cal. 1997) (informal adjudication procedure used to order cleanup of toxic waste site; statute explicitly precludes use of "adjudicatory hearing").
12. Doe v. Leavitt, 552 F.3d 75 (1st Cir. 2009). As a form of informal adjudication, an agency's interpretation of a statute is entitled to deference, although the court refrained from identifying whether *Skidmore* or *Chevron* deference was the appropriate standard. *See also* Melissa M. Berry, *Beyond Chevron's Domain: Agency Interpretations of Statutory Procedural Provisions,* 30 Seattle U. L. Rev. 541 (2006).

9.03 PROCEDURES IN INFORMAL ADJUDICATION

9.031 Departures from formal adjudication

Informal adjudication procedures depart from the formal adjudicatory model in many respects.[13] Subject to constraints imposed by due process,[14] or by particular statutes or procedural regulations, an agency is free to provide any procedure (or no procedure) in conducting informal adjudication. Thus, informal adjudication may include decisions by informal conferences or based exclusively on an exchange of written documents, ex parte contacts,[15] active involvement by the decisionmaker in the investigation and prosecution of the agency's case,[16] loose evidentiary standards, and generally a relaxation of the formalities associated with formal adjudication.[17] Particular informal adjudication processes may make no provision for confrontation of evidence or oral presentation of

---

13. *See* Verkuil, *supra* note 4, at 760–79 (only two of 42 informal adjudication schemes studied contained all 10 of the due process requirements spelled out in *Goldberg v. Kelly*).

14. *See* Chapter 2, §§ 2.04, 2.05.

15. In U.S. Lines, Inc. v. Fed. Mar. Comm'n, 584 F.2d 519 (D.C. Cir. 1978), the court banned ex parte contacts in an informal adjudication setting. However, this decision is of doubtful precedential value since courts are not permitted to supplement procedures mandated by the APA. *See* § 9.033. But the 2007 Model Code of Judicial Conduct and 1989 Model Code of Judicial Conduct for Administrative Law Judges (*see* Chapter 7, § 7.041) would seem to prohibit the administrative law judiciary (if it would be involved in an informal adjudication) from engaging in ex parte communications. In an exceptional case, an ex parte communication made in the course of informal adjudication might offend due process. See Sangamon Valley Television Corp. v. United States, 269 F.2d 221 (D.C. Cir. 1959) (in a proceeding that involved "conflicting private claims to a valuable privilege" ex parte communications and private gifts to agency officials violated "basic fairness").

16. *But see* Finer Foods, Inc. v. USDA, 274 F.3d 1137, 1140 (7th Cir. 2001) (decision in informal adjudication should be made by someone without a stake in the outcome).

17. *See Federal Administrative Law Developments—1970*, 1971 DUKE L.J. 149, 195 ("'informal adjudication' . . . covers a wide spectrum of conferences, discussions, and settlements outside the framework of a formal hearing").

evidence through witnesses; there may be no discovery and no transcript of the proceedings.[18]

Some informal adjudications employ procedures similar to those used in notice and comment rulemaking, such as by giving interested parties notice of the agency's proposed order and allowing written or oral comments but not conducting formal adjudicatory procedures.[19] If the agency chooses (or is required by statute or regulation) to hold public hearings, these may actually be open meetings at which all interested persons can express their views on the matter without cross-examination or formal consideration of evidence.[20]

Given the dearth of specific requirements in the APA regarding due process in informal adjudication compared to the far stricter requirements of formal adjudication, federal agencies will generally use "more efficient" informal adjudication when given the choice.[21]

---

18. *See generally* Ward v. Johnson, 690 F.2d 1098, 1105 (4th Cir. 1982) (describing differences between formal and informal adjudication). *Ward's* specific holding, that prison disciplinary committee members are entitled to absolute immunity as judges, was rejected in Cleavinger v. Saxner, 474 U.S. 193 (1985). The Supreme Court, in concluding that prison guards conducting disciplinary hearings were not the functional equivalent of judges, relied in part on the absence of a cognizable burden of proof or verbatim transcript of the proceedings and the inmate's inability to hire counsel, summon witnesses, cross-examine the other side's witnesses, or conduct discovery.

19. *See, e.g.,* Aircraft Owners & Pilots Ass'n v. FAA, 600 F.2d 965, 966 (D.C. Cir. 1979) (characterizing as "informal adjudication" a procedure under which the FAA investigated and solicited comments on the risks to aviation posed by a newly constructed television broadcast tower).

20. *See* Izaak Walton League of Am. v. Marsh, 655 F.2d 363–65 (D.C. Cir.), *cert. denied*, 454 U.S. 1092 (1981). This case interpreted a regulation issued by the Army Corps of Engineers that called for at least one public meeting to be held in connection with preconstruction planning of authorized projects. The court required the Corps to hold an informal nonadjudicatory public meeting as part of the process of constructing locks and dam on the Mississippi River. It had to receive public comments and respond to objections in those comments.

21. Berry, *supra* note 12, at 586. In Dominion Energy Brayton Point v. Johnson, 443 F.3d 12, 15 (1st Cir. 2006), the Environmental Protection Agency cited increased efficiency to explain its move from formal to informal adjudication of elements of the Clean Water Act. *See also* Clark County v. FAA, 522 F.3d 437 (D.C. Cir. 2008); S. Utah Wilderness Alliance v. Bureau of Land Mgmt., 425 F.3d 735 (10th Cir. 2005).

9.032 Informal adjudication: Particular statutes or rules

Particular agency statutes often detail the procedures that agencies must follow before issuing orders. Courts sometimes interpret these statutes broadly to provide procedural protections for the parties or to facilitate judicial review,[22] but will generally not impute a quasi-judicial procedure if one is not established by law.[23] In addition, agency procedural rules often provide for obligatory procedures that would not otherwise be required by statute. The agency must follow these procedural rules if adopted for the protection of the public rather than the convenience of the agency.[24] If the rule exists for the convenience of the agency itself, however, it may generally waive the enforcement of that rule on itself.[25]

Illustrations:

1. By statute, no person can harvest timber on federal land without first obtaining a permit from Agency. The statute gives Agency substantial discretion in deciding whether to issue a permit and in prescribing permit terms. The statute also provides that before granting or denying a permit, Agency must notify the applicant and the public of Agency's initial decision and hold "an oral hearing at which the applicant and other interested persons are afforded an opportunity to present evidence, data and views regarding the application." P applies for a permit that Agency proposes to grant. Members of the public protest. Agency grants

---

22. *See Izaak Walton League*, 655 F.2d at 363–65.
23. *See, e.g.*, Empresa Cubana Exportadora de Alimentos Productos Varios v. Dep't of Treasury, 606 F. Supp. 2d 59, 70 (D.D.C. 2009) (finding that if neither the APA nor the agency statute provided for a quasi-judicial procedure prior to licensing, there was no grounds to impute one).
24. United States ex rel. Accardi v. Shaughnessy, 347 U.S. 260 (1954) (president could not dictate decision of board to which he had delegated decisional power); Service v. Dulles, 354 U.S. 363, 372, 386 (1957); Vitarelli v. Seaton, 359 U.S. 535, 539 (1959); Nader v. Bork, 366 F. Supp. 104 (D.D.C. 1973) (president could not fire special counsel).
25. Am. Farm Lines v. Black Ball Freight Serv., 397 U.S. 532 (1970); *In re* Long-Distance Tel. Serv. Fed. Excise Tax, 539 F. Supp. 2d 287 (D.D.C. 2008). *Cf.* ACLU v. Miami-Dade Sch. Bd., 439 F. Supp. 2d 1242, 1292 (S.D. Fla. 2006) (finding that a rule of convenience may not be waived by the agency if that waiver would cause prejudice to those that would object to the agency's actions).

the application without any further process. A court may set aside the grant of the application and require Agency to hold a public hearing before granting the application.

2. Assume the same facts as Illustration 1 except Agency holds an oral hearing before granting the application. It allows members of the public to present oral statements and to submit written briefs, but it refuses to allow members of the public to cross-examine the expert witnesses who offered testimony on behalf of P. Neither the APA nor due process requires a hearing.[26] A court will probably uphold Agency's discretionary decision to deny cross-examination.

9.033 The *Vermont Yankee* rule in informal adjudication

Absent constraints imposed by due process or agency-specific statutes or procedural rules, federal courts may not require agencies engaged in either rulemaking[27] or adjudication[28] to provide procedural protections that the agency decides not to provide. Some cases have mandated additional procedures for agencies to follow in informal adjudication in order to assure a fair decision and facilitate judicial review, but these cases are of doubtful validity.[29]

---

26. *See* Chapter 2, § 2.05 (due process); Chapter 3, § 3.01 (APA).
27. Vt. Yankee Nuclear Power Corp. v. Natural Res. Def. Council, Inc., 435 U.S. 519 (1978) (lower court prohibited from requiring agency to follow rulemaking procedures beyond those set forth in the APA); *see also* Gonzalez-Oropeza v. Attorney General, 321 F.3d 1331 (11th Cir. 2003); Am. Radio Relay League v. FCC, 524 F.3d 227 (D.D.C. 2008).
28. Pension Benefit Guar. Corp. v. LTV Corp. 496 U.S. 633, 655–56 (1990) ("The determination in this case, however, was lawfully made by informal adjudication, the minimal requirements for which are set forth in the APA"); Neighborhood Ass'n of the Back Bay v. Fed. Transit Admin., 463 F.3d 50, 60 (1st Cir. 2006) ("[W]e are required to presume that the FTA abided by the statutory requirements in the absence of any showing that it did not do so." In this case, the enabling statute required the agency to undertake an independent analysis of historical facts to determine historic preservation status, but did not require any particular form of record or report of the determination.); W. Ref. Sw. v. FERC, 636 F.3d 719 (5th Cir. 2011).
29. *See* Am. Trading Transp. Co. v. United States, 841 F.2d 421 (D.C. Cir. 1988); Indep. U.S. Tanker Owners Comm. v. Lewis, 690 F.2d 908 (D.C. Cir.

The freedom of an agency to establish its own procedural rules does not completely insulate it from judicial review, however. A federal court may still entertain a case alleging that an agency failed to abide by its own established procedural rules.[30]

Illustration:

3. A federal statute requires sponsors of federally funded undertakings to consider their impact on historically or archaeologically important sites. The statute and associated regulations give little guidance as to the form of this consideration. In preparation for a construction project, Agency hires an archaeologist to dig several sample pits near a local Native American tribe's lands to determine whether the proposed line will go through the tribe's ancient burial grounds. Upon finding only scattered minor artifacts, the archaeologist determines that the burial grounds will be undisturbed, and excavation proceeds. The tribe pursues an injunction requiring the agency to consult with it before continuing with the project. The court will most likely reject the request for an injunction on the grounds that the statute merely requires the agency to make the impact determination, and neither requires it to follow any particular procedure nor requires it to reach any particular decision.[31]

1982). In both cases, the court held that the procedures employed by the Maritime Administration were flawed and produced inadequate records for judicial review. Both courts apparently held, without relying on statutory authority, that notice and comment procedures were required in the particular informal adjudications under review, and the *Am. Trading* court, without citing APA § 555(e), found the agency's explanation of its decision to be inadequate.

30. *See, e.g.,* Mendoza v. Attorney General, 327 F.3d 1283, n. 7 (11th Cir. 2003) (noting that *Vt. Yankee* does not apply when a petitioner is challenging an agency's alleged failure to follow its own rules of procedure when it failed to review his appeal.

31. *See* Narragansett Indian Tribe v. Warwick Sewer Auth., 334 F.3d 161 (1st Cir. 2003).

9.04 PROCEDURES SET FORTH IN APA § 555

APA § 555 contains the minimal procedures applicable to informal adjudication.[32] The provisions set forth in Section 555 apply to both formal and informal adjudication.

9.041 Right to counsel

A person compelled to appear before an agency is entitled to be represented by counsel.[33] In addition, a party is entitled to appear in person or by or with counsel.[34] If a person knowingly waives his or her right to counsel, it does not constitute a denial of due process.[35]

9.042 Right to appear

If the "orderly conduct of public business permits," interested persons who are not parties to the proceeding may "appear" for the presentation and determination of various controversies.[36]

9.043 Conclusion of matter in reasonable time

Agencies are to conclude matters within a reasonable time.[37] A court might require an agency to decide a matter if it appears to be stalling or

---

32. *LTV Corp.*, 496 U.S. at 655.
33. APA § 555(b).
34. *Id. See* Chapter 5, § 5.07. In general, the right to counsel is fundamental to a finding of procedural due process in both formal and informal settings. Woods v. Willis, 09-CV-2412 (N.D. Ohio Sept. 27, 2010). *But see* Veterans for Common Sense v. Shinseki, 644 F.3d 845, 858 (9th Cir. 2011) (a veteran has no right to retain paid counsel when applying for VA benefits, but he or she does have a right to counsel if entering the formal or informal appellate processes upon denial of those benefits).
35. *See, e.g.,* Sutera v. TSA, 708 F. Supp. 2d 304, 316 (E.D.N.Y. 2010) (citing cases).
36. APA § 555(b). See Chapter 4, § 4.051.
37. "With due regard for the convenience and necessity of the parties or their representatives and within a reasonable time, each agency shall proceed to conclude a matter presented to it." APA § 555(b). *See, e.g.,* 47 U.S.C. 251(d) (requiring the Federal Communications Commission to establish regulations implementing interconnection requirements within six months of the passage of the Telecommunications Act of 1996). *See also* Norton v. S. Utah Wilderness Alliance, 542 U.S. 55, 60–63 (2004).

unduly procrastinating.[38] While the court may compel the agency to act, it has no power to specify what action must be taken or what result must be reached.[39]

9.044 Legal authorization for investigations

Agencies may not engage in investigations except as legally authorized to do so.[40]

The Attorney General's Manual on the APA states that this provision "merely restates a principle of good administration." Department of Justice, *Attorney General's Manual on the Administrative Procedure Act* 65.
38. See APA § 706(1) (reviewing court shall "compel agency action unlawfully withheld or unreasonably delayed."). *See also* Telecomm. Research & Action Ctr. v. FCC, 750 F.2d 70, 79–80 (1987) (D.C. Cir. 1984) (factors to consider in assessing claim of unreasonable delay); Farmworker Justice Fund, Inc. v. Brock, 811 F.2d 613 (D.C. Cir.), *vacated as moot*, 817 F.2d 890 (D.C. Cir. 1987) (requiring agency to adopt regulation that it had decided to defer); Cobell v. Babbitt, 91 F. Supp. 2d 1, 46–48 (D.D.C. 1999) (requiring agency to take expeditious action in Indian trust fund dispute); Cordoba v. McElroy, 78 F. Supp. 2d 240, 244–45 (S.D.N.Y. 2000) (possible violation of § 555(b) in failing to process Immigration and Nationalization Services application because of agency backlog).
39. *S. Utah Wilderness Alliance*, 542 U.S. at 65.
40. APA § 555(c) ("Process, requirement of a report, inspection, or other investigative act or demand may not be issued, made, or enforced except as authorized by law."). *See also* § 9.05. While the language of this provision reads as a limitation on agency powers, it is most commonly invoked by agencies in defense or justification of their inaction or lack of cooperation with investigative requests. *See* Weaver's Cove Energy v. Allen, 587 F. Supp. 2d 103, 110 (D.D.C. 2008) (a document produced by the Coast Guard is a "Navigation Review" rather than a "Preliminary Investigation Report" because the statute does not authorize the Coast Guard to engage in a formal investigation under the circumstances at hand); Danner v. U.S., 208 F. Supp. 2d 1166, 1172 (E.D. Wash. 2002) (the IRS was under no obligation to turn over requested documents to plaintiffs because the statute did not expressly authorize it to "make a report" of those documents as required by APA § 555).

9.045 Copy of transcript

Persons compelled to submit testimony are ordinarily entitled to a transcript.[41]

9.046 Subpoenas

Section 555(d) provides for subpoenas and their judicial enforcement.[42]

9.047 Prompt notice of denial of applications

Agencies must give prompt notice of the denial of an application in connection with any agency proceeding.[43] An "agency proceeding" refers to adjudication, rulemaking, or licensing.[44] The prompt notice may be given in writing or orally.[45] It is unclear whether "in connection with any agency proceeding" refers to a preexisting agency proceeding or whether filing a petition with an agency initiates a proceeding so that the agency must respond to the petition.

---

41. APA § 555(c) ("A person compelled to submit data or evidence is entitled to retain or, on payment of lawfully prescribed costs, procure a copy or transcript thereof, except that in a non-public investigatory proceeding the witness may for good cause be limited to inspection of the official transcript of his testimony.").

42. *See* Chapter 4, § 4.04. In general, subpoenas issued by agencies as part of informal adjudicatory and investigative processes are subject to the same procedures and judicial review as subpoenas issued as part of formal adjudicatory procedures. *See, e.g.,* U.S. Dep't of Educ. v. NCAA, 481 F.3d 936 (7th Cir. 2007); SEC v. Wall St. Transcript Corp., 422 F.2d 1371 (2d Cir. 1970); Wilmot v. Doyle, 403 F.2d 811 (9th Cir. 1968).

43. APA § 555(e) ("Prompt notice shall be given of the denial in whole or in part of a written application, petition, or other request of an interested person made in connection with any agency proceeding.").

44. APA § 551(12). Section 555(e) "has no application to matters which do not relate to rulemaking, adjudication, or licensing. Generally, it is not applicable to the mass of administrative routine unrelated to those proceedings." *Attorney General's Manual, supra* note 37, at 70.

45. *Id.*

9.048 Statement of reasons for denial

A brief statement of reasons must accompany the denial of a petition.[46] The statutory language appears to contemplate a general statement,[47] and some decisions allow for very general reasons supporting denials.[48] However, some courts have required a more detailed statement, apparently to facilitate judicial review under the arbitrary and capricious test.[49] No explanation is required if the denial is self-explanatory.[50] Regardless, the statement must contain some reasoning, not just conclusion. A flat refusal

---

46. APA § 555(e) provides: "Except in affirming a prior denial or when the denial is self-explanatory, the notice [of denial of an application] shall be accompanied by a brief statement of the grounds for denial." *See* Roelofs v. Sec'y of the Air Force, 628 F.2d 594, 599–601 (D.C. Cir. 1980) (requiring statement of reasons for denial of petition to have general discharge upgraded to honorable discharge); King v. United States, 492 F.2d 1337, 1343–45 (7th Cir. 1974) (requiring parole board to give reasons for parole denial).

47. The statement of reasons "while simple in nature, must be sufficient to advise the party of the general basis of the denial." *Attorney General's Manual, supra* note 37, at 70.

48. For example, in Estate of French v. FERC, 603 F.2d 1158, 1161–62 (5th Cir. 1979), the court held that the following sufficed to explain FERC's denial of a petition: "Based upon a review of your request and the supplemental data submitted upon Staff request, it appears that the Estate has the financial ability to make the required refunds. Accordingly, your request for relief is denied." The court rejected arguments that the agency should have included factual and legal conclusions in its explanation.

49. For example, the Tenth Circuit has stated that the statement "must be sufficiently detailed that the reviewing tribunal can appraise the agency's determination under the appropriate standards of review. . . . [T]he statement of grounds must be sufficiently detailed that we can determine whether the [agency] considered the relevant factors and that the choice it made based on those factors is a reasonable one." Friends of the Bow v. Thompson, 124 F.3d 1210, 1214 (10th Cir. 1997). *See also* Washington v. Office of the Comptroller of the Currency, 856 F.2d 1507, 1513 (11th Cir. 1988) (agency explanation disapproved because it was generic and did not address particulars of case).

50. APA § 555(e). Similarly, no explanation is required if the denial affirms a previous denial since it is assumed the applicant has knowledge of the grounds for denial. *Attorney General's Manual, supra* note 37, at 70.

to revisit an issue without explanation may be considered arbitrary and capricious under APA § 706.[51]

9.05 SOURCE OF AGENCY AUTHORITY

APA § 558(b) provides that an agency may not act or impose a sanction (or issue a substantive rule or order) except as prescribed by law.[52] The APA defines the term "sanction" broadly,[53] and Section 558(b) applies whether the sanction is punitive or remedial.[54] However, it empowers an agency to impose a sanction not expressly authorized by statute that is designed to protect the integrity of its own processes.[55]

Section 558(b) states an obvious and well-accepted principle of administrative law: An agency is a creature of limited power. It can take action only pursuant to authority granted by some superior source. Normally, it derives its authority from a statute,[56] but in many cases the authority of the agency to impose a sanction or take other action is implied rather than expressed in the governing statute.[57]

---

51. Butte County v. Hogen, 613 F.3d 190 (D.C. Cir. 2010). This holding may be inconsistent with the general principle that an agency head may simply adopt the earlier decision of a lower-level decisionmaker. *See* Chapter 6, § 6.0351.
52. APA § 558(b) provides: "A sanction may not be imposed or a substantive rule or order issued except within jurisdiction delegated to the agency and as authorized by law."
53. APA § 551(10) defines "sanction" as: "[T]he whole or a part of an agency— (A) prohibition, requirement, limitation, or other condition affecting the freedom of a person; (B) withholding of relief; (C) imposition of penalty or fine; (D) destruction, taking, seizure, or withholding of property; (E) assessment of damages, reimbursement, restitution, compensation, costs, charges, or fees; (F) requirement, revocation, or suspension of a license; or (G) taking other compulsory or restrictive action."
54. Am. Bus. Ass'n v. Slater, 231 F.3d 1, 6 (D.C. Cir. 2000).
55. *See* Touche, Ross & Co. v. SEC, 609 F.2d 570, 582 (2d Cir. 1979) (agency has power to impose disciplinary rule on attorneys practicing before it). This case was distinguished, and apparently cited with approval, in *Am. Bus. Ass'n*, 231 F.3d at 7.
56. However, it is possible that the authority could be derived from some other source of law such as a treaty or court decision. The Attorney General's Manual points out that Congress changed the word "statute" to "law" in order to broaden the potential sources of authority on which an agency's power could be based. *Attorney General's Manual, supra* note 37, at 88.
57. *Id.* at 89.

9.06 LICENSING PROCEDURES

APA § 558 contains a number of procedural protections that concern licensing. Under the APA, the definition of licensing is quite broad;[58] it covers any form of administrative permission[59] and applies to both formal and informal adjudications. There is currently some ambiguity regarding the "license" status of federal agency decisions that do not directly grant permission for a private act but instead serve an indirect or implicit gate-keeping function toward that act.[60] Historically, reliance upon Section 558 has been relatively rare.[61]

Section 558 licensing provisions cover three separate and mutually exclusive[62] phases:

- applications
- withdrawals
- renewals

---

58. APA § 551(8) defines a license as "the whole or part of an agency permit, certificate, approval, registration, charter, membership, statutory exemption or other form of permission." *See, e.g.*, Pillsbury Co. v. United States, 18 F. Supp. 2d 1034, 1037–38 (Ct. Int'l Trade 1998) (permission to file claim for customs duty drawback on expedited basis is a "license").
59. Horn Farms v. Johanns, 397 F.3d 472, 478–79 (7th Cir. 2005) (suggesting the licensing rules apply whenever federal approval is required for some act, but not if there is no agency standing in a gatekeeping role). The APA definition covers both temporary and permanent permissions. Pan-Atlantic S.S. Corp. v. Atl. Coast Line R.R., 353 U.S. 436, 439 (1957) (temporary authority to operate as common carrier); Atl. Richfield Co. v. United States, 774 F.2d 1193, 1200 (D.C. Cir. 1985) (temporary permission to use ship in domestic commerce).
60. Ursack, Inc. v. Sierra Interagency Black Bear Grp., 639 F.3d 949 (9th Cir. 2011) (citing N.Y. Pathological & X-Ray Labs., Inc. v. INS, 523 F.2d 79 (2d Cir. 1975)). The *Ursack* decision stated that the *Horn Farms* decision improperly applied § 558 of the APA by adopting too strict a definition of "license." In this case, a federal agency approval that is not strictly necessary for company to manufacture its product is still a "license" if revoking that approval would have a substantial impact on the market for that product. N.Y. *Pathological* had a similar holding regarding an agency decision that substantially reduced a clinic's patient base.
61. *See, e.g.*, WILLIAM F. FUNK, ET AL., FEDERAL ADMINISTRATIVE PROCEDURES SOURCEBOOK 8 (4th. ed. 2008).
62. Attorney General's Manual, *supra* note 37, at 89.

Illustrations:

4. By statute, a company must first obtain permission from Agency in order to manufacture ice axes made of Alloy X within the United States. This permission is later revoked without notice or opportunity for appeal. If the company challenges the revocation, it will almost certainly be treated as a "license" by the courts because Agency serves as a gatekeeper for the manufacture of the ice axes.

5. There are no restrictions on manufacturing ice axes made of Alloy X, but no materials made of Alloy X may be carried within national parks without express prior authorization from Agency. If revocation of this authorization is challenged by the manufacturer, whether the court treats the authorization as a license will depend on whether it follows the reasoning of the *Horn Farms* court or the *Ursack* court. The *Horn Farms* reasoning is that the authorization does not constitute a license, because the authorization has no bearing on the manufacturer's ability to legally manufacture or market the ice axes. The *Ursack* reasoning is that since the authorization to use the ice axes in national parks is a major selling point for the manufacturer, revocation of that authorization will have a negative impact on the manufacturer's ability to market its product, and thus may be a "constructive" license.

9.061 Applications

Section 558(c) requires that applications for licenses required by law[63] be disposed of within a reasonable time.[64] Agencies must determine applications for licenses either through the formal process of Sections 556 and 557, when the APA's formal adjudication provisions apply,[65] or through informal adjudication when formal adjudication provisions

---

63. *See, e.g.,* Perry v. Delaney, 74 F. Supp. 2d 824, 838 (C.D. Ill. 1999) (credentials needed to serve as security guards were not "required by law," so this provision was not applicable).

64. APA § 558(c) provides: "When application is made for a license required by law, the agency, with due regard for the rights and privileges of all the interested parties or adversely affected persons and within a reasonable time, shall set and complete proceedings required to be conducted in accordance with sections 556 and 557 of this title or other proceedings required by law and shall make its decision."

65. *See* Chapter 3, § 3.01.

do not apply. Section 558(c) does not in itself compel formal procedure with respect to an application.[66]

The requirement in Section 558(c) that an application be acted upon promptly appears to have little practical effect.[67] It is conceivable, however, that a court could require that an agency take action on a license application if the agency appeared to be stalling.[68] Section 558(c) also requires that in license application proceedings, the agency shall act "with due regard for the rights and privileges of all the interested parties or adversely affected persons." This provision also appears to have little practical effect.

Illustration:

6. Company seeks approval for a recapitalization from Agency, which is required to determine the request "after an opportunity for a public hearing." Agency must dispose of the application

---

66. *See* City of West Chicago v. U.S. Nuclear Regulatory Comm'n, 701 F.2d 632, 644 (7th Cir. 1983) (section 558 does not independently require formal adjudicatory hearing). *West Chicago* disapproves U.S. Steel Corp. v. Train, 556 F.2d 822, 833–34 (7th Cir. 1977). *But see* N.Y. Pathological & X-Ray Labs., Inc. v. INS, 523 F.2d 79 (2d Cir. 1975) (denial of a license application automatically requires APA formal adjudication). The *N.Y. Pathological* decision is probably incorrect since § 558(b) does not mandate formal adjudication (when it is not otherwise required), but instead provides in the alternative for formal adjudication or "other proceedings required by law." *See* Seacoast Anti-Pollution League v. Costle, 572 F.2d 872, 878 n.11 (1st Cir.), *cert. denied*, 439 U.S. 824 (1978) (disagreeing with *U.S. Steel* case); Gallagher & Ascher Co. v. Simon, 687 F.2d 1067, 1072–76 (7th Cir. 1982) (disagreeing with *N.Y. Pathological*); *Attorney General's Manual, supra* note 37, at 89. *See also* Chapter 3, notes 8 and 11 (discussing *Citizens Awareness Network* case).

67. In the originally enacted version of the APA, the term "reasonable dispatch" was used. This is merely a statement of fair administrative procedure and varies with the circumstances. *Attorney General's Manual, supra* note 37, at 90. An early committee draft of the provision provided that a license would be deemed granted if not acted on in 60 days, but this was dropped in favor of the term "reasonable dispatch." *Id.* The present language "within a reasonable time" replaced the term "reasonable dispatch."

68. *See* § 9.043.

within a reasonable time, but it is unlikely that Agency will be compelled to follow the APA's formal adjudication provisions.[69]

9.062 Withdrawal

APA § 558(c) provides for notice and a second chance before institution of proceedings for the withdrawal, suspension, revocation, or annulment (collectively referred to as "withdrawal" of a license).[70] This provision applies whether the agency proceedings that follow the notice and second chance will be formal or informal adjudication, and only to agency action withdrawing a license prior to its expiration, not to the expiration of a license according to its terms.[71]

---

69. The proceeding would be considered adjudication rather than rulemaking. While the approval of a reorganization is defined as a rule, APA § 551(4), the fact that agency "permission" is required makes the proceeding "licensing" and "licensing" is treated as "adjudication." APA § 551(6), (8), (9). Current cases indicate that the formal adjudication provisions would not be triggered by a statute calling for a "public hearing"(rather than a "hearing on the record"), particularly when the issues are of the sort best resolved through submission of written documents or written expert opinions. *See* Chapter 3, § 3.01. APA § 558(c) does not of itself mandate formal adjudication. *See supra* note 55.

70. APA § 558(c) provides: "Except in cases of willfulness or those in which the public health, interest, or safety requires otherwise, the withdrawal, suspension, revocation or annulment of a license is lawful only if, before the institution of agency proceedings therefor, the licensee has been given"—(1) notice by the agency in writing of the facts or conduct which may warrant the action; and (2) opportunity to demonstrate or achieve compliance with all lawful requirements." In general, licensees are entitled to due process before a license is withdrawn. Jifry v. FAA, 370 F.3d 1174 (D.C. Cir. 2004) (two Saudi Arabian pilots without property or presence in the United States had their airman certificates revoked after the FAA determined they posed a security risk). The *Jifry* court indicated in dicta that nonresident aliens might not have due process rights at all, but did not rule as such on the grounds that all applicable due process had been followed regardless of whether the plaintiffs were entitled to it. *See also* People's Mojahedin Org. of Iran v. Dep't of State, 327 F.3d 1238 (D.C. Cir. 2003).

71. Miami MDS Co. v. FCC, 14 F.3d 658, 659 (D.C. Cir. 1994); Atl. Richfield Co. v. United States, 774 F.2d 1193, 1200–1 (D.C. Cir. 1985); Bankers Life & Cas. Co. v. Callaway, 530 F.2d 625, 634–35 (5th Cir. 1976), *cert. denied*, 429 U.S. 1073 (1977). However, § 558(c) does contain a provision applicable to the renewal of expired licenses. *See* § 9.063.

9.0621 Notice of facts warranting withdrawal

Section 558(c)(1) requires an agency to notify a party of the facts or conduct that would warrant withdrawal of the license before the agency institutes withdrawal proceedings. This notice must be in writing but need not take any special form. In general, a notice is sufficient if it "warns the licensee of the parameters of acceptable conduct and thereby prevents unfair surprise."[72] In assessing the adequacy of a warning, the key consideration is whether it is sufficient to allow the licensee to remediate the problem and achieve compliance so as to avoid withdrawal.[73] For example, the notice requirements for a license suspension were met where an agency employee prepared a report detailing the violations and discussed that report with the licensee.[74] But a warning that occurred 10 years before the current problems arose would not satisfy the notice requirements.[75]

9.0622 Opportunity to demonstrate or achieve compliance

Section 558(c)(2) requires that the licensee have an opportunity to demonstrate or achieve compliance with all lawful licensing requirements after the warning notice. This is the so-called "second chance" provision. It requires some sort of opportunity (not necessarily a hearing) whereby the licensee can demonstrate that it has remediated the problem to which the warning had alerted it. If the violations are not corrected before a second inspection, the agency can institute withdrawal proceedings without further warnings.[76] This provision does not apply to the agency's denial of an application for an initial license, even if the ground for the denial is that the applicant committed misconduct under a previous license.[77]

---

72. Air N. Am. v. Dep't of Transp., 937 F.2d 1427, 1438 (9th Cir. 1991).
73. *Id.* at 1437. The *Air N. Am.* case upheld revocation of a license based on a notice that occurred 18 months before. However, the *Air N. Am.* case seems questionable because the notice did not inform the licensee of particular violations but rather consisted of a general notice of legal requirements applicable to all licensees. Instead, it would seem that § 558(c) requires a particularized notice of deficiencies.
74. Moore v. Madigan, 990 F.2d 375, 379 (8th Cir), *cert. denied*, 510 U.S. 823 (1993).
75. Hutto Stockyard, Inc. v. USDA, 903 F.2d 299, 304 (4th Cir. 1990).
76. *Moore*, 990 F.2d at 380. In *Moore*, the court found it irrelevant that the violations may have been corrected shortly after the second inspection.
77. *See* George Steinberg & Son, Inc. v. Butz, 491 F.2d 988, 993 (2d Cir. 1974).

9.0623 *Multiple or ongoing violations*

A licensee is generally entitled to only one second chance to demonstrate or achieve compliance, even if it receives multiple notices due to persistent, ongoing, or repeated similar violations. The additional notices would not trigger an additional second chance each time, otherwise an agency could never render an adverse decision because each new violation would provide another chance for the licensee to comply.[78]

9.0624 *Exceptions: Willfulness or public health, interest, or safety*

Under Section 558(c), the agency need not furnish a licensee with a warning and a second chance when the party's conduct is willful or when public health, interest, or safety is at stake.

Willfulness is established by repeated violations, intentional wrongdoing, or gross neglect of a known duty, but not by simple negligence.[79] To take advantage of the willfulness exception to the "warning" and "second chance" requirements, the agency must make a finding at the time it institutes proceedings that a violation was willful,[80] and its finding of willfulness must be supported by substantial evidence.[81]

The "public health, interest, or safety" exception contemplates an unusual or emergency circumstance.[82] An agency cannot dispense with

---

78. Buckingham v. USDA, 603 F.3d 1073 (9th Cir. 2010).
79. *See, e.g.,* Potato Sales Co. v. USDA, 92 F.3d 800, 805–06 (9th Cir. 1996); Capital Produce Co. v. United States, 930 F.2d 1077, 1080 (4th Cir. 1991); *Hutto Stockyard*, 903 F.2d at 304. Another line of cases states a different definition: a party acted willfully if he "1) intentionally does an act which is prohibited, irrespective of evil motive or reliance on erroneous advice, or 2) acts with careless disregard of statutory requirements." Goodman v. Benson, 286 F.2d 896, 900 (7th Cir. 1961); Capitol Packing Co. v. United States, 350 F.2d 67, 77–78 (10th Cir. 1965) (citing many cases).
80. *See* Anchustegui v. USDA, 257 F.3d 1124, 1129 (9th Cir. 2001) (agency instituting withdrawal proceedings without first claiming that violations were willful); Pillsbury Co. v. United States, 18 F. Supp. 2d 1034, 1038 (Ct. Int'l Trade 1998).
81. *Hutto Stockyard*, 903 F.2d at 304 (ALJ found violations were not willful; no substantial evidence supports judicial officer's finding that they were willful).
82. Tucson Rod & Gun Club v. McGee, 25 F. Supp. 2d 1025, 1030–31 (D. Ariz. 1998) (bullets leaving containment area of shooting range pose public safety risk).

notice merely because it deems that "the public interest" requires revocation of a license since that would obviously be true in every case in which an agency seeks to withdraw a license.[83]

Illustrations:

7. Agency threatens to withdraw School's status as an approved school for immigrant alien students because School negligently failed to comply with Agency's requirements that School report any students who failed to attend classes. Agency may not institute proceedings for the withdrawal of School's license without first giving School reasonable notice of the violation and an opportunity to achieve compliance with the requirements of the governing statute and regulations.[84]

8. Company intentionally manipulates the market price of wheat futures on the Chicago Board of Trade. Agency regulates trading in commodity futures. The procedural requirements of Section 558(c) are not applicable, so Agency may institute proceedings for the suspension of Company's license without a prior warning or opportunity for a second chance.[85]

9.063 Renewal

The APA provides that a license does not expire until an agency acts on a timely and sufficient renewal application.[86] The rationale of this provision is that "it is only fair where a licensee has filed his application for a renewal or a new license in ample time prior to the expiration of his license, and where the application itself is sufficient, that his license

---

83. *See* Air N. Am. v. Dep't of Transp., 937 F.2d 1427, 1437 n.8 (9th Cir. 1991).
84. *See* Blackwell Coll. of Bus. v. Attorney General, 454 F.2d 928, 933–34 (D.C. Cir. 1971).
85. *See* Cargill, Inc. v. Hardin, 452 F.2d 1154, 1173 (8th Cir. 1971).
86. APA § 558(c) provides: "When the licensee has made timely and sufficient application for a renewal or a new license in accordance with agency rules, a license with reference to an activity of a continuing nature does not expire until the application has been finally determined by the agency." *See* Pan-Atlantic S.S. Corp. v. Atl. Coast Line R. R., 353 U.S. 436 (1957) (water carrier whose 180-day temporary license expired before the Interstate Commerce Commission could finish processing its renewal is protected from expiration of license).

should not expire until his application shall have been determined by the agency."[87]

Generally, this provision applies to a license for activity of a continuing nature (such as a broadcasting or common carrier license) rather than a permit to build a particular project.[88] It applies mainly in the situation in which an agency fails to process a renewal application before the license expires due to delays in agency proceedings or the agency's resource constraints.[89] It also requires that a renewal application be "sufficient," meaning that it must contain all necessary consents.[90]

Illustrations:

9. By statute Agency may grant "temporary authority" to a common carrier by water to institute service for which there is an urgent need, but such authority is valid for only 180 days. The statute contemplates that during the 180-day period, Agency will conduct hearings to determine whether the temporary authority should be made permanent. Agency granted W Corp. temporary authority to operate between cities A and B and began proceedings to determine whether to make the authority permanent. It did not complete those proceedings during the 180-day period, so it extended W's authority until it completed the proceedings. R Corp., which competes with W, believes that W's authority must lapse after 180 days and could not be temporarily extended. A court will hold that Agency is authorized to extend the temporary authority.[91]

---

87. *Attorney General's Manual, supra* note 37, at 91. Similarly, in *Pan-Atlantic S.S. Corp.*, 353 U.S. at 444–45, the dissenting opinion stated that the rationale of this provision is "that of protecting those persons who already have regularly issued licenses from the serious hardships occasioned both to them and to the public by expiration of a license before the agency finds time to pass upon its renewal." The dissenters thought that § 558(b) was inapplicable in the particular case because it contradicted provisions in the Interstate Commerce Act.

88. Miami MDS Co. v. FCC, 14 F.3d 658, 659–60 (D.C. Cir. 1994) (construction permit with stated expiration date–renewal provision of § 558(c) is inapplicable); Bankers Life & Cas. Co. v. Callaway, 530 F.2d 625, 634 n.13 (5th Cir. 1976) (alternative ground), *cert. denied*, 429 U.S. 1073 (1977).

89. *Id.* at 634.

90. *Id.* at 633–34 (application to renew dredge and fill permit insufficient because it lacked necessary local consents).

91. *Pan-Atlantic S.S. Corp.*, 353 U.S. 436.

10. In order to dredge and fill a lake, Company required a permit
from Agency. The permit was granted on the condition that if the
work were not completed by December 31, the permit would be
forfeited. The work was not completed by December 31. Company
applied for an extension of the permit. Agency was not required
to allow continuation of the work covered by the expired permit
pending its decision on the extension application.[92]

---

92. *Bankers Life & Cas. Co.*, 530 F.2d 625.

Chapter 10

ADMINISTRATIVE LAW JUDGES

10.01 OVERVIEW

This chapter considers the role of the administrative law judge (ALJ) in administrative adjudication.[1] The APA specifies the powers of ALJs (§ 10.02) and provides that ALJs will serve as presiding officers in almost all formal adjudications (§ 10.03). The APA and other sections of the U.S. Code also provide for a broad array of protections for the independence of ALJs. These include regulation of the selection process (§ 10.04), prohibition on assignment of inconsistent duties (§ 10.05), protection of ALJ tenure (§ 10.06), provisions concerning compensation (§ 10.07) and case rotation (§ 10.08), prohibition on performance ratings (§ 10.09), and special provisions concerning ex parte contact and command influence (§ 10.10).

10.02 ALJ POWERS

The APA confers substantial powers on ALJs in the course of presiding at hearings.[2] For example, subject to published rules of the agency, ALJs are empowered to administer oaths, issue subpoenas, receive

---

1. *See generally* Russell L. Weaver & Linda D. Jellum, *Neither Fish Nor Fowl: Administrative Judges in the Modern Administrative State*, 28 WINDSOR YEARBOOK ON ACCESS TO JUSTICE 243 (2010); Morell E. Mullins, *Manual for Administrative Law Judges*, 23 J. OF THE NAT'L. ASS'N OF ALJs 1 (2004).
2. APA § 556(c)(1)–(11). As a result of these powers, plus the APA's provisions for the integrity and independence of the ALJ's position, the Supreme Court held that the similarities between adjudication before ALJs and before federal district judges are "overwhelming." Fed. Mar. Comm'n v. S.C. Ports Auth., 535 U.S. 743, 759 (2002).

relevant evidence, take depositions, and regulate the course of the hearing, assuming that the agency has such powers. While an agency can define these powers in its procedural rules,[3] the powers arise from the APA "without the necessity of express agency delegation" and "an agency is without the power to withhold such powers" from its ALJs.[4]

10.03 PRESIDING OFFICERS OTHER THAN ALJS

In general, ALJs preside over hearings subject to the APA's formal adjudication provisions, provided that the agency head has chosen not to preside.[5] Of course, there are a large number of agency employees (sometimes referred to as administrative judges or AJs), bearing a variety of titles, who preside over hearings that are not governed by the APA. Some of these hearings are as formal as those governed by the APA; some are quite informal.[6] These judges do not enjoy the APA's protections of decisional independence, although statutes or agency regulations may provide comparable protection.[7]

The APA provides that statutes can override the requirement that ALJs must preside at formal hearings. It provides: "This subchapter does not supersede the conduct of specified classes of proceedings, in whole or in part, by or before boards or other employees specially provided for by or designated under statute."[8] Such statutes need not specifically designate who the non-ALJ presiding officer would be; it is sufficient if the statute authorizes the agency to designate a specific employee or a specific

---

3. U.S. Dep't of Justice, *Attorney General's Manual on the Administrative Procedure Act* 75.

4. *Attorney General's Manual, supra* note 3, at 74.

5. *See* APA § 556(b), providing that the agency or one or more members of the body that make up the agency may preside. Otherwise, an ALJ shall preside.

6. *See* Paul R. Verkuil, *A Study of Informal Adjudication Procedures*, 43 U. Chi. L. Rev. 739 (1975).

7. *See* Michael Asimow, *The Spreading Umbrella: Extending the APA's Adjudication Provisions to All Evidentiary Hearings Required by Statute*, 56 Admin. L. Rev. 1003, 1005–08 (2004); Paul H. Verkuil et al., *The Federal Administrative Judiciary*, 2 ACUS Rec. & Rep. 779, 788–90, 843–73 (1992); Paul H. Verkuil, *Reflections Upon the Federal Administrative Judiciary*, 39 UCLA L. Rev. 1341 (1992); John H. Frye III, *Survey of Non-ALJ Hearing Programs in the Federal Government*, 44 Admin. L. Rev. 261 (1992).

8. APA § 556(b).

class of employees to conduct the hearings.[9] In order to allow an agency to utilize presiding officers other than ALJs in reliance on this "savings clause," the statute that so provides must be express and clear.[10] Non-ALJ hearing officers must follow the other procedural safeguards of the APA to the same extent as ALJs, unless the statute permitting the designation of non-ALJ hearing officers is otherwise inconsistent with the APA.[11]

Illustration:

1. As permitted by statute, Agency allows its District Director to preside over a hearing regarding a customhouse broker's license. The District Director also investigated the case and wrote a report in compliance with the agency's regulations. Although the District Director is allowed to preside over the hearing by reason of the savings clause in APA § 556(b), the combination of investigative and adjudicating functions violates APA § 554(d). The fact that the savings clause allows the District Director to preside over the hearing instead of an ALJ does not allow him to violate other APA provisions.[12]

10.04 THE SELECTION PROCESS

10.041 General rule

The Office of Personnel Management (OPM), the central personnel agency of the federal government, holds periodic competitions for

---

9. *See Attorney General's Manual, supra* note 3, at 71–72 (giving numerous examples).
10. *Id.* at 72 ("a statutory provision which merely provides for the conduct of hearings by any officers or employees the agency may designate, does not come within the exception so as to authorize the agency to dispense with hearing examiners appointed in accordance with section 11"). *See* APA § 559 (subsequent statutes may not be held to supersede or modify the APA unless it does so expressly); Marcello v. Bonds, 349 U.S. 302, 310 (1955) ("Exemptions from the terms of the Administrative Procedure Act are not lightly to be presumed"). *See also* Borg-Johnson Elecs. v. Christenberry, 169 F. Supp. 746, 753 (S.D.N.Y. 1959) ("The provisions for the appointment of impartial, independent Hearing Examiners are the very heart and soul of the Administrative Procedure Act and variations therefrom should not be countenanced except where a statute expressly provides for a Hearing Examiner appointed in another manner").
11. *Attorney General's Manual, supra* note 3, at 72.
12. Twigger v. Schultz, 484 F.2d 856, 859 (3d Cir. 1973).

placement of applicants on the ALJ register. To be eligible for hire, an applicant must meet the minimum qualifications set by OPM. If the minimum qualifications are met, the applicant participates in an examination procedure and is then issued a final rating. Agencies wishing to hire ALJs must select from the top three candidates rated by OPM.[13]

OPM has discretionary power to create and modify the selection criteria and examinations. OPM's action in creating or modifying selection standards can be invalidated only if its actions are found to be arbitrary.[14]

Illustration:

2. X is a candidate for a position as an ALJ. X takes part in the examination process, is given a rating by the OPM, and is put on a register. OPM subsequently decides to modify its selection procedure, and since some of the candidates had not yet been rated, it disregards the register and rerates all of the candidates. X is then given a rating lower than his previous one. OPM's action is within its discretion.[15]

10.042 Qualifications

To be eligible for an ALJ position, applicants must meet OPM's minimum qualifications for experience in administrative hearings.[16] OPM has

---

13. 5 U.S.C. § 3318.
14. Meeker v. Merit Sys. Prot. Bd., 319 F.3d 1368 (Fed. Cir. 2003) (upholding OPM's change in ranking procedures which dropped the requirement that applicants had to get a 70 percent ranking to remain in the pool); Nash v. ICC, 225 F.2d 42 (D.C. Cir. 1955); Steinberg v. Ramspeck, 208 F.2d 823 (D.C. Cir. 1953); Friedman v. Devine, 565 F. Supp. 200 (D.D.C. 1982). Applicants have very limited rights regarding the ALJ hiring process. *See* Ramspeck v. Fed. Trial Examiners Conference, 345 U.S. 128, 133 (1953) ("The position of [administrative law judge] is not a constitutionally protected position. It is a creature of congressional enactment. [Applicants] have no vested right to positions as examiners.").
15. *See Steinberg*, 208 F.2d 823.
16. The current requirements are set forth in http://www.opm.gov/qualifi cations/alj/alj.asp. An ALJ must have seven years of experience in trials or formal administrative hearings. Applicants for ALJ positions must be currently licensed to practice under state law (but the licensure requirement has been suspended for incumbent ALJs). 5 C.F.R. § 930.204(b)(2) (2011)). Prior legal experience is necessary for an ALJ position because it provides maturity, a reliable record, experience with problems likely

broad discretion in interpreting its own regulations governing these criteria, but an arbitrary interpretation is an abuse of discretion.[17]

10.043 Supplemental qualifications

Applicants who meet the initial requirements are assigned a score on a supplemental qualifications statement according to the level of their experience. The score is based on the applicant's knowledge of rules of evidence and trial procedure, analytical ability, decisionmaking ability, oral communication ability and judicial temperament, writing ability, and organizational skills.

10.044 Examination procedures

Applicants who meet initial qualifications participate in a written examination and an interview. OPM also sends questionnaires to an applicant's professional contacts.

10.045 Final ratings

Applicants are assigned a final numerical rating on a scale of 0 to 100. The rating is based on a weighted sum of the scores from the supplemental qualifications statement and the three examination procedures. If the applicant is a veteran, 5 points are added to the score; 10 points are added if the veteran is disabled.[18] Applicants are then added to the register.

---

to be encountered as an ALJ, and first-hand knowledge of rules of the operation of the courts. Amiel T. Sharon & Craig B. Pettibone, *Merit Selection of Federal Administrative Law Judges*, 70 JUDICATURE 216, 218 (1987).

17. *See* Dugan v. Ramsay, 727 F.2d 192 (1st Cir. 1984) (OPM abused discretion in not counting trial preparation days for cases that settled as trial experience); Friedman v. Devine, 565 F. Supp. 200 (D.D.C. 1982) (OPM did not abuse discretion in finding that preparation of agency Advice and Appeals Memoranda did not count as trial experience).

18. The "veterans preference" has encountered severe criticism. It exacerbates the problem that the ALJ selection process is seen as relying too heavily on numerical grades. *See* Daniel J. Gifford, *Federal Administrative Law Judges: The Relevance of Past Choices to Future Directions*, 49 ADMIN. L. REV. 1, 56–57 (1997). The veterans preference has also been criticized for disadvantaging female applicants. Statistical studies demonstrate that the average scores of men and women before the addition of veterans points are roughly the same. However, since more men than women are veterans, there is a sharp divergence after adding the veterans points.

OPM certifies three eligible applicants to the employing agency for consideration for each vacancy (the "rule of three"). An agency must select one of these candidates (though not necessarily in the order in which they are ranked).[19]

10.046 Transfer

Agencies often prefer to avoid hiring ALJs off the register. Instead, they hire ALJs laterally from other agencies. Lateral transfers are allowed after an ALJ has served at least one year in the agency making the original hire.[20]

10.05 INCONSISTENT FUNCTIONS

ALJs "may not perform duties inconsistent with their duties and responsibilities as administrative law judges."[21] However, in Social Security hearings, where the government is not represented by counsel, an ALJ's duties include gathering evidence for both sides, then deciding the case. The Supreme Court upheld this procedure under due process; it did not discuss whether performing all of these duties violates the APA.[22]

The average score of men rises almost 3 points, while the average score of women rises only 1/10 of 1 point. *See* Verkuil et al., *supra* note 7, at 945–46.

19. The "rule of three" has been criticized, along with the veterans preference, as giving ratings and examination scores too much importance. *See* Verkuil et al., *supra* note 7, at 941; Gifford, *supra* note 18, at 56.

20. 5 C.F.R. § 930.204(h) (2011). About 75 percent of the ALJs employed by the federal government hear benefits cases for the Social Security Administration (SSA). Therefore, most agencies prefer to hire from the abundance of experienced SSA ALJs, rather than hiring off the register. As a result, only the SSA significantly relies on the OPM selection process to hire its ALJs. *See* Verkuil, et al., *supra* note 7, at 942–43.

21. 5 U.S.C. § 3105 (2006).

22. *See* Richardson v. Perales, 402 U.S. 389, 410 (1971): "[We are not persuaded] by the advocate-judge-multiple-hat suggestion. It assumes too much and would bring down too many procedures designed, and working well, for a governmental structure of great and growing complexity. The [ALJ] . . . does not act as counsel. He acts as an examiner charged with developing the facts."

10.06 TENURE

10.061 General rule

An ALJ may be removed or disciplined only for good cause established by the Merit Systems Protection Board (MSPB) after opportunity of hearing before the board.[23]

10.062 What constitutes good cause[24]

10.0621 General rule

Actions by an ALJ that undermine confidence in the administrative adjudicatory process constitute good cause for disciplinary action.[25] The MSPB drew this standard from the ABA's Model Code of Judicial Conduct,[26] which was revised in 2007 to apply to "members of the administrative law judiciary."[27]

---

23. An agency can take disciplinary action against an ALJ "only for good cause established and determined by the MSPB on the record after opportunity for hearing." 5 U.S.C. § 7521 (2006). The MSPB rules for hearings concerning discipline against ALJs are set forth in 5 C.F.R. § 1201.137 et seq. (2011). Only an ALJ can hear an MSPB case involving an ALJ. 5 C.F.R. § 1201.140(a) (2011). MSPB has no jurisdiction over a chief ALJ's removal and demotion to regular ALJ status. Butler v. SSA, 331 F.3d 1368 (Fed. Cir. 2003). For comprehensive treatment of MSPB hearings, *see* Robert G. Vaughn, Merit Systems Protection Board Rights and Remedies (1995 and annual supplements).
24. *See generally* Mullins, *supra* note 1, at 115–21; Vaughn, *supra* note 23, at § 10.06. *See also* Brennan v. HHS, 787 F.2d 1559, 1561–63 (Fed. Cir. 1986) (stating that the APA intentionally did not define "good cause" in the APA, instead leaving that task to the judiciary, and noting that the Supreme Court rejected equating "good cause" with the "good behavior" standard applicable to Art. III judges). The MSPB often cites *Brennan*.
25. Long v. SSA, 635 F.3d 526 (Fed. Cir. 2011); SSA v. Davis, 19 M.S.P.B. 279, 282 (1984), *aff'd*, 758 F.2d 661 (Fed. Cir. 1984).
26. *Long*, 635 F.3d at 533.
27. MODEL CODE OF JUDICIAL CONDUCT Application sec. I.B (2007). *See supra* Chapter 7, note 1.

10.0622 Misconduct or incompetence

Misconduct or incompetence constitutes good cause for removal of an ALJ. Misconduct includes conduct that disrupts the workplace or violates generally accepted rules of conduct.[28] Misconduct can also include conduct in an ALJ's private life that undermines confidence in the adjudicative process.[29] An ALJ was disciplined for incompetence where the record showed a high rate of significant adjudicatory errors.[30] MSPB is entitled to receive *Chevron* deference for its interpretation of the term "good cause."[31]

Illustrations:

3. P is an ALJ for Agency. P makes unwanted advances and lewd comments to women on the agency staff. This conduct is violative of generally accepted rules of conduct, grossly offensive to many employees, and disrupts the workplace. Agency has good cause to remove P.[32]

4. Q is an ALJ for Agency. The chief ALJ at Agency reprimands Q for failing to properly perform his duties. Q files a grievance about the chief ALJ's action, claiming purposeful harassment. Q did not act inappropriately and cannot be disciplined for good cause.

5. Assume the same facts in Illustration 4, except Q files 100 grievances against the chief ALJ, intentionally placing a heavy burden on those responsible for processing grievances. Q has misused

---

28. This includes serious misconduct such as sexual harassment as well as other rude and inconsiderate behavior. SSA v. Carr, 78 M.S.P.B. 313 (1998), *aff'd*, 185 F3d 1318 (Fed. Cir. 1999); SSA v. Burris, 39 M.S.P.B. 51, 59 (1988), *aff'd*, 878 F.2d 1445 (Fed. Cir), *cert. denied*, 493 U.S. 855 (1989); *Davis*, 19 M.S.P.B. at 282.

29. *Long*, 635 F.3d at 533–38 (domestic abuse leading to calls to the police and neighbor involvement could be considered misconduct).

30. SSA v. Anyel, 58 M.S.P.B. 261, 267–71 (1993).

31. *Long*, 635 F.3d at 534–35.

32. *See* SSA v. Carter, 35 M.S.P.B. 466 (1985); *Davis*, 19 M.S.P.B. at 282: "Honesty, integrity, and other essential attributes of good moral character are foremost among the qualities that . . . judges ought to possess if public confidence in the legal profession and the judiciary is to be promoted and preserved."

the grievance system, which constitutes good cause for disciplinary action.[33]

6. R is an ALJ for Agency. He pushed and hit his domestic partner and chased her through the neighborhood. The police were called, but eventually the criminal case against R was dismissed. A number of neighbors became involved in the fracas. The incident raises serious questions about whether R is suited to being an ALJ, specifically his judicial temperament, demeanor, self-control, and judgment. There was good cause to dismiss him.[34]

10.0623 Insubordination

Deliberate insubordination by an ALJ is good cause for adverse action.[35] Insubordination includes refusal to follow proper agency orders, such as refusal to schedule or to hear assigned cases or refusal to deliver legal documents.[36]

Illustrations:

7. S is an ALJ for Agency. The head of Agency orders S to hand over files from a case he suspects S handled with bias. S refuses to deliver the files. Agency has good cause for adverse action against S.[37]

8. T is an ALJ for Agency. Agency makes some management changes within the agency that T disagrees with. T refuses to abide by

---

33. *See Burris*, 39 M.S.P.B. at 57.
34. *Long*, 635 F.3d at 533–38. However, a concurring opinion in *Long* indicated substantial doubts about the result. It states that an agency was not free to ferret out misconduct in a federal employee's private life. The concurring opinion also criticized MSPB for failing to articulate standards to define when private conduct may result in disciplinary action and suggested that the absence of such standards could lead to reversal in subsequent cases. *Id.* at 538–39.
35. *See* SSA v. Manion, 19 M.S.P.B. 298, 303 (1984): "Agencies must have the power to discipline an ALJ for an insubordinate and unreasonable refusal to carry out his primary function of hearing and deciding cases."
36. *See id.*; SSA v. Boham, 38 M.S.P.B. 540 (1988); SSA v. Arterberry, 15 M.S.P.B. 320 (1983); *Burris*, 39 M.S.P.B. at 56.
37. *See In re* Chocallo, 1 M.S.P.B. 605 (1980), *vacated on other grounds*, 673 F.2d 551 (D.C. Cir.), *cert. denied*, 459 U.S. 857 (1982).

office procedures concerning the delivery of mail to support staff, which prevented the staff from properly logging cases. Because T is being deliberately disobedient, Agency has good cause to take adverse action against her.[38]

10.0624 Physical incapacity

Complete disability of an ALJ, so that he or she cannot perform his or her adjudicatory duties, constitutes good cause for removal, particularly where the agency demonstrates that it needs to fill the position with an employee available for duty on a regular basis.[39]

10.0625 Violation of statute or regulations

Violation of statute or regulations may be good cause for adverse action against an ALJ.[40]

Illustration:

9. X is an ALJ for Agency. X abuses the free mail privilege by using official envelopes for private matters in violation of a criminal statute. Agency has good cause to discipline X.[41]

10.0626 Performance during adjudicatory proceeding

An ALJ can be disciplined on the basis of his or her performance during the course of an adjudicatory proceeding.[42] A knowing refusal to

---

38. *See* SSA v. Brennan, 27 M.S.P.B. 242 (1985), *aff'd*, 787 F.2d 1559 (Fed. Cir.), *cert. denied*, 479 U.S. 985 (1986).

39. Benton v. United States, 488 F.2d 1017 (1973); SSA v. Mills, 73 M.S.P.B. 463, 467–72 (1996), *aff'd without op.*, 124 F.3d 228 (Fed. Cir. 1997). Obviously, such action must be consistent with requirements imposed by the Americans with Disabilities Act and other legislation protecting disabled persons.

40. HHS v. Haley, 20 M.S.P.B. 365 (1984) (use of government vehicle for other than official purposes in violation of statute).

41. *Burris*, 39 M.S.P.B. at 63.

42. SSA v. Glover, 23 M.S.P.B. 57, 76 (1984); SSA v. Goodman, 19 M.S.P.B. 321, 330 (1984); SSA v. Anyel, 58 M.S.P.B. 261, 268 (1993): "[E]xempting administrative law judges from any performance-based action 'could easily erode the public confidence' in administrative adjudications that the APA 'was designed, in large part, to maintain.'"

follow clear precedents can constitute good cause.[43] Similarly, unacceptably low productivity can be good cause for disciplinary action, although MSPB cases have imposed a difficult burden of proof on an agency that seeks to discipline an ALJ on low productivity grounds.[44] In order to support discipline, misconduct during a hearing must rise "to the level of serious improprieties, flagrant abuses, or repeated breaches of acceptable standards of judicial behavior."[45]

Illustration:

10. Y is an ALJ for Agency. Y has a case disposition rate of about 50 percent of the national average. However, there is no evidence that the national average is a measurement of reasonable productivity, or that Y's cases were similar in difficulty to those decided by other ALJs. Consequently, MSPB will determine that Agency lacked good cause to remove Y.[46]

10.0627 Reduction in force

A reduction in force (RIF) constitutes good cause to remove an ALJ.[47] The requirement of a hearing before the MSPB does not apply to RIFs.[48] RIFs can occur by reason of lack of funds, personnel ceilings, reorganiza-

---

43. *Anyel*, 58 M.S.P.B. at 267 (high rate of adjudicatory errors indicates incompetence).

44. In *Goodman*, 19 M.S.P.B. at 331, the MSPB held that the number of cases a judge decided each year was insufficient to establish unacceptably low productivity "in the absence of evidence demonstrating the validity of using [the agency's] statistics to measure comparative productivity." Even in cases in which the agency appeared to demonstrate low productivity by a proper statistical presentation, MSPB required an in-depth analysis of how particular cases heard by the ALJ compared to cases heard by other ALJs. Verkuil et al., *supra* note 7, at 935, 1020. *See also* SSA v. Balaban, 20 M.S.P.B. 675 (1984).

45. SSA v. Carr, 78 M.S.P.B. 313, 328 (1998).

46. *See* cases in note 44.

47. Ramspeck v. Fed. Trial Exam's Conference, 345 U.S. 128, 143 (1953). *See* 5 C.F.R. § 930.210 (2011).

48. 5 U.S.C. § 7521(b)(B) (2006); 5 C.F.R. § 930.211(c) (2011).

tions, decrease of work, or similar reasons.[49] In case of a RIF, ALJs with the lowest number of "retention credits" are dropped.[50]

10.063 What does not constitute good cause

10.0631 Interference with ALJ independence

If a disciplinary action by an agency is arbitrary, politically motivated, or based on reasons that constitute an improper interference with the performance by an ALJ of his or her judicial functions, the charge cannot constitute good cause.[51] Improper interference with ALJ performance includes interference with the writing of opinions[52] or interference with the way in which an ALJ conducts hearings. It has been held that the decisional independence of the administrative judiciary is constitutionally protected.[53]

Illustration:

11. B is an ALJ for Agency. B continually criticizes Agency in his written decisions. Agency orders B to stop his criticism, but B refuses. B cannot be disciplined for insubordination because the charge improperly interferes with B's duty as an ALJ.[54]

---

49. *Ramspeck*, 345 U.S. at 142.
50. "Retention credits" are based on length of service, so an agency has no power to select which ALJs are let go.
51. Brennan v. HHS, 787 F.2d 1559, 1563 (Fed. Cir. 1986) (discipline for failing to follow office administrative procedures did not interfere with decisional independence); SSA v. Goodman, 19 M.S.P.B. 321, 328 (1984); SSA v. Manion, 19 M.S.P.B. 298 (1984); SSA v. Mills, 73 M.S.P.B. 463, 468 (1996).
52. SSA v. Burris, 39 M.S.P.B. 51, 61 (1998), *aff'd*, 878 F.2d 1445 (Fed. Cir.) *cert. denied*, 493 U.S. 855 (1989): "The ability of an administrative law judge to write decisions free from improper agency pressure is at the very core of an administrative law judge's decisional independence."
53. Perry v. McGinnis, 209 F.3d 597, 603–08 (6th Cir. 2000) (termination of state ALJ because of agency's disagreement with his decisions states claim of First Amendment violation); Harrison v. Coffman, 35 F. Supp. 2d 722 (E.D. Ark. 1999) (same).
54. *See Burris*, 39 M.S.P.B. at 60.

10.0632 *Efficiency of the service*

The standard of "good cause" is not the same as the standard of "efficiency of the service," which is used in connection with adverse action against other government employees.[55]

10.064 Disciplinary actions

10.0641 *Removal*

Removal is the involuntary separation of an employee from his position, whether or not for disciplinary reasons.[56]

Illustration:

12. D is an ALJ for Agency. Agency retires D for disability against his will. Although D is not dismissed for disciplinary reasons, the retirement is involuntary, and it therefore constitutes a removal. D is entitled to an APA hearing before the MSPB, and good cause must be shown before D is removed.[57]

10.0642 *Constructive removal*

An agency "constructively" disciplines or removes an ALJ if it engages in actions that prevent the impartial exercise of the ALJ's judicial functions.[58] The determination of whether a constructive removal has

---

55. In adverse actions against other government employees, good cause is often determined by establishing a nexus between an employer's misconduct and the efficiency of the service. That is, if an employee's misconduct affects how efficiently an agency runs, disciplinary action can be taken. 5 U.S.C. § 7513 (2006). However, "efficiency of the service" is not a factor in determining good cause in § 7521 actions and there does not need to be any separate showing of "nexus." *See* Long v. SSA, 635 F.3d 526, 536 (Fed. Cir. 2011); *Goodman*, 19 M.S.P.B. at 331; SSA v. Davis, 19 M.S.P.B. 279, 281–82 (1984).

56. "Removal" indicates involuntary separation from a position. Benton v. United States, 488 F.2d 1017, 1020 (1973).

57. *Id.*

58. Matter of Doyle, 29 M.S.P.B. 170, 175 (1985); Matter of Perry, 39 M.S.P.B. 446, 448 (1989); Bennett v. SSA, 72 M.S.P.B. 116, 119 (1996). As long as the agency's actions do not affect the ALJ's ability to function as an independent decisionmaker, they are permissible. *In re Sannier*, 45 M.S.P.B. 420,

occurred is based on whether a reasonable person, considering the totality of the circumstances, would consider the actions to constitute interference with the judge's independence. However, an ALJ's independence does not provide immunity from appropriate supervision. Reasonable efforts to increase production levels or other administrative policies disliked by ALJs do not interfere with judicial independence or impartial decisionmaking.[59]

MSPB changed course and determined that it had no jurisdiction to adjudicate constructive removal cases.[60] However, this decision was overturned on appeal on procedural grounds. The court indicated that MSPB's interpretation was reasonable but could be implemented only by adoption of a regulation after APA notice and comment.[61] The regulations now permit ALJs to raise constructive discharge claims before MSPB.[62] The ALJ has the burden to establish that a constructive removal has occurred (as distinguished from cases of actual removal, in which the agency has the burden to establish that good cause is present).

Illustrations:

13. Agency is suffering from low production rates. This results in staffing shortages and public criticism of Agency's ALJs. Agency restricts ALJ transfers to new locations. This measure does not constitute constructive removal because it does not prevent the impartial exercise of ALJ judicial functions.[63]

14. G is an ALJ for Agency. Agency orders G to attend a program designed to help him with his perceived deficiencies at work. Agency's actions do not affect G's judicial independence, and G has not been constructively removed.[64]

---

425 (1990), *aff'd*, 931 F.2d 856 (Fed. Cir. 1991). *See* VAUGHN, *supra* note 23, at 9-31 to 9-32.
59. Nash v. Bowen, 869 F.2d 675, 680 (2d Cir. 1989); Lawson v. HHS, 64 M.S.P.B. 673, 681 (1984).
60. Tunik v. SSA, 93 M.S.P.B. 482 (2003).
61. Tunik v. Merit Sys. Prot. Bd., 407 F.3d 1326 (Fed. Cir. 2005).
62. 5 C.F.R. § 1201.142 (2011).
63. *See In re Sannier*, 45 M.S.P.B. at 426.
64. *See* Stephens v. Merit Sys. Prot. Bd., 986 F.2d 493, 493 (Fed. Cir. 1993).

10.0643 Suspension

Conduct that constitutes good cause for disciplinary action may be deserving of suspension, instead of removal, if mitigating circumstances exist.[65]

10.0644 Reduction in grade/pay level

A reduction in grade or pay can be challenged in an MSPB proceeding. A reduction in pay is a reduction in the rate of pay fixed by law or administrative action for the position held by an employee.[66]

Illustration:

15. N is an ALJ for Agency. N submits a travel voucher for Agency to pay. Agency refuses to pay. This is not a reduction in pay deserving of a hearing in front of MSPB.[67]

10.0645 Choice of discipline

In reviewing adverse action against an ALJ, MSPB can consider whether the particular method of discipline chosen by the agency was an abuse of discretion. Agencies must consider all relevant factors, including not only the gravity of the offense, but such other matters as mitigating circumstances, the frequency of the offense, and whether the action accords with justice in the particular situation. If the agency explains why it imposed more severe discipline despite mitigating factors, its decision merits more deference from MSPB than if it fails to do so.[68]

10.07 COMPENSATION

OPM sets the compensation of ALJs independent of agency recommendations and ratings. OPM has the right to determine the pay level at which each ALJ is placed and the qualifications required for appointment

---

65. *See, e.g.*, SSA v. Glover, 23 M.S.P.B. 57, 80 (1984).
66. In re Doyle, 41 M.S.P.B. 31, 34 (1989); Lawson v. HHS, 64 M.S.P.R. 673, 680 (1984); White v. SSA, 76 M.S.P.B. 447, 459 (1997).
67. *See* Matter of Doyle, 29 M.S.P.B. 170 (1985).
68. Douglas v. VA, 5 M.S.P.B. 313, 330–31 (1981). *See id.* at 331–32, listing 12 relevant factors to consider in deciding the severity of discipline. The case also decides that MSPB has authority to mitigate a penalty rather than remanding to the agency to reconsider the penalty.

to each level.[69] Once an ALJ is appointed to a designated level, the method of advancement is governed solely by the provisions of 5 U.S.C. § 5372.[70]

Illustration:

16. Y is a dual-position ALJ, which means that she hears cases designated to her grade level as well as cases designated to the level above her. All dual-position ALJs are paid at the lower level. OPM decides to promote some of the dual-position ALJs to the higher level. Y is not promoted, but she is doing the same work as the dual-position ALJs who are promoted. A court could find that OPM's promotion process is arbitrary and violative of the APA.[71]

10.08 ROTATION

"Administrative law judges shall be assigned to cases in rotation so far as practicable."[72] A major goal of the APA was to give ALJs independence from agency pressure in deciding cases and to assure fair and unbiased adjudication. Congress therefore provided for ALJs to be assigned in rotation so that agencies could not choose which ALJ they wanted for which case. However, Congress added the qualifier "so far as practicable."[73] The

---

69. 5 U.S.C. § 5372(b)(2) (2006).
70. That is, Congress determined that the method of raising an ALJ's salary (as well as the maximum pay of an ALJ) should not vary by agency, but it left the fixing of the initial salaries to the OPM. Sprague v. King, 23 F.3d 185, 189 (7th Cir. 1994).
71. *See* Gray v. OPM, 771 F.2d 1504, 1506 (D.C. Cir. 1985).
72. 5 U.S.C. § 3105 (2006). Under a consent decree applicable to SSA, cases must be assigned on a "true rotational basis" to the extent practicable. In determining practicability, the chief ALJ can properly consider, among other things, the extent to which an ALJ has an extensive backlog of pending cases. Cases may be assigned on a geographic basis only if the geographic areas are rotated among the ALJs on an equitable basis. Bono v. SSA, No. 77-0B19-CV-W-4 (W.D. Mo. 1979).
73. The Attorney General's Committee Report, upon which the APA was based, did not recommend assigning ALJs to cases in rotation. It instead recommended giving the chief ALJ for each agency the duty to assign cases. U.S. Attorney General's Committee on Administrative Procedure, *Final Report* 199, S. Doc. No. 8, 77th Cong., 1st Sess. (1941); Gifford, supra note 18, at 41–42.

assignment of ALJs cannot be made with the intent or effect of interfering with ALJ independence or otherwise depriving a party of a fair hearing.[74]

Illustrations:

17. Where ALJs are assigned to different classifications based on their qualifications, OPM can permit agencies to assign ALJs to cases according to that classification. Thus it is possible that different ALJs in the same agency could hear different types of cases. Although this system does not mechanically rotate cases among ALJs, it is allowable under the APA.[75]

18. In order to prevent backlog, Agency assigns cases to ALJs according to how many cases an ALJ has in his or her docket. The more cases an ALJ has, the less likely it is that he or she will be assigned new cases, even if this violates a strict mechanical rotation. A court could find that Agency's method of assigning cases would not violate the APA.[76]

19. Z is an ALJ for Agency. Z presides over a benefits hearing for Agency. The case is appealed and is reversed and remanded. The chief ALJ assigns Z to hear the case on remand. Z demonstrates no bias or incompetence. Z's assignment to the case does not violate the rotation provision of the APA.[77]

10.09 PERFORMANCE RATINGS AND PRODUCTION QUOTAS

10.091 Performance ratings

ALJs are not subject to performance ratings by their agency.[78] Of course, an agency is permitted to review the work of its judges since

---

74. Sykes v. Bowen, 854 F.2d 284, 288 (8th Cir. 1988); Borg-Johnson Elecs. v. Christenberry, 169 F. Supp. 746, 754 (S.D.N.Y. 1959) (substitution of non-ALJ for ALJ).

75. *See* Ramspeck v. Fed. Trial Exam's Conference, 345 U.S. 128, 140 (1953).

76. *See* Chocallo v. Bureau of Hearings & Appeals, 548 F. Supp. 1349, 1370 (E.D. Pa. 1982), aff'd, 716 F.2d 889 (3d Cir.), *cert. denied*, 464 U.S. 983 (1983).

77. *See Sykes*, 854 F.2d at 287.

78. "An agency may not rate the job performance of an administrative law judge." See 5 U.S.C. §§ 4301(2)(D), 4302 (2006, 2010 Supp.); 5 C.F.R. § 930.206(a) (2011). *See generally* James P. Timony, *Performance Evaluation of*

the agency is entitled to initiate an action before the MSPB to discipline the judges for a variety of reasons.[79] However, such review of an ALJ's work product must not be conducted in such a manner that it constitutes improper pressure on the judge to adjudicate cases in a certain manner.

10.092 Management initiatives for improvement of ALJ performance

10.0921 Quotas versus goals

Agencies may not implement production quotas, under which ALJs are subject to discipline for failing to produce a specified number of decisions per month. However, an agency is permitted to set reasonable production goals for ALJs.[80] Reasonable goals intended to increase the production levels of ALJs are not an infringement of decisional independence. Note, however, that it is difficult for an agency to discipline an ALJ on account of low productivity;[81] therefore, the agency may have little power to enforce its production goals.

Under a consent decree applicable to the Social Security Administration (SSA), the agency is prohibited from setting either quotas or goals, although the agency is permitted to modify this policy upon prior good faith consultation with representatives of its ALJs.[82] The consent decree

---

Federal Administrative Law Judges, 7 ADMIN. L. J. OF AM. UNIV. 629 (1993); Jeffrey S. Lubbers, *The Federal Administrative Judiciary: Establishing an Appropriate System of Performance Evaluation for ALJs*, 7 ADMIN. L. J. OF AM. UNIV. 589 (1993); L. Hope O'Keeffe, *Administrative Law Judges, Performance Evaluation, and Production Standards: Judicial Independence versus Employee Accountability*, 54 GEO. WASH. L. REV. 591, 604 (1986).

79. *See* Ass'n of Admin. Law Judges v. Heckler, 594 F. Supp. 1132, 1140 (D.D.C. 1984) (agencies may identify low producers by gathering information on their productivity).

80. *See In re Sannier v. M.S.P.B.*, 931 F.2d 856, 858 (Fed. Cir. 1991) (production targets or goals do not constitute constructive removal of ALJs since they do not compromise their judicial independence); Nash v. Bowen, 869 F.2d 675, 681 (2d Cir. 1989) ("in view of the significant backlog of cases, it was not unreasonable to expect ALJs to perform at minimally acceptable levels of efficiency. Simple fairness to claimants awaiting benefits required no less. Accordingly we agree with the district court that the decisional independence of ALJs was not in any way usurped by the Secretary's setting of monthly production goals.").

81. *See* text at note 44.

82. Bono v. SSA, No. 77-0B19-CV-W-4 (W.D. Mo. 1979).

allows the agency to maintain records on individual ALJ's total disposi-
tions and reversal rates for management purposes only; those figures are
not published.[83]

10.0922 Review programs

Agencies may employ programs to review ALJ decisions outside the
usual appeals process in order to improve the quality of ALJ decisionmaking, so long as such programs do not directly interfere with "live"
decisions. Such review programs can help ensure a reasonable degree of
uniformity among ALJ decisions.[84]

10.0923 Reversal rate policies

A policy that is designed to coerce ALJs into lowering the rates at
which they uphold private party claims would constitute an infringement of the decisional independence of ALJs.[85] It is unclear whether an

---

83. *Id.*
84. Review programs do not interfere with the decisional independence of
    ALJs, since "an ALJ is a creature of statute and, as such, is subordinate to
    [agency heads] in matters of policy and interpretation of law." *Nash,* 869
    F.2d at 680.
85. The most famous management reform program was the Bellmon Review
    Program, which was conducted by the SSA during the 1980s. The pro-
    gram targeted ALJs who had the highest percentage of decisions against
    the agency and tried to reform their decisionmaking process. Some ALJs
    charged SSA with violating their decisional independence. Disability
    and benefits claimants also charged SSA with violating their due pro-
    cess rights by denying them impartial ALJs. Some ALJs and claimants
    were successful. *See* Ass'n of Admin. Law Judges v. Heckler, 594 F. Supp.
    1132, 1143 (D.D.C. 1984) (holding that the original Bellmon Review Pro-
    gram affected ALJ decisional independence and therefore violated the
    APA); Barry v. Heckler, 620 F. Supp. 779 (1985) (holding that the Bellmon
    Amendment unfairly denied claimant his right to an impartial ALJ in
    violation of due process); W.C. v. Bowen, 807 F.2d 1502 (9th Cir. 1987)
    (holding that the Bellmon Review Program was unlawfully adopted in
    violation of the APA). *See also* Barry v. Bowen, 825 F.2d 1324, 1330 (9th Cir.
    1987) ("Every court that has addressed the issue [of the legitimacy of the
    Bellmon Review Program] has concluded that the program [had a] perni-
    cious effect."); in Salling v. Bowen, 641 F. Supp. 1046, 1056 (W.D. Va. 1986),
    the court said: "If there ever was a chilling of judicial independence, this
    is it. This is like threatening a lawyer with disbarment if he takes a case

agency can adopt a policy that identifies particular ALJs with unusually high reversal rates in order to improve decisional quality and consistency; such programs skate dangerously close to coercion.[86]

10.10 EX PARTE COMMUNICATIONS AND COMMAND INFLUENCE

APA § 554(d)(1) imposes a special ex parte contact rule applicable to ALJs. APA § 554(d)(2) imposes a special rule preventing supervision of an ALJ by agency employees engaged in investigative or prosecuting functions. These provisions are further discussed in Chapter 7, § 7.06.

---

of a controversial nature. This is the same as saying that every law judge in the country should be deciding a certain percentage of cases against the claimant."

86. *Nash*, 869 F.2d at 681, found sufficient evidence in the record to affirm a district court decision that held that SSA's "Quality Assurance Program" was not designed to reduce reversal rates, only to improve decisional quality and consistency. However, the court acknowledged that such programs can come dangerously close to coercing ALJs to lower their reversal rates.

Chapter 11

ATTORNEYS' FEES UNDER THE EQUAL ACCESS TO JUSTICE ACT

11.01 THE "AMERICAN RULE" AND ITS EXCEPTIONS

The "American rule" regarding attorneys' fees requires that each party pay its own fees.[1] This is the default rule applicable to suits involving the federal government; however, there are numerous exceptions. A court can award attorneys' fees in cases of bad faith or other misconduct

---

1. 28 U.S.C. § 2412(a)(1) (2006); Alyeska Pipeline Serv. Co. v. Wilderness Soc'y, 421 U.S. 240 (1975); Unbelievable, Inc. v. NLRB, 118 F.3d 795 (D.C. Cir. 1997) (NLRB has no power to order that private party pay agency's litigation costs even though party acted in "egregious bad faith.").

219

by the government[2] or the creation of a common fund as in a class action.[3] Moreover, a large number of specific federal statutes provide that prevailing parties are entitled to a fee award, including in some cases an award against the government.[4] Finally, the Equal Access to Justice Act[5] (EAJA) is perhaps the most widely applicable exception, providing that a prevailing party can recover attorneys' fees against the federal government.

11.02 THE EQUAL ACCESS TO JUSTICE ACT[6]

EAJA, which was enacted in 1980[7] and subsequently amended several times, provides for the recovery by a prevailing party (other than the government) of reasonable attorneys' fees and other expenses such as expert witness fees or investigation costs. (§§ 11.03–11.06) Eligible claimants are basically those individuals or small businesses that lack sufficient assets to litigate against the government without help. (§ 11.07)[8] There is a $125 per hour cap on recovery of attorneys' fees (adjusted for inflation). (§ 11.08)

---

2. See 28 U.S.C. § 2412(b) (2006). This section waives sovereign immunity and permits the award of attorneys' fees against the government to the same extent that any other party would be liable under the common law. Thus the government could be liable for fees if it acted in "bad faith, vexatiously, wantonly, or for oppressive reasons." F.D. Rich Co. v. United States *ex rel.* Indus. Lumber Co., 417 U.S. 116, 129 (1974). Recovery under the bad faith standard requires a showing of "subjective bad faith," meaning that a position was advanced or maintained for an improper purpose such as harassment. Griffin Indus., Inc. v. EPA, 640 F.3d 682 (6th Cir. 2011). Fees awarded under § 2412(b) are not subject to the $125 per hour cap imposed by EAJA. *See* Newmark v. Principi, 283 F.3d 172, 174–78 (3d Cir. 2002). However, § 2412(b) is less inclusive than EAJA because it covers costs incurred in federal court litigation, but not costs incurred during litigation before an agency.
3. *See* Brzonkala v. Morrison, 272 F.3d 688, 691–92 (4th Cir. 2001) (finding common-benefit theory inapplicable to case invalidating federal Violence Against Women Act).
4. *See, e.g.,* IRC, 26 U.S.C. § 7430 (2006); FOIA, 5 U.S.C. § 552(a)(4)(E) (2006, 2011 Supp.); Civil Rights Attorney's Fees Act, 42 U.S.C. § 1988 (2006). Discussion of these statutes is beyond the scope of this book.
5. 5 U.S.C. § 504; 28 U.S.C. § 2412(d).
6. *See generally* Harold J. Krent, *Fee Shifting Under the Equal Access to Justice Act—A Qualified Success,* 11 Yale L. & Pol. Rev. 458 (1993).
7. Pub. L. No. 96-481, 94 Stat. 2325 (1980).
8. The fee awarded under EAJA belongs to the litigant, not to the attorney, and so can be reduced or wiped out if the government can set off its

The prevailing party is entitled to such recovery unless the government's position was "substantially justified" or "special circumstances make an award unjust." (§ 11.09)

The purposes of EAJA are "encouraging private parties to vindicate their rights and curbing excessive regulation and the unreasonable exercise of Government authority."[9]

EAJA applies in three distinct situations:

- A private party prevails in formal agency adjudication.[10] (§ 11.04)
- A private party prevails in federal court litigation.[11] (§ 11.05)
- The government recovers less than its previous demand from a private party in either agency formal adjudication or federal court litigation.[12] (§ 11.06)

11.03 PREVAILING PARTIES

To recover fees under EAJA, the private party must be a "prevailing party." A party prevails when "actual relief on the merits of his claim materially alters the legal relationship between the parties by modifying the defendant's behavior in a way that directly benefits the plaintiff."[13]

A prevailing party must prevail on the merits of at least some of its claims *through a judgment or consent decree.* Under *Buckhannon,* a party is not entitled to a fee award simply because litigation brought about the desired effect through a voluntary change in defendant's conduct.[14] In *Buckhannon,* the plaintiff challenged a state statute, claiming it was preempted by federal law. The state legislature then repealed the statute.

---

claims against the litigant against the fee. Astrue v. Ratliff, 130 S. Ct. 2521 (2010).

9. Comm'r v. Jean, 496 U.S. 154, 164–65 (1990); Krent, *supra* note 6, at 458.
10. 5 U.S.C. § 504.
11. 28 U.S.C. § 2412(d)(1)(A).
12. 5 U.S.C. § 504(a)(4); 28 U.S.C. § 2412(d)(1)(D).
13. Farrar v. Hobby, 506 U.S. 103, 111–12 (1992). A temporary victory is insufficient; plaintiff must obtain an "enduring change in the legal relationship" between the party and the government. Sole v. Wyner, 551 U.S. 74 (2007).
14. Buckhannon Bd. & Care Home, Inc. v. W. Va. Dep't of Health & Human Res., 532 U.S. 598, 603–10 (2001); Perez-Arellano v. Smith, 279 F.3d 791 (9th Cir. 2002) (applying *Buckhannon* to EAJA). The *Buckhannon* rule does not apply to fee awards under the Freedom of Information Act. 5 U.S.C. § 552(a)(4)(E)(ii) (2006, 2011 Supp.).

Although the lawsuit was a "catalyst" for the statutory change, this was not sufficient to make plaintiff a "prevailing party," because the lawsuit did not actually require the state legislature to act. Countless cases under EAJA and other federal fee-shifting statutes have struggled with the *Buckhannon* requirement.[15]

11.04 FORMAL AGENCY ADJUDICATION

Under Section 504,[16] a prevailing private party is entitled to recover the costs of "adversary adjudication," which means formal agency adjudication under the APA,[17] i.e., only those adjudications in which a statute[18] specifies that the APA is applicable to the hearing or calls for a "hearing on the record."[19] EAJA does not apply to cases of adjudication (however adversarial or formal they may be) to which the APA formal adjudication provisions do not apply. For example, because immigration proceedings are not governed by the APA (even though they entail a hearing on the record), EAJA does not apply to such cases.[20]

---

15. *See, e.g.,* Aronov v. Napolitano, 562 F.3d 84 (1st Cir. 2009) (stipulated judicial remand order is settlement, not consent decree, 3–2 decision); Goldstein v. Moatz, 445 F.3d 747 (4th Cir. 2006) (no "tactical mooting" exception to *Buckhannon* so government can agree to provide the requested relief to avoid a likely judicial decision against it); Carbonell v. INS, 429 F.3d 894 (9th Cir. 2005) (voluntary stipulation allowing plaintiff a stay of deportation was incorporated into a judicial decree and thus became judicially enforceable). *See generally* Catherine R. Albiston & Laura Beth Neilsen, *The Procedural Attack on Civil Rights: The Empirical Reality of Buckhannon for the Private Attorney General*, 54 UCLA L. Rev. 1087 (2007).
16. 5 U.S.C. § 504 (2006, 2011 Supp.).
17. *Id.* § 504(b)(1)(C)(i).
18. In Collord v. Dep't of Interior, 154 F.3d 933, 935–37 (9th Cir. 1998), the court held that EAJA applied to a hearing that was required by due process rather than the APA. *See* Chapter 3, § 3.02, which questions the current viability of this approach.
19. *See* Chapter 3, § 3.01. *But see* Five Points Rd. Joint Venture v. Johanns, 542 F.3d 1121 (7th Cir. 2008); Aageson Grain & Cattle v. USDA, 500 F.3d 1038 (9th Cir. 2007); Lane v. USDA, 120 F.3d 106, 108–9 (8th Cir. 1997). These cases hold that for purposes of EAJA recoveries, the APA applies to hearings conducted by USDA's National Appeals Division (NAD) (even though the statute does not call for a hearing "on the record" and the NAD does not use ALJs).
20. Ardestani v. INS, 502 U.S. 129, 132–39 (1991).

EAJA does not cover adjudication for the purposes of ratemaking or granting or renewing a license.[21] It applies only in cases in which the government "is represented by counsel or otherwise."[22] For example, because the government is not represented by counsel or otherwise in Social Security cases, Section 504 of EAJA is normally inapplicable to the agency adjudicative phase of Social Security cases.[23]

Under Section 504, the decision about fee recovery is made by the adjudicative officer (normally an ALJ) who presided at the merits hearing.[24] The agency heads have power to make the final decision at the agency level. The private party can appeal the agency's decision concerning fee recovery but the government cannot appeal.[25]

Illustrations:

1. L's license is revoked by Agency. At an adversarial hearing in which Agency is represented by counsel, the ALJ overturns Agency's determination. The Agency heads uphold this determination. L incurs attorneys' fees and other costs of $50,000 in winning back his license. The APA is not applicable to Agency licensing cases because no statute calls for a hearing on the record. A court

---

21. 5 U.S.C. § 504(b)(1)(C)(i) (2006, 2011 Supp.); *see* W. Watersheds Project v. Interior Bd. of Land Appeals, 624 F.3d 983 (9th Cir. 2010) (case involving renewal of grazing permits did not qualify for EAJA fee recoveries).
22. 5 U.S.C. § 504(b)(1)(C)(i) (2006, 2011 Supp.).
23. Sullivan v. Hudson, 490 U.S. 877, 891–92 (1989). However, 28 U.S.C. § 2412(d) is applicable to costs incurred by a claimant who prevails on judicial review of a negative determination by SSA. Normally, only the costs at the judicial review stage can be recovered under § 2412. There is a narrow exception: Where the reviewing court retains jurisdiction over a case remanded to SSA, the court can also award fees for the costs of post-remand proceedings before SSA. *Sullivan*, 490 U.S. 883–93 (allowing post-remand costs before SSA where district court remanded but retained jurisdiction). An attorney who prevails in court is entitled to whichever fee is larger—the fee prescribed by EAJA or that prescribed by the Social Security Act. 42 U.S.C. § 406(b) (2006, 2011 Supp.) (providing for a reasonable fee paid out of the benefits awarded, but not to exceed 25 percent of past due benefits). See Gisbrecht v. Barnhart, 535 U.S. 789 (2002); Jeter v. Astrue, 622 F.3d 371 (5th Cir. 2010) (contingency fee cannot produce a "windfall").
24. 5 U.S.C. § 504(b)(1)(D) (2006, 2011 Supp.).
25. *Id.* § 504(c)(2).

would probably hold that EAJA does not entitle L to recover attorneys' fees.[26]

2. Assume the same facts as Illustration 1 except that L is seeking a new license. Assume further that a statute requires that Agency provide a hearing on the record. Section 504 of EAJA does not apply to adjudications for the purpose of granting a license.

11.05 FEDERAL COURT LITIGATION AGAINST THE FEDERAL GOVERNMENT

Under 28 U.S.C. § 2412(d), a court shall award to a prevailing party fees and expenses incurred in any civil action (except a case sounding in tort)[27] brought by or against the United States, *including judicial review of agency action.*[28]

Where a party who lost at the agency level prevails on judicial review, Section 2412(d) permits an award of costs incurred at the judicial review level, whether or not the dispute concerned formal agency adjudication. Moreover, Section 2412(d) provides for recovery of costs at *both* the agency and judicial levels, but *only* if Section 504 would have permitted a recovery of costs at the agency level. In other words, EAJA allows recovery of costs incurred at the agency level only in cases of agency formal adjudication, whether the private party won at the agency level or lost at the agency level but prevailed on judicial review.[29]

Illustrations:

3. Assume the same facts as Illustration 1 (a license revocation to which APA formal adjudication requirements do not apply), except that L loses before Agency. However, L prevails on judicial review. Assuming other requirements are satisfied, EAJA applies.

---

26. *But see* Collord v. Dep't of Interior, 154 F.3d 933, 935–37 (9th Cir. 1998), which states that EAJA applies to cases in which a hearing is required by due process.
27. An action for negligence and breach of fiduciary duty against directors of a failed bank sounds in tort so EAJA is inapplicable. Resolution Trust Co. v. Gaudet, 192 F.3d 485, 487 (5th Cir. 1999).
28. 28 U.S.C. § 2412(d) (2006, 2011 Supp.).
29. 28 U.S.C. § 2412(d)(3) (2006, 2011 Supp.).

L can recover his attorneys' fees incurred on judicial review, but not the costs incurred before Agency.[30]

4. Assume the same facts as Illustration 3, except that a statute requires Agency to furnish a hearing on the record before revoking a license. Assuming other EAJA requirements are satisfied, L can recover his attorneys' fees incurred at both the judicial review and administrative levels.

11.06 ENFORCEMENT ACTIONS BROUGHT BY THE GOVERNMENT

Sections 504(a)(4) and 2412(d)(1)(D) apply to enforcement actions brought by the government against a private party, either in an agency formal adjudication or in court. The right to recover fees is triggered if (1) the government's demand was substantially in excess of the judgment finally obtained by the government (by reason of an agency decision or judicial judgment), and (2) the government's demand was unreasonable when compared with such judgment. These provisions were added by 1996 amendments to EAJA.[31] This provision gives a right to recovery of fees to a *nonprevailing* party. It does not, however, remove the requirement that a *prevailing party* show that the government's position was not substantially justified.[32]

In such cases, the agency or the court can award fees and other expenses related to defending against the excessive demand unless the private party has committed a willful violation of law or otherwise acted in bad faith, or special circumstances make an award unjust.[33]

An action to recover civil penalties falls under these sections. In addition, other sorts of demands might be covered. For example, an agency might demand that a party cease and desist from a wide range

---

30. *But see Collord*, 154 F.3d at 935–37, holding that if APA formal adjudication provisions are triggered by due process, the hearing before Agency would be adversary adjudication and L could recover fees incurred before Agency.

31. Pub. L. No. 104-121, 110 Stat. 863, § 232(a) (1996). *See generally* Judith E. Kramer, *Equal Access to Justice Act Amendments of 1996: A New Avenue for Recovering Fees from the Government*, 51 ADMIN. L. REV. 363 (1999).

32. Park Manor Ltd. v. HHS, 495 F.3d 433, 437 (7th Cir. 2007).

33. 5 U.S.C. § 504(a)(4); 28 U.S.C. § 2412(d)(1)(D) (2006, 2011 Supp.) *See* Kramer, *supra* note 31, at 379–88.

of activities; at the hearing or trial, the decisionmaker issues a cease and desist order for only a small part of these activities. If the original demand is considered unreasonable in comparison with the judgment, EAJA might apply.

Illustration:

5. Agency asserts that B owes a civil penalty of $1 million. By statute, Agency adjudicates civil penalty cases and must employ APA formal adjudication. After a hearing, it is determined that B owes a penalty of only $5,000. It is further determined that B's conduct was not willful. B incurs attorneys' fees of $50,000 in resisting Agency's penalty demand. Assuming that the other requirements of EAJA are met, a court might find that the government's demand was unreasonable when compared to the ultimate judgment and therefore rule that B is entitled to recover attorneys' fees under EAJA.

11.07 ELIGIBLE CLAIMANTS

11.071 Parties eligible for fee awards

Both Sections 504 and 2412(d) permit awards of attorneys' fees only to a limited class of parties who are considered to need assistance in litigating against the government.[34] Broadly speaking, awards can be made only to an individual whose net worth did not exceed $2 million at the time the action or agency adjudication was filed[35] or to a business, organization,[36] or local government unit that did not have a net worth exceeding $7 million when the action was filed *and* that did not have more than 500 employees. However, tax-exempt charitable organizations qualify regardless of their net worth.[37]

---

34. 28 U.S.C. § 2412(d)(2)(B); 5 U.S.C. § 504(b)(1)(B) (2006, 2011 Supp.).
35. A decedent's estate is treated as an individual under this provision, but the determination of whether its net worth exceeded $2 million on the date of filing must include distributions made to beneficiaries prior to filing. Estate of Woll by Woll, 44 F.3d 464 (7th Cir. 1994).
36. A trade association whose assets were less than $7 million qualified even though its members were corporations having assets vastly greater than that amount. Tex. Food Indus. Ass'n v. USDA, 81 F.3d 578, 580–82 (5th Cir. 1996).
37. 28 U.S.C. § 2412(d)(2)(B); 5 U.S.C. § 504(b)(1)(B) (2006, 2011 Supp.). In addition, agricultural cooperatives qualify regardless of their net worth.

In the case of EAJA recoveries where the agency has made an excessive monetary demand (§11.06), a "small entity" is also an eligible claimant.[38]

Illustrations:

6. Agency seeks to revoke C's license. C is a business partnership having a net worth of $4 million and 515 employees at the time Agency's action was filed. C prevails before Agency and the license is not revoked. C is not entitled to a recovery of fees under EAJA because it has more than 500 employees.

7. Assume the same facts as Illustration 6, except that C is a tax-exempt charity with a net worth of $9 million. C is not entitled to a recovery of fees under EAJA. Charities are not subject to the $7 million net worth requirement, but are subject to the requirement that they not have more than 500 employees.

11.072 Deadlines

In order to be an eligible claimant, the prevailing party must satisfy the strict timing provisions of EAJA. A party seeking an award of fees must submit an application containing an itemized statement to the agency or court within *30 days* of final disposition of the matter, meaning from the time that the decision at issue is no longer subject to appeal.[39]

---

38. 5 U.S.C. § 504(b)(1)(B); 28 U.S.C. § 2412(d)(2)(B) (2006, 2011 Supp.). The phrase "small entity" is defined in 5 U.S.C. § 601 (2006) and refers to a "small business concern" (meaning one that is not dominant in its field of operation) as well as a "small organization," or "small government jurisdiction." *See* Kramer, *supra* note 31, at 377–78.

39. 5 U.S.C. § 504(a)(2) (2006, 2011 Supp.); Adams v. SEC, 287 F.3d 183 (D.C. Cir. 2002) (time for seeking fees from agency runs out 30 days after the time for appeal of decision has expired). Under 28 U.S.C. § 2412(d)(1)(B), the application must be submitted within 30 days of final judgment in the action. The term "final judgment" means a judgment that is "final and not appealable." *Id.* § 2412(d)(2)(G). The judgment of a court of appeals is no longer "appealable" when the 90-day time for filing a petition for certiorari has expired. Al-Harbi v. INS, 284 F.3d 1080, 1082–84 (9th Cir. 2002). The application of these timing provisions has caused much difficulty in Social Security cases remanded from federal courts to SSA. *See* Shalala v. Schaefer, 509 U.S. 292, 297–98 (1993) (30-day period under § 2412(d) runs from date that district court decision remanding case to Social

Even if every element of the right to recover under EAJA is not stated in the application, it can be amended to add the missing allegation under the "relation back" doctrine since the government was adequately placed on notice within the 30-day period that it would have to defend the EAJA claim.[40] In an extreme case, the doctrine of equitable tolling might apply if the plaintiff was reasonably ignorant of the filing requirement and the government was not prejudiced.[41]

11.08 AMOUNT OF RECOVERY

The amount that can be recovered by a prevailing party under EAJA includes the cost of expert witnesses, the costs of necessary studies or tests, and reasonable attorney fees,[42] but not the salaries of regular employees of the prevailing party who worked on the case.[43] The prevailing party who is compelled to expend additional resources litigating about fees ("fees on fees" or "supplemental fees") is entitled to recover fees expended in doing so.[44]

Security without retaining jurisdiction becomes final and nonappealable); Melkonyan v. Sullivan, 501 U.S. 89, 93–94 (1991) (30-day period runs from post-remand judgment of district court, where court remanded to agency while retaining jurisdiction). *Schaefer*, 509 U.S. at 300–02, makes clear that a claimant who wins a remand from the court (without retaining jurisdiction) is a "prevailing party" for EAJA purposes regardless of what happens during the subsequent proceedings before the agency on remand.

40. Scarborough v. Principi, 541 U.S. 401 (2004).
41. Townsend v. SSA, 486 F.3d 127, 132 (6th Cir. 2007) (counsel should have known that government's motion for relief from judgment was filed too late so that it did not delay a final decision—equitable tolling did not apply).
42. 28 U.S.C. § 2412(d)(2)(A); 5 U.S.C. § 504(b)(1)(A) (2006, 2011 Supp.). Section 504 (but not § 2412) covers the cost of "reasonable attorney or agent fees." Thus the cost of a lay representative may be recovered. Cook v. Brown, 68 F.3d 447, 451 (Fed. Cir. 1995) (fees paid to lay representative recoverable under § 504 but not § 2412). A pro se litigant cannot recover fees under EAJA. Krecioch v. United States, 316 F.3d 684, 688 (7th Cir. 2003).
43. Fanning, Phillips, & Molnar v. West, 160 F.3d 717, 720–22 (Fed. Cir. 1998).
44. *See* Comm'r v. Jean, 496 U.S. 154, 158–66 (1990) (prevailing party entitled to recover fees incurred in litigating about fees regardless of whether the government had "substantial justification" for its position resisting payment of the fees). Supplemental fees should be denied to the extent that

However, attorney fees cannot exceed $125 per hour unless it is determined that an increase in the cost of living since 1996 or a special factor (such as limited availability of qualified attorneys for the proceedings involved) justifies a higher fee. In the case of § 504, the payment of any amount in excess of $125 per hour must be provided for by regulation.[45] In the case of § 2412, however, such amounts are determined by the court independently of agency regulations.

The $125 per hour figure (even as adjusted for inflation) is far below the amount currently charged by big city law firms. Nevertheless, it is difficult to avoid the cap on the basis of a "special factor." The exception for "limited availability" does not refer to whether there is a scarcity of attorneys willing to work for $125 per hour. Instead, it refers to attorneys whose availability is limited because they possess some distinctive knowledge or specialized skill needed in the particular litigation. For example, a specialty such as patent law or knowledge of foreign law or language might qualify.[46]

The term "special factor" does not include the novelty and difficulty of the issues, the undesirability of the case, the quality of work and ability of counsel, the general market rates, or the results obtained, nor does it include the contingent nature of the fee.[47]

---

the original fee application was unsuccessful. *Id.* at 163 n. 10; Wagner v. Shinseki, 640 F.3d 1255 (Fed. Cir. 2011).

45. 5 U.S.C. § 504(b)(1)(A) (2006, 2011 Supp.).

46. Pierce v. Underwood, 487 U.S. 552, 572 (1988). This language in *Pierce* has given rise to uncertainty when applied to attorneys in specialized fields that lack a technical background such as is needed to practice patent law. Most decisions have indicated that mere specialization is not enough. *See* F.J. Vollmer Co. v. Magaw, 102 F.3d 591, 598–99 (D.C. Cir. 1996) (specialization in firearms law does not qualify for enhancement because no specialized training); Perales v. Casillas, 950 F.2d 1066, 1078 (5th Cir. 1992) (same for immigration law). However, the Ninth Circuit does permit enhancement because the attorney has developed expertise through a specialized field of law practice needed in the litigation. *See* Pirus v. Bowen, 869 F.2d 536, 542 (9th Cir. 1989) (specialization in Social Security); Love v. Reilly, 924 F.2d 1492, 1496 (9th Cir. 1991) (same for environmental law). One compromise position, adopted by the First and Seventh Circuits, allows enhancement upon a showing that "a particular . . . kind of case. . . requires for competent counsel someone from among a small class of specialists who are available only for more than" the inflation-adjusted $125 figure. Mathews-Sheets v. Astrue, 653 F.3d 560, 565 (7th Cir. 2011).

47. *Pierce*, 487 U.S. at 573. Under attorney fee statutes other than EAJA that contain no hourly cap, attorneys frequently argue that the market rate

The $125 figure can also be increased by reason of increases in the cost of living since 1996 (the time when the revised $125 cap became effective).[48] However, the inflation adjustment is measured at the time the legal services were rendered, not at the time the fee award was made.[49] Under EAJA, the cost of paralegals is reimbursed at their prevailing market rates, not at the amount the attorney actually paid the paralegals.[50]

Normally, the EAJA recovery is based on the "lodestar" amount, meaning the product of a reasonable hourly rate (not exceeding the cap) times the number of hours reasonably expended on the entire case. It is essential that detailed time sheets be submitted. If the hours spent on a matter seem excessive or nonessential given the difficulty of the case, the court will reduce them.[51]

---

should be enhanced because of special circumstances present in the case. The Supreme Court is quite hostile to such claims. Enhancement can occur only if the hourly rate failed to take account of the attorney's true market value, which requires specific proof; or if the attorney had to make an extraordinary outlay of expenses (calculated by applying a standard rate of interest to the outlays); or if there is exceptional delay in payment of the fees (again measured by a standard rate of interest). Perdue v. Kenny A., 130 S. Ct. 1662 (2010) (fact that attorneys had done an outstanding job with an apparently unwinnable case that restructured an entire government institution is insufficient to grant fee enhancement).

48. Presumably this adjustment should be made by calculating the increase in the Department of Labor's cost of living index from 1996 to the date the work is done. *See* Tchemkou v. Mukasey, 517 F.3d 506, 512 (7th Cir. 2008), which granted fees for work done in 2006 at the rate of $161.85 per hour. However, some decisions indicate that the party seeking fees must make an additional showing, either of an increase in the lawyer's costs of providing the service or that "a lawyer capable of handling the challenge . . . could not be found in the relevant geographical area to handle such a case" for less than the inflation-adjusted $125 figure. *Mathews-Sheets*, 653 F.3d at 563–65.

49. Hubbard v. United States, 480 F.3d 1327, 1334 (Fed. Cir. 2007).

50. Richlin Sec. Serv. Co. v. Chertoff, 553 U.S. 571 (2008). The Court "assumed" but did not actually decide that the same result would apply under § 2412. Dictum in the case suggests that the same rule should apply to all of the "fees and other expenses reimbursable under EAJA"—that is, reimbursement at market rates (or at the client's cost if market rates could not be determined). *Id.* at 576–78.

51. *See, e.g.,* Fabi Constr. Co. v. Sec'y of Labor, 541 F.3d 407 (D.C. Cir. 2008) (reducing fee request by 25 percent because of inadequate detail in time sheets); Role Models Am., Inc. v. Brownlee, 353 F.3d 962, 970–74 (D.C. Cir.

If a party prevails on some but not all claims, it may be appropriate to scale down the amount of fees recoverable. First, if the party failed to prevail on claims that were unrelated to the claims on which he succeeded, a reduction is appropriate. Second, a reduction is appropriate if the success achieved seems less than commensurate with the number of hours expended.[52] A fee award can be reduced if the party establishes a lack of substantial justification for some claims but not others. Moreover, any fee award can be reduced to the extent that the prevailing party engaged in conduct that unduly and unreasonably protracted the final resolution of the matter in controversy.[53] The trial court has considerable discretion in this situation, given the difficult problem of allocating the time between successful and failed claims and claims with and without substantial justification.[54]

Illustration:

8. After an APA formal adjudication, Agency rules that D's broker-dealer license should not be revoked. D was represented by Attorney who bills D at her normal rate of $300 per hour. All competent securities lawyers charge $300 per hour. Assuming that the other requirements of EAJA apply, Agency will be required to pay Attorney's fees, but the cap will probably apply since Attorney lacks specialized technical training even though she is an expert in securities law.[55] Thus D can be reimbursed at a rate of not more than $125 per hour (adjusted for inflation since 1996).

2004) (cutting the number of hours in half for a variety of reasons including lack of detail in time sheets, excessiveness of hours, duplicative and redundant staffing, and inessential chores like meeting with the press).

52. Hensley v. Eckerhart, 461 U.S. 424, 434 (1983); F.J. Vollmer Co. v. Magaw, 102 F.3d 591, 599–600 (D.C. Cir. 1996) (reimbursement of only 70 percent of hours where plaintiff is only partially successful).

53. 5 U.S.C. § 504 (b)(1)(E); 28 U.S.C. § 2412(d)(1)(C).

54. *See Fabi Constr. Co.*, 541 F.3d 407 (scaling down $450,000 claim for fees to $56,250 to account for winners and losers and mixed finding of substantial justification for the winners). In another case, allocation between claims that were and were not substantially justified was unnecessary when the government's position on the "more prominent" issue was substantially justified. Gatimi v. Holder, 606 F.3d 344 (7th Cir. 2010).

55. *See* note 46, recognizing a split in authority on this issue.

11.09 SUBSTANTIAL JUSTIFICATION

Under both §§ 504 and 2412(d), the government has the burden to show that its "position" was "substantially justified."[56] For this purpose, the government's "position" includes both its litigating position before the agency or the court and also the original action (or failure to act) on which the subsequent administrative and judicial litigation was based.[57] The determination is whether the government's action, taken as a whole, is justified, considering both the government's original action and its litigating position.[58]

"Substantially justified" means that the government's position had a "reasonable basis in both law and fact."[59] A decision is "substantially justified" if the agency position was grounded in a reasonable basis in truth for the facts alleged, a reasonable basis in law for the theory propounded,[60] and a reasonable connection between the facts alleged and the legal theory advanced.[61]

The government's position can be found to be "substantially justified" even if the government lost the case because its action was found not to be supported by substantial evidence or to be arbitrary and capricious.[62]

---

56. *F.J. Vollmer Co.*, 102 F.3d at 595.
57. 5 U.S.C. § 504(b)(1)(E); 28 U.S.C. § 2412(d)(2)(D) (2006, 2011 Supp.).
58. United States v. Marolf, 277 F.3d 1156 (9th Cir. 2002) (fee award justified because government's underlying position was unreasonable even though its litigating position was reasonable); United States v. Real Prop. at 2659 Roundhill Drive, 283 F.3d 1146 (9th Cir. 2002) (government's underlying action was reasonable but its litigation position was unreasonable because it ignored new Supreme Court case).
59. The government's position is substantially justified if it is "justified in substance or in the main—that is, justified to a degree that could satisfy a reasonable person. That is no different from . . . [having] a reasonable basis both in law and fact." Pierce v. Underwood, 487 U.S. 552, 565 (1988).
60. An agency's unsuccessful statutory interpretation can pass the substantial justification test even if it is "non-obvious," given that it was not at odds with existing case law and found some support in legislative history. The fact that it was asserted as a "post-hoc rationalization" before the court of appeals did not mean that it lacked substantial justification. Hill v. Gould, 555 F.3d 1003 (D.C. Cir. 2009) (agency's position that mute swan was not a migratory species because it is not native to North America was wrong but had substantial justification).
61. Bricks Inc. v. EPA, 426 F.3d 918, 922 (7th Cir. 2005).
62. *See id.* at 923 (although substantial evidence was lacking, the case was a close one on the facts); Sotelo-Aquije v. Slattery, 62 F.3d 54, 58 (2d Cir.

Nevertheless, the preceding merits determination is highly relevant to the subsequent substantial-justification determination; it is difficult for the government to prevail if the antecedent merits determination found its conduct to be unreasonable.[63]

In determining substantial justification, objective factors are relevant but not determinative. Thus the fact that the government settled the case on unfavorable terms does not establish a lack of substantial justification since it might reflect such factors as a change in governmental policy.[64] Nor is it established by the fact that the decisionmaker decided the case at the pleadings stage, since this may evidence only that the judge was efficient.[65] Whether other courts have rejected the government's position is also relevant but not determinative.[66] Instead, all facts and circumstances must be weighed to determine whether the government's position had a "reasonable basis in both law and fact."[67]

Appellate courts review decisions of lower courts under § 2412(d) on the "substantial justification" issue under an abuse of discretion standard.[68] This gives considerable power to the lower court judge. However, courts reviewing agency EAJA determinations under § 504 do so under the normal rules of scope of review such as the substantial evidence test.[69]

Illustration:

9. F is charged with an unfair labor practice by Agency. The general counsel of Agency issued a complaint based on evidence

---

1995) (decision could lack substantial evidence yet still be substantially justified). However, if the government's case survived a motion to dismiss and a summary judgment motion, it is presumed that its position was substantially justified. United States v. Thouvenot, Wade & Moerschen, Inc., 596 F.3d 378 (7th Cir. 2010).

63. *Sotelo-Aquije*, 62 F.3d at 58 (government has "high hurdle" to overcome antecedent finding that its position was unsupported by substantial evidence); F.J. Vollmer Co. v. Magaw, 102 F.3d 591, 595 (D.C. Cir. 1996); Hess Mech. Corp. v. NLRB, 112 F.3d 146, 149 (4th Cir. 1997) (general counsel's issuance of complaint based on very weak testimonial evidence that was rejected by ALJ—agency lacked substantial justification).
64. *Pierce*, 487 U.S. at 568.
65. *Id.* at 568–69.
66. *Id.* at 569.
67. *Id.* at 565.
68. *Id.* at 557–63.
69. United Bhd. of Carpenters & Joiners v. NLRB, 891 F.2d 1160, 1162 (5th Cir. 1990).

provided by G who stated that F discharged G because of G's efforts to organize a union. F claimed that G was discharged because of poor performance on the job. Other than G's statement that he was discharged for union activities, no evidence supported G's position. Overwhelming evidence supported F's position. Agency's ALJ ruled in favor of F that no unfair labor practice occurred and the agency heads affirmed. An ALJ could rule that Agency's position lacked substantial justification and therefore could award attorneys' fees to F, assuming that other EAJA requirements are met.[70]

---

70. Hess Mech. Corp. v. NLRB, 112 F.3d 146, 149 (4th Cir. 1997).

Chapter 12

ADJUDICATION UNDER THE
2010 MODEL STATE APA

12.01 OVERVIEW

In July 2010, the Uniform Law Commission (ULC)[1] approved a new Model State Administrative Procedure Act (MSAPA or Act).[2] This is the ULC's fourth model state act,[3] and it attempts to capture into the model's language events and developments impacting administrative procedure that were not anticipated when prior models were drafted.[4] The ULC analyzed case law, legal articles, agency policies and guidance documents, prior versions of the MSAPA, the federal APA, and states' administrative procedures to develop a model to address both intended and unintended consequences of administrative practice to date.[5] The 2010 MSAPA is the result of six years of active review of the model, and includes commentary to describe the changes made and to clarify

---

1. The Uniform Law Commission (ULC), also known as the National Conference of Commissioners on Uniform State Laws (NCCUSL), gathers qualified representatives appointed from the 50 states and other jurisdictions to "research, draft[,] and promote enactment of uniform state laws in areas of state law where uniformity is desirable and practical." http://www.uniformlaws.org/Narrative.aspx?title=About%20the%20ULC (last visited Feb. 22, 2012).
2. Revised Model State Admin. Procedure Act (2010) [hereinafter 2010 MSAPA], *available at* http://www.law.upenn.edu/bll/archives/ulc/msapa/2010_final.htm (last visited Feb. 22, 2012).
3. 2010 MSAPA Prefatory Note. Shortly after Congress enacted the federal APA in 1946, the NCCUSL promulgated the 1946 MSAPA. John Gedid, *An Introduction to the 2010 Model State Administrative Procedure Act, in Symposium, Modernizing Agency Practice: The 2010 Model State Administrative Procedure Act*, 20 WIDENER L.J. 697, 698–99 (2011). The NCCUSL later revised the MSAPA in 1961 and again in 1981. *See infra* § 12.02.
4. Gedid, *supra* note 3, at 697–98.
5. Gedid explains that the growth in electronic media, state experiments in new statutory devices, ongoing state adaptation and experimentation with earlier model acts, studies of the federal APA, the creation of central panels, studies by the American Bar Association's Section of Administrative Law and Regulatory Practice, as well as academic literature have "invariably provoke[d] comment, analysis, and discussion[, providing] a rich source of insight and information about the strengths and weaknesses of state APA innovations." *Id.* at 698–99. Additionally, "appellate case law in forty years has identified problems of ambiguity, omission, and contradiction in state APAs." *Id.* at 699.

the drafters' intent.[6] The Act seeks to promote fairness, accessibility, and efficiency.[7] The drafters concluded that, because "notions of best statutory practices evolve, as the result of experience and academic commentary, . . . it makes sense for states to revisit and update older versions of their APAs."[8] Essentially, "[t]he function of the MSAPA is to facilitate that process by crystallizing new concepts of best practices for the convenience of state lawmakers."[9] In that light, this chapter summarizes the distinctions in adjudication provisions between the 2010 MSAPA and the federal APA, which may indicate where federal practice incrementally might be headed.

12.02 EVOLUTION OF THE MODEL ACT[10]

The original MSAPA was drafted in 1946.[11] It "incorporated basic principles with only enough elaboration of detail to support essential features of an administrative procedure act . . . because 1) agencies . . . perform[ed] widely diverse tasks . . . and 2) the legislatures of different states ha[d] taken dissimilar approaches to virtually identical problems."[12] The 1961

---

6. The drafters first discussed proposed revisions to the MSAPA in November 2004. NCCUSL, *Proposed Revisions to the Model State Administrative Procedure Act of 1981, First Discussion Draft for the Meeting of the Committee*, Nov. 12–14, 2004, *available at* http://www.law.upenn.edu/bll/archives/ulc/msapa/Nov2004Draft.htm (last visited Feb. 22, 2012). Almost six years later, the proposed revisions were "Approved and Recommended for Enactment in All the States" at the 119th Annual Conference held July 9–16, 2010. 2010 MSAPA Prefatory Note. *See also* Michael Asimow, *Contested Issues in Contested Cases: Adjudication Under the 2010 Model State Administrative Procedure Act, in Symposium, Modernizing Agency Practice*, 20 Widener L.J. 707 (2011).
7. Gregory L. Ogden, *Overview of the 2010 Revised Model State Administrative Procedure Act*, 36 Admin. & Reg. L. News 3 (Winter 2011).
8. Asimow, *supra* note 6, at 708.
9. *Id.*
10. This brief history is a summary of the 2010 MSAPA Prefatory Note. For a history of the federal APA, see George B. Shepherd, *Fierce Compromise: The Administrative Procedure Act Emerges from New Deal Politics*, 90 Nw. U. L. Rev. 1557 (1996).
11. Interestingly, the NCCUSL presented the 1946 MSAPA following the promulgation of the federal APA. Gedid, *supra* note 3, at 697–98. Drafters of both acts communicated with each other regularly. 2010 MSAPA Prefatory Note.
12. 2010 MSAPA Prefatory Note.

revision followed after some "maturing of thought" gave way to "goals [of] fairness to the parties involved and creation of procedure that [wa]s effective from the standpoint of government," resulting in a model act of "basic principles" and "essential major features."[13] By 1981, greater experience in administrative law and the growth in state government called for another revision, which led to a more detailed model. The 2010 revision was undertaken as a result of "a substantial body of legislative action, judicial opinion[,] and academic commentary that explain, interpret[,] and critique the 1961 and 1981 Acts and the [f]ederal Administrative Procedure Act[,] . . . represent[ing] best practices in the states."[14] Experts "designed [the 2010 Act] to ensure fairness in administrative proceedings, increase public access to the law administered by agencies, and promote efficiency in agency proceedings by providing for extensive use of electronic technology."[15] "The 2010 Act provides for a uniform minimum set of procedures . . . [and] creates only procedural rights and imposes only procedural duties."[16]

12.021 Overview of the 2010 MSAPA

The 2010 MSAPA contains eight articles,[17] which apply "a uniform minimum set of procedures to be followed by agencies subject to the act."[18] "When specific state laws are inconsistent with the provisions of the 2010 Act, those specific state laws will be controlling."[19] The MSAPA is more detailed than the federal APA, but, upon review, the language appears to be clearer and less cumbersome. New and modified definitions expand the Act's applicability.[20] The Act explicitly governs formal agency

---

13. *Id.*
14. *Id.*
15. Ogden, *supra* note 7, at 3.
16. 2010 MSAPA Prefatory Note.
17. The eight articles are as follows: Article 1: General Provisions; Article 2: Public Access to Agency Law and Policy; Article 3: Rulemaking, Procedural Requirements and Effectiveness of Rules; Article 4: Adjudication in Contested Case; Article 5: Judicial Review; Article 6: Office of Administrative Hearings; Article 7: Rules Review; Article 8: Miscellaneous Provisions. 2010 MSAPA Prefatory Note. *See also* Ogden, *supra* note 7, at 3, 27 (summarizing the eight articles).
18. 2010 MSAPA Prefatory Note.
19. *Id.*
20. For example, the word "agency" was altered from previous model acts to apply to "as many state actors in the executive branch . . . as possible," given the variances in applicability of an administrative procedure act

proceedings, as well as proceedings for judicial review and civil enforcement of agency action,[21] informal hearings are not covered.[22] The Act also attempts to plug gaps in administrative procedure that courts have identified, where administrative statutes and regulations have been silent.[23]

12.022 Adjudication provisions

Adjudication in the MSAPA applies to formal adjudication.[24] The Act defines adjudication as "the process for determining facts or applying law pursuant to which an agency formulates and issues an order."[25]

---

when agencies lobby the legislature to create exceptions. 2010 MSAPA § 102(3) cmt. The term "agency head" separates the person or persons with final decisional authority from the agency as a whole. *Id.* § 102(5) & cmt. These terms allow for consistent procedures across agencies through one administrative procedure act.

21. By comparison, the 1981 Model State Administrative Procedure Act applied to almost any state agency action regardless of statutory provisions. Asimow, *supra* note 6, at 713–14. Revised Model State Admin. Procedure Act (1981), *available at* http://www.nmcpr.state.nm.us/acr/presentations/1981MSAPA.htm (last visited Feb. 22, 2012).

22. *See* Asimow, *supra* note 6, at 720 ("[T]he 2010 MSAPA does not contain any provision for informal or summary hearings, only for full-bore formal hearings."); *id.* at 720 n.65 ("The 2010 MSAPA does not contain a conference or informal hearing model as an alternative to a formal hearing . . . ."). Although licensing generally is informal adjudication, it is covered under the MSAPA. 2010 MSAPA § 419. *See* Chapter 9 §§ 9.0231, 9.06 (explaining licensing procedures as informal adjudication).

23. *See, e.g.,* Moore v. VA, 475 F.2d 1283, 1286 (D.C. Cir. 1973) ("[I]n the absence of special statutory provision, and in the absence of special administrative regulation, no procedure for discovery is normally available in a federal administrative proceeding. . . ."); N.Y. State Dep't of Law v. FCC, 984 F.2d 1209, 1218–19 (D.C. Cir. 1993) (explaining that the APA grants an agency substantial discretion regarding settlement discussions, and does not automatically require notice of settlement discussions to all interested parties); Nat'l Welfare Rights Org. v. Finch, 429 F.2d 725 (D.C. Cir. 1970) (allowing intervention despite the lack of any statutory provision).

24. *See* Asimow, *supra* note 6, at 720 (explaining that Article 4 applies only to formal adjudication). *See also supra* note 22 (explaining that the 2010 MSAPA does not apply to informal adjudication).

25. 2010 MSAPA § 102(1). The comment to section 102 states that the word "adjudication" is intended to be read in conjunction with the terms "contested case," "evidentiary hearing," and "order."

Adjudication is "formal" when the law calls on an agency to follow certain procedures for receiving evidence and issuing an order based on the evidence received. The MSAPA maintains the federal APA's definitional distinction between "adjudication" and "rulemaking"—adjudication is particular agency action toward an identified party that results in an order, while rulemaking is general agency action that results in a rule.[26] Article 4 governs adjudication procedures and cross-references other relevant articles within the Act.[27] Article 6 presents adjudication procedures in a central hearing agency.[28]

12.03 RIGHT TO A HEARING

12.031 The "contested case" requirement

A contested case is "an adjudication in which an opportunity for an evidentiary hearing is required by the federal constitution, a federal

---

26. APA § 551(7) (adjudication); APA § 551(5) (rulemaking). Chapter 1, § 1.04 states, "In common usage [under the federal APA], adjudication means agency action of particular or individualized applicability, while rulemaking means agency action of general applicability." But that section also explains the confusing overlap between adjudication and rulemaking in the federal APA. Under the MSAPA, an order is "an agency decision that determines or declares the rights, duties, privileges, immunities, or other interests of a specific person." 2010 MSAPA § 102(23). The term "order" was updated to conform "with modern law in rejecting the right/privilege distinction in constitutional law. The addition of the language 'or other interests' is intended to clarify this change and to include entitlements." *Id.* § 102(23) cmt. Orders are further distinguished as "final," "initial," and "recommended," all of which are newly defined in the Act. *See* discussion *infra* § 12.043.
27. 2010 MSAPA § 401.
28. *Id.* §§ 601–607. A central hearing agency (often referred to as a "central panel") is an independent agency established solely to hear administrative adjudications. More than half of U.S. jurisdictions have a central panel. John Hardwicke & Thomas E. Ewing, *The Central Panel: A Response to Critics*, 24 J. NAT'L ASS'N OF ADMIN. L. JUDGES 231 (2004) (reviewing experiences of some central panels). Although no federal central panel currently exists, including the function of central panels in this discussion ensures the spectrum of administrative procedure is presented. *See generally* 2010 MSAPA art. 6.

statute, or the constitution or a statute of th[e] state."[29] Because the 2010 MSAPA establishes only the minimal procedural requirements,[30] the trigger for formal adjudication in a "contested case" is either constitutional or statutory language calling for "an *opportunity* for an evidentiary hearing."[31] The federal APA's trigger for formal adjudication is statutory language calling for a determination "*on the record* after opportunity for an agency hearing."[32]

12.032 Emergency adjudication

The MSAPA's section 407 establishes procedures for emergency adjudication in contested cases of imminent peril to the public health, safety, or

---

29. 2010 MSAPA § 102(7). Evidentiary hearing, in turn, means "a hearing for the receipt of evidence on issues on which a decision of the presiding officer may be made in a contested case." *Id.* § 102(11).

30. *See supra* text at note 18. According to the MSAPA's drafters, "Hearings that are required by procedural due process guarantees serve to protect life, liberty[,] and property *interests,* which arise where a statute creates a justified expectation or legitimate entitlement. [For this reason, t]his section includes more than what were described as 'rights' under older common law." 2010 MSAPA § 401 cmt. (emphasis in original).

   "Section 401 . . . does not apply to investigatory hearings, a hearing that merely seeks public input or comment, pure administrative process proceedings such as tests, elections, or inspections, and situations in which a party has a right to a de novo administrative or judicial hearing." *Id.* § 401 cmt.; *see also id.* § 102(7) cmt. ("Article Four does not apply to informal adjudications, which are not contested cases.").

31. 2010 MSAPA § 102(7) (emphasis added). Section 401 "looks to external sources such as statutes and constitutions to determine when a party is entitled to a hearing." *Id.* § 401 cmt. The drafters tried to "clarify those situations in which there is a right to a hearing. Instead of a judicial search for a right, duty[,] or privilege, the opportunity for a hearing must be created by law . . . or constitution." ULC, *Issues Memo for Annual Meeting 2006, Key Issues* § 102(5), *available at* http://www.law .upenn.edu/bll/archives/ulc/msapa/2006_issuesmemo.htm (last visited Feb. 22, 2012). The expanded definition "is consistent with the line of cases that identify constitutionally protected interests that occurred as part of the expansion of procedural due process beginning in the 1970's." *Id.*

32. APA § 554(a) (emphasis added). *See also* Chapter 3, § 3.01 (discussing the ways that the circuits have interpreted statutes that call for a hearing without using the phrase, "on the record").

welfare.[33] The federal APA provides emergency procedures for licensing in "cases of willfulness or those in which public health, interest, or safety requires otherwise."[34] In contrast to the federal APA, which does not articulate procedures for emergency adjudication,[35] section 407 requires advance notice and an opportunity to be heard *if practicable*,[36] and the emergency order must also briefly explain the factual and legal reasons for invoking emergency adjudication.[37] Additionally, at the conclusion of emergency adjudication, the MSAPA requires formal adjudication as soon as practicable after the presiding officer issues the emergency order.[38]

12.033 Licensing

The MSAPA follows most of the federal APA's language governing license hearings, except for the notice requirement.[39] Under MSAPA section 419, emergency action under licensing is not excused from notice before ordering summary suspension of a license.[40] By comparison, an

---

33. 2010 MSAPA § 407(b). The comment to § 407 states that it does not apply to cease and desist orders, emergency adjudications, or other urgent action pursuant to express authority of another statute. Such hearings may still need to comply with federal and state due process requirements. *See* Chapter 2, § 2.04 ("The general rule is that due process must be provided *before* the deprivation . . ., but there are numerous exceptions to this rule.").
34. APA § 558.
35. *See* Chapter 9, § 9.0623. Although the federal APA does not specify procedures for emergency adjudication, it discusses a similar concept under licensing for situations involving willfulness or public health, safety, or interest. Due process, however, requires many of the same emergency adjudication procedures that the 2010 MSAPA expressly requires. *See also infra* § 12.033.
36. 2010 MSAPA § 407(c) (emphasis added). This notice and opportunity to be heard "may be oral or written and may be by telephone, facsimile, or other electronic means." *Id.*
37. *Id.* § 407(d).
38. The MSAPA emergency order is effective for only 180 days or until the effective date of an order in the adjudication following the emergency order, whichever is shorter. *Id.* § 407(f)–(g).
39. *Compare id.* § 419(b) (requiring notice before proceedings begin), *with* APA § 558(c) (agency need not furnish a licensee with notice and second chance).
40. If imminent, summary suspension may be ordered pending proceedings. 2010 MSAPA § 419(b).

agency is not required to provide notice when the licensee's conduct is willful or threatens public health, interest, or safety.[41]

Section 419 requires licensing proceedings be "promptly instituted and concluded," whereas the federal APA requires an agency to set and complete licensing proceedings "with due regard for the rights and privileges of all the interested parties or adversely affected persons and within a reasonable time."[42] Finally, the federal APA's second chance language is slightly altered in the MSAPA: While the federal APA gives licensees an "opportunity to *demonstrate* or *achieve* compliance with all lawful requirements,"[43] the MSAPA gives licensees "an opportunity to show compliance with all lawful requirements."[44]

12.04 HEARING PROCEDURES

The MSAPA's section 403 sets the minimum procedural requirements for hearings in nonemergency contested cases. The section applies to all agencies unless a statute says otherwise;[45] however, agencies may adopt more stringent procedures.[46] While most other provisions of the MSAPA parallel the federal APA, the obvious changes in procedure relate to the presiding officer's authority. For example, both the federal APA and the

---

41. APA § 558(c). *See supra* notes 34–35.
42. APA § 558(c).
43. *Id.* § 558(c)(2) (emphasis added). *See* Air N. Am. v. Dep't of Transp., 937 F.2d 1427, 1438 & n.8 (9th Cir. 1991) (explaining APA § 558(c)).
44. 2010 MSAPA § 419(b).
45. *Id.* § 403 cmt. By applying these basic provisions to all agencies, the drafters intended to establish procedural consistency across agencies. Again, section 403 does not supersede conflicting state or federal statutes. Procedures for emergency adjudication fall under section 407. *See supra* § 12.032.
46. 2010 MSAPA § 403 comment. Although the MSAPA allows agencies to adopt more stringent procedures, the drafters sought to create minimum standards for fair hearing procedures that would apply to all agencies. The drafters noted that "[i]n many states, individual agencies have lobbied the legislature to remove various requirements of the state [APA] from them. The result . . . is a multitude of divergent agency procedures[, which] create problems for litigants, the bar[,] and the reviewing courts." *Id.* The drafters also commented that because these minimum procedures apply only to contested cases under section 401, they believe that these minimum procedures "do not spread quasi judicial procedures widely, and do not create any significant agency loss of efficiency or increased cost." *Id.*

MSAPA anticipate nontraditional hearing alternatives,[47] but the MSAPA does not expressly limit a presiding officer's procedural authority to the published rules of the agency.[48] The MSAPA also mandates open hearings in contested cases, but authorizes a presiding officer to close a hearing.[49] By comparison, the federal APA does not expressly contemplate open hearings.[50] Finally, the federal APA entitles parties to "a reasonable opportunity to submit . . . proposed findings and conclusions; or exceptions to . . . decisions; and supporting reasons for the [documents filed]."[51] In contrast, the MSAPA entitles parties to "a timely opportunity to file pleadings, motions, and objections," and allows parties to submit briefs, proposed orders, or proposed findings of facts and conclusions of law at the presiding officer's discretion.[52]

12.041 Pre-hearing requirements

12.0411 Notice

To commence formal adjudication under the MSAPA, notice must meet specific requirements, just as is required by the federal APA.[53] The

---

47. The federal APA and MSAPA address alternate dispute resolution (ADR) in different ways. The federal APA allows presiding employees to inform parties as to the availability of ADR and hold settlement conferences. APA § 556(c)(6)–(7). The MSAPA, however, authorizes the presiding officer to refer the case to mediation or other dispute resolution procedure. 2010 MSAPA § 403(c). For more about the use of ADR in federal administrative adjudications, *see* Chapter 8.
48. *Compare* MSAPA § 403, *with* APA § 556(c). The MSAPA expands on a presiding officer's authority, seeking to provide more consistency in procedures across agencies.
49. 2010 MSAPA § 403(f)–(g).
50. In practice, however, adversarial administrative proceedings are open to the public and presiding officers are authorized to close hearings for compelling reasons. For a more thorough review of the openness doctrine in federal administrative proceedings, *see* Chapter 5, § 5.03.
51. APA § 557(c)(1)–(3).
52. *Id.* § 557(c); 2010 MSAPA § 403(c).
53. Notice requirements for administrative proceedings must satisfy both the federal APA and due process. *See* Chapter 4, § 4.02 (discussing the extent to which notice is required under APA section 554(b)). The MSAPA demands notice "when the agency takes an action as to which the person has a right to a contested case hearing." 2010 MSAPA § 403. The MSAPA newly defines "notice" and "notify." The drafting committee's

MSAPA distinguishes notice requirements, which clarify ambiguities in the federal APA about who is entitled to notice, and how notice is satisfied. Accordingly, notice is due to a person "when the agency takes an action as to which the person has a right to a contested case hearing,"[54] and the notice must be in writing.[55]

Before a hearing commences, the MSAPA requires the agency to notify the person of the agency action, the person's rights, the procedure, and the time limit to file a contested-case petition.[56] The notice also must include a copy of the agency procedures governing the case.[57]

After a contested case hearing has commenced, i.e., while a case is pending, the MSAPA's notice requirements change according to who initiated the case.[58] As with the federal APA, all notices in a contested case under the MSAPA must include the time, place, and nature of the hearing, the legal authority and jurisdiction under which the hearing is to be held, and the matters of fact and law asserted.[59] In a contested case initiated by a person other than the agency, the MSAPA requires that the

---

comment indicates that the definition for "notify" is similar to the definition of "notice" in the Uniform Arbitration Act section 2(a), and the Uniform Computer Information Transactions Act section 02(a)(49), based on the provisions of Uniform Commercial Code § 1-201(26). The drafters explained that the definition of "notify" is consistent with due process of law requirements. 2010 MSAPA § 102(22) cmt. (citing Mullane v. Cent. Hanover Bank, 339 U.S. 306, 314–16 (1950); Goldberg v. Kelly, 397 U.S. 254, 267–68 (1970); Dusenberry v. United States, 534 U.S. 161, 168–70 (2002); Ho v. Donovan, 569 F.3d 677, 680–81 (7th Cir. 2009)).

54. In contrast, notice under the federal APA applies to "[p]ersons entitled to notice of an agency hearing." APA § 554(b). "The [federal] APA does not identify which 'persons' are entitled to notice and there is little authority on the issue." *See* Chapter 4, § 4.021 (explaining how various sources "must be analyzed to determine who is entitled to notice of agency hearings").

55. 2010 MSAPA § 403(b).

56. *Id.* § 403.

57. *Id.* § 403(b). Notice before a contested case proceeding has commenced requires agencies to include all formal and informal procedures published by the agency, procedures pursuant to the governing statute, and standard procedural rules. *Id.* § 403 cmt. The federal APA does not specifically require the agency to provide the parties with a copy of the agency's procedures, but, if it does not do so, then it might be precluded from using that procedure. *See, e.g.,* APA § 552(a)(2).

58. 2010 MSAPA § 405.

59. APA § 554(b)(1)–(3); 2010 MSAPA § 405(b)–(c).

agency provide notice that the case has commenced within five days after filing[60] and include contact information and the names and addresses of any other person receiving the notice.[61] In a contested case initiated by an agency, the agency's notice must include statements about default, the right to a hearing, and instructions in plain English about how to request a hearing.[62] The MSAPA also authorizes the presiding officer to provide notice of "other matters that the presiding officer considers desirable to expedite the proceedings,"[63] which is not within the presiding officer's purview in the federal APA. Finally, the MSAPA allows for a hearing or pre-hearing conference only if 30 days have passed since the agency issued the notice.[64]

12.0412 Discovery

Discovery is generally unavailable in administrative hearings under the federal APA absent a statute or regulation requiring it.[65] The MSAPA allows, on written notice at least 30 days before the hearing, for a party to obtain information about witnesses, evidence, investigative reports, exculpatory material, and other materials for good cause that will or may be presented at the hearing.[66] On petition and for good cause, the

---

60. Even in cases initiated by a person other than the agency, the burden is on the agency to provide proper notice under both Acts. *See* Chapter 4, § 4.028 (discussing APA's notice requirement when a party other than the agency is the moving party).
61. 2010 MSAPA § 405(b). The five-day time period is a recommendation; states could select a different time period.
62. *Id.* § 405(c).
63. *Id.* § 405(e).
64. *Id.* § 405(d). The 30-day time period is a recommendation; states could select a different time period.
65. *See* Chapter 4, § 4.03 (discussing when agencies may allow discovery). *See* NLRB v. Valley Mold Co., 530 F.2d 693 (6th Cir. 1976) ("The [federal APA] does not confer a right to discovery in federal administrative proceedings.") (citing Frilette v. Kimberlin, 508 F.2d 205, 208 (3d Cir. 1974), *cert. denied*, 421 U.S. 993 (1975)).
66. 2010 MSAPA § 411(b). Parties must supplement responses if information is acquired after evidence is produced. *Id.* § 411(c). On petition, a protective order may be issued for exempt, privileged, confidential, or protected information, or for material that would result in annoyance, embarrassment, oppression, or undue burden or expense to any person. 2010 MSAPA § 411(d).

presiding officer must order discovery in compliance with the rules of civil procedure; refusal to comply with the order may be enforced in accordance with the rules of civil procedure.[67] However, by regulation, agencies may restrict discovery for specific cases or programs if discovery would complicate or interfere with certain hearing processes, or if relevant information can be sufficiently shared to ensure a fair proceeding.[68] In addition, the MSAPA gives presiding officers the flexibility to apply more extensive discovery if needed.[69]

12.0413 Subpoenas

Administrative subpoenas are treated the same under the MSAPA and the federal APA[70]—on request and upon a showing of general relevance and reasonable scope of evidence for use at the hearing.[71] Subpoenas are available to both agencies and private parties through the agency's statutory subpoena power. To the extent that the law authorizes an agency to issue subpoenas, this authority may be delegated to the presiding officer.[72] Like other methods of discovery, subpoena service and enforcement follow the methods prescribed in civil actions, unless otherwise dictated by law or agency regulation.[73]

12.0414 Intervention

The federal APA defines no standard or right for intervention.[74] When no statute or agency rule addresses intervention, the decision to allow third parties to intervene falls within the agency's discretion, but only if

---

67. *Id.* § 411(e)–(f).
68. *Id.* § 411(g).
69. *Id.* § 411.
70. *Id.* § 410; APA § 556(c)–(d). Agency subpoenas authorized by law, under the federal APA, apply to both formal and informal adjudication. *Id.* § 555(d). Because the MSAPA applies to formal adjudication, no provision addresses agency subpoena powers for informal adjudication.
71. 2010 MSAPA § 410(a); APA § 555(d); *see* Chapter 4, § 4.041 (discussing federal APA provisions for administrative subpoenas).
72. 2010 MSAPA § 410(a).
73. 2010 MSAPA § 410(b).
74. *See* Chapter 4, § 4.051 (discussing intervention in agency proceedings under the federal APA).

"the orderly conduct of public business permits."[75] The MSAPA, in turn, delineates intervention standards in formal adjudication.[76] As courts have interpreted under the federal APA, the MSAPA also requires a presiding officer to grant a timely[77] petition for intervention if a case is contested, if the petitioner has a right to initiate or intervene in the case, or if the petitioner has an interest that may be adversely affected and that is not adequately represented in the contested case hearing.[78] Under the federal APA, an agency may deny intervention if it would delay, burden, or fail to assist in the decisionmaking. Unlike the federal APA, the MSAPA gives the presiding officer discretion to grant intervention under a permissive statutory right to intervene or if the claim or defense is based on the same transaction or occurrence as the case. Although both the MSAPA and federal APA may allow an intervener for limited purposes, one element that stands out in the MSAPA is when a presiding officer imposes conditions on an intervener or allows provisional intervention;[79] these conditions, on request, can be heard separately from the contested case hearing. The federal APA allows an intervener, as an interested party, to have an

---

75. Courts generally rely on other statutes or rules to authorize interventions. *See* Chapter 4 §§ 4.051, 4.052 (citing cases). Under the federal APA, a party "includes a person or agency named as a party, or properly seeking and entitled as of right to be admitted as a party, in an agency proceeding, and a person or agency admitted by an agency as a party for limited purposes." APA § 551(3). An intervener may qualify as a party, and "all interested parties" have certain rights in federal APA adjudications. *Id.* § 554(c). Further, the federal APA allows an "interested person" to "appear before the agency . . . for the presentation, adjustment, or determination of an issue, request, or controversy in a proceeding." *Id.* § 555(b).

76. 2010 MSAPA § 409.

77. A "timely" petition is one that allows both the intervener sufficient time to prepare for hearing and the existing parties sufficient time to respond to the intervener's petition. *See id.* § 409 cmt. Under the federal APA, timeliness operates similar to the Federal Rules of Civil Procedure. *See* Chapter 4, § 4.055 (discussing timeliness of motions to intervene).

78. 2010 MSAPA § 409(a). Under the federal APA, intervention is reviewed for abuse of discretion. *See* Chapter 4, § 4.052 (discussing intervention through statutes and rules).

79. The presiding officer may also later revoke the provisional intervention. 2010 MSAPA § 409(c)–(d).

opportunity to partake in informal settlement proceedings.[80] Because the MSAPA does not contemplate informal adjudications, no such provision is included in the MSAPA. The 2010 Act also follows the rules of civil procedure requiring the presiding officer to promptly give notice upon receiving a petition for intervention.[81]

12.042 Hearing requirements

The MSAPA mirrors hearing provisions in the federal APA: An independent hearing officer or administrative law judge presides over hearings, manages the process, protects the rights of pro se litigants, takes official notice of certain facts, and issues decisions supported by reliable, probative, and substantial evidence.[82] The MSAPA, however, does not delegate hearing procedures or evidentiary rules to individual agencies.[83] The act touches on technological innovations that have impacted the legal process, which were unimaginable in 1946. For example, a presiding officer may conduct all or part of a hearing or pre-hearing conference by alternative method, such as by telephone or video conference, if the method will not affect the presiding officer's ability to decide witness credibility.[84] The MSAPA also codifies the public's

---

80. *See* Chapter 4, § 4.051 (citing APA § 554(c) as providing for informal settlement or adjustment of controversies as an alternative to formal adjudicatory proceedings).
81. 2010 MSAPA § 409(a) cmt.
82. APA § 556; 2010 MSAPA § 402. *See also* Chapter 5, §§ 5.05 (discussing the rules of evidence), 5.064 (discussing a presiding officer's obligation to protect pro se litigants).
83. *Compare* APA § 556(c), (c)(11), *with* 2010 MSAPA § 404.
84. *See* 2010 MSAPA § 403(e). The Act allows for "telephone, television, video conference, or other electronic means," if the presiding officer finds the method will not impair reliable determination of credibility. If parties cannot be seen by an alternative method, all parties must consent to use of the alternative method. State courts are split on whether the due process clause requires live, in-person hearings when material issues of fact call for credibility determinations. *See id.* § 403 cmt. (citing Whiteside v. State, 20 P.3d 1130 (Alaska 2001) (finding that a telephone hearing for driver license revocation involving a credibility determination violated due process) and Babcock v. Emp't Div., 72 Or. App. 486, 696 P.2d 19, 21 (1985) (concluding that audible indicia of a witness demeanor is sufficient for credibility)).

right of access to administrative hearings, which is not discussed in the federal APA,[85] and grants the presiding officer authority to close hearings in certain circumstances.[86] Another notable difference is that the MSAPA does not explicitly follow the federal APA's default rule as to the burden of proof, which allocates the burden to the proponent of the order.[87] Moreover, the MSAPA allows a presiding officer to issue orders without taking evidence when the party bearing the burden of proof defaults.[88]

12.0421 *Evidence*

The federal APA's evidentiary standards do not change in the MSAPA—evidence must be relevant, reliable, probative, and substantial.[89] The MSAPA provides greater detail as to what constitutes acceptable evidence in administrative hearings, which changes the practice under the federal APA of allowing agencies to develop their own evidentiary rules.[90] The MSAPA dictates that testimony must be made under oath or affirmation; that copies of documents are acceptable, so long as parties can compare the copies to the originals if requested; that parties may make offers of proof if evidence is excluded; and that evidence may be received if it will expedite the hearing without substantial prejudice

---

85. The 2010 MSAPA allows the presiding officer to "conduct all or part of an evidentiary hearing or a prehearing conference by telephone, television, video conference, or other electronic means," unless a witness needs to be seen by all others in the proceeding. 2010 MSAPA § 403(e). The Act requires all hearings to be open to the public and conducted in the presiding officer's presence, unless the presiding officer exercises his or her discretion to close. *Id.* § 403(f). *See also* Chapter 5, § 5.03.
86. *See* Chapter 5 § 5.03 (discussing the public's right of access in administrative proceedings under the APA).
87. APA § 556(d). *See also* Chapter 5, § 5.04 (discussing burden of proof). The MSAPA addresses burden of proof as it relates to review. MSAPA § 508(a) (1).
88. 2010 MSAPA § 412(c). The Act also discusses the burden of proof under judicial scope of review. *See id.* § 508(a)(1).
89. *Id.* § 404; APA § 556(c)(3), (d). *See also* Chapter 5, § 5.05 (discussing rules of evidence).
90. Except for sections 556(c)(3) and 556(d), the APA does not provide further discussion of evidence. Agencies may adopt their own evidentiary rules, unless a statute says otherwise, and courts must consider evidentiary standards on a case-by-case basis. *See* Chapter 5, § 5.05.

to the parties.[91] Under both the federal APA and MSAPA, evidence need not always be presented orally—agencies may adopt procedures for written evidence.[92] The MSAPA continues to authorize reliance on hearsay evidence.[93] Evidence must become part of the hearing record; a presiding officer may not consider anything not in the hearing record to decide the case.[94] As courts have interpreted in the federal APA, the MSAPA also allows a presiding officer to conduct closed hearings for confidential evidence;[95] to take official notice of judicially cognizable facts, as well as "scientific, technical, or other facts within the specialized knowledge of the agency;"[96] and to use his or her own "experience, technical competence, and specialized knowledge . . . to evaluate the evidence in the hearing record."[97]

---

91. 2010 MSAPA § 404(3)–(5). When a party defaults, under the MSAPA, the presiding officer is not required to take evidence if the defaulting party bears the burden of proof. *Id.* § 412(c).
92. In some cases under the APA, a party may have to specifically request an oral hearing. In other cases, the party requesting an oral hearing may have to show that material facts are in dispute. *See* Chapter 5, § 5.08.
93. The 2010 MSAPA offers two alternative approaches to evidence. 2010 MSAPA § 413(f). One of these alternatives, the residuum rule, is not authorized by the federal APA. Chapter 5, § 5.05. The residuum rule allows presiding officers to rely solely on hearsay to support their decisions in contested cases. *See infra* § 12.0431 (discussing how evidentiary standards affect decisions).
94. 2010 MSAPA § 404(6). *But see infra* § 12.052 for a discussion of 2010 MSAPA § 408, which allows agency heads acting as presiding officers to communicate ex parte with an employee or representative of the agency in specific circumstances.
95. 2010 MSAPA § 404(6). Generally, the presiding officer may conduct a closed hearing to discuss confidential information in a hearing record, issue necessary protective orders, and seal all or part of the hearing record.
96. *Id.* § 404(7). A party must be notified at the earliest practicable time of the facts proposed for official notice and their sources, and afforded an opportunity to contest any officially noticed fact before the decision becomes final.
97. *Id.* § 404(8).

12.0422 *Right to counsel*

While the MSAPA and federal APA expressly allow a party to be represented, they do so differently.[98] The federal APA entitles any person compelled to appear for an administrative hearing to representation (but not always for the entire proceeding). The MSAPA, on the other hand, merely allows a party—at the party's expense—to be represented by counsel, or to be advised, accompanied, or represented by another individual unless prohibited by state law.[99]

12.043 Post-hearing requirements

12.0431 *Decisions*

After a contested case hearing, the presiding officer must issue an order.[100] An order is "an agency decision that determines or declares the rights, duties, privileges, immunities, or other interests of a specific person."[101] The MSAPA allocates decisionmaking authority and obligations much like the federal APA.[102] If the presiding officer is the agency

---

98. *Compare id.* § 403(h) ("Unless prohibited by law of this state other than this [Act], a party, at the party's expense, may be represented by counsel or may be advised, accompanied, or represented by another individual."), *with* APA § 555(b) ("A person compelled to appear in person before an agency or representative thereof is entitled to be accompanied, represented, and advised by counsel or, if permitted by the agency, by other qualified representative. A party is entitled to appear in person or by or with counsel or other duly qualified representative in an agency proceeding."). The commentary to section 403(h) notes that the MSAPA does not expressly confer a right to self-representation in contested cases, but states have the option of providing such a right.
99. 2010 MSAPA § 403(h).
100. *Id.* § 413(a)–(b). The Act distinguishes three types of orders: a final order, an initial order, and a recommended order.
101. *Id.* § 102(23). The term "order" was updated to conform "with modern law in rejecting the right/privilege distinction in constitutional law. The addition of the language 'or other interests' is intended to clarify this change and to include entitlements." *Id.* § 102(23) cmt.
102. *See* APA § 557(b)–(d) (calling on the hearing officer to issue the initial or recommended decision).

head, then the presiding officer issues a final order.[103] If the presiding officer has been delegated final decisional authority, then the presiding officer issues an initial order that becomes final unless reviewed by the agency head sua sponte or on petition of a party.[104] If the presiding officer has not been delegated final decisional authority, then the presiding officer issues a recommended order,[105] and the agency head is responsible for issuing the final order. When a central hearing agency[106] hears cases for agencies, an ALJ is the default presiding officer unless the agency head assigns otherwise.[107]

---

103. 2010 MSAPA § 413(a); APA §§ 556(e), 557(b). Under the 2010 MSAPA, a final order is

> the order issued by the agency head sitting as the presiding officer in a contested case, the order issued following the agency head review of a recommended order, the order issued following the agency head review of an initial order, or the order issued by the presiding officer when the presiding officer has been delegated final decisional authority with no subsequent agency head review.

2010 MSAPA § 102(12). In comparison, the federal APA defines an order as "the whole or a part of a final disposition, whether affirmative, negative, injunctive, or declaratory in form, of an agency in a matter other than rule making but including licensing." APA § 551(6).

104. 2010 MSAPA § 413(b); APA § 557(b). The MSAPA defines initial order as "an order that is issued by a presiding officer with final decisional authority if the order is subject to discretionary review by the agency." 2010 MSAPA § 102(16). For a discussion about initial and other preliminary decisions under the federal APA, *see* Chapter 6, § 6.032.

105. 2010 MSAPA § 413(b); APA § 557(b). The 2010 MSAPA defines recommended order as "an order issued by a presiding officer if the officer does not have final decisional authority and the order is subject to review by the agency head." 2010 MSAPA § 102(28).

106. A central hearing agency, commonly referred to as a central panel or office of administrative hearings, is a separate agency established exclusively to hear administrative proceedings. Under the 2010 MSAPA, Article 6 creates an Office of Administrative Hearings.

107. 2010 MSAPA § 606(a). The National Conference of Administrative Law Judiciary opposed section 606(a) because it did not delegate final decisionmaking authority on ALJs from an Office of Administrative Hearings—that is, authority to issue a final decision without review by the agency head. *See* American Bar Association Resolution 112 (Feb. 2011), submitted by the National Conference of Administrative Law Judiciary, *available at* http://www.americanbar.org/content/dam/aba/

The MSAPA gives the presiding officer the discretion to allow parties to submit briefs, proposed findings of fact and conclusions of law, and proposed orders before issuing an order.[108] This practice differs from the federal APA, which entitles the parties to an opportunity to submit proposed findings and conclusions, exceptions to decisions, and reasons to support their submissions, and also requires that the record reflect the presiding officer's ruling on all of the submissions.[109]

Decisions in administrative proceedings under both the MSAPA and federal APA require that the factual findings "be based exclusively on the evidence and matters officially noticed in the hearing record."[110] Both acts also mandate that decisions be prepared electronically and made available in writing, and that agencies follow the prescribed publication requirements.[111] As to a decision's factual finding, the MSAPA offers two alternatives for relying on hearsay. Alternative A adopts the residuum rule, which allows hearsay to be used to supplement or explain other evidence, but is insufficient to support a factual finding unless it would be admissible in a civil case.[112] Alternative B accepts hearsay to support

---

migrated/2011_build/house_of_delegates/112_2011_my.authcheckdam .pdf (last visited Feb. 22, 2012).

108. 2010 MSAPA § 413(d).

109. APA § 557(c). Under the federal APA, the opportunity to file proposed findings, conclusions, or exceptions applies before the presiding officer issues an initial or tentative order. *See* Chapter 6, § 6.033.

110. 2010 MSAPA § 413(e). *But see infra* § 12.052 for discussion of MSAPA § 408, which allows agency heads acting as presiding officers to communicate ex parte with an employee or representative of the agency in specific circumstances.

111. *Compare* 2010 MSAPA § 202(a)(8)–(9) ("Unless the record is exempt from disclosure under law . . . , an agency shall publish on its Internet website and . . . make available through the regular mail each final order in a contested case . . . ; and the index of final orders"), *with* APA § 552 (FOIA) (requiring agencies to "make available for public inspection and copying final opinions, including concurring and dissenting opinions, as well as orders, made in the adjudication of cases"). The Freedom of Information Act also identifies how agencies are to respond to special cases, such as handling private information and publishing information using computer telecommunications. *See also* 2010 MSAPA art. 2 (codifying public access to agency law and policy).

112. 2010 MSAPA § 413(f) Alternative A & cmt. *See also supra* § 12.0421 (comparing evidence under the federal APA and the 2010 MSAPA).

a factual finding if it is "reliable, probative, and substantial evidence."[113] The federal APA does not impose the residuum rule on federal agencies. Agencies generally have broad discretion under the federal APA to rely on hearsay so long as admitting the hearsay does not violate due process.[114]

12.0432 Agency head review of initial orders

Under the MSAPA, an agency head has the same authority as under the federal APA in exercising its decisionmaking powers except as to limiting the issues subject to review as provided by law or as specified by the agency head on notice to the parties.[115] The initial order becomes the agency's final decision unless appealed.[116] More specifically, however, the MSAPA requires the agency head to consider the hearing record or parts designated by the parties, as well as the presiding officer's opportunity to observe witnesses and determine credibility.[117] Under the MSAPA, the final order must identify differences from the initial order and must state the facts of record that support the differences with the initial order's facts of record, the law that supports differences in legal conclusions, and policy reasons that support any difference in the exercise of discretion.[118]

---

113. 2010 MSAPA § 413(f) Alternative B & cmt. *See also supra* § 12.0421 (comparing evidence under the federal APA and the 2010 MSAPA).
114. *See* Chapter 5, § 5.052.
115. *See* APA § 557(b) ("[O]n appeal from or review of the initial decision, the agency has all the powers which it would have in making the initial decision except as it may limit the issues on notice or by rule."); 2010 MSAPA § 414(e) ("When reviewing an initial order, the agency head shall exercise the decision-making power that the agency head would have had if the agency head had conducted the hearing that produced the order, except [as] limited by law . . . or by order . . . on notice to the parties."). For a discussion of a federal agency head's role in initial and other preliminary decisions under the federal APA, *see* Chapter 6, §§ 6.023, 6.0352, 6.0353.
116. The federal APA makes the presiding officer's initial decision the agency's final decision by operation of law. APA § 557(b). As a result, initial decisions must include "findings and conclusions, and the reasons or basis therefor, on all the material issues of fact, law, or discretion presented on the record; and the appropriate rule, order, sanction, relief, or denial thereof." *Id.* § 557(c).
117. 2010 MSAPA § 414(e).
118. *Id.* § 414(g).

12.0433 *Agency head review of recommended orders*

For recommended orders, the MSAPA functions like the APA. The agency head may issue a final order disposing of the case or may remand the case with instructions.[119] Like agency head reviews of initial decisions, the final order must specify and explain differences between the recommended order and final order, and include or incorporate by reference the findings of fact and conclusions of law in the recommended order.[120]

12.0434 *Hearing record*

The MSAPA and the federal APA define hearing record similarly— essentially all materials related to a contested case proceeding—except that, in addition to a transcript, the MSAPA requires a recording of the proceeding.[121] Under the MSAPA, the presiding officer is responsible for a proper hearing record, which includes the authority to seal all or part of a hearing record as required.[122] Both the MSAPA and federal APA allow for the submission of written evidence exclusively in a contested case in lieu of an oral presentation[123] and require that decisions be based on the record.[124]

---

119. *Id.* § 415(c).
120. *Id.* § 415(d).
121. *Compare* 2010 MSAPA § 406(b) (listing the items that make up a hearing record: a recording of the proceeding; notices; pre-hearing orders; motions, briefs, or other filings; evidence admitted; officially noticed matters; proffers, as well as relevant objections and rulings; proposed findings, orders, or exceptions; transcripts of the proceeding prepared at the direction of the agency; recommended order, final order, or order on reconsideration; and any ex parte matters placed on the record), *with* APA § 556(e) ("The transcript of testimony and exhibits, together with all papers and requests filed in the proceeding, constitutes the exclusive record for decision. . . ."), *and* APA § 557(c) ("The record shall show the ruling on each finding, conclusion, or exception presented. All decisions . . . are a part of the record. . . .").
122. 2010 MSAPA §§ 403(i), 404(6).
123. *Id.* § 406; APA § 557(d).
124. 2010 MSAPA § 401 cmt. APA § 557(d).

12.0435 Default, reconsideration, and stay

The MSAPA allows an agency to dispose of a case without a hearing by stipulation, settlement, consent order, or default.[125] An agency may also reconsider a matter[126] and is authorized to stay a decision pending the final outcome of a case.[127] Conversely, the federal APA does not specify procedures for defaults, reconsiderations, or stays.[128] The MSAPA retains declaratory orders as set out in the federal APA "to terminate a controversy or remove uncertainty."[129]

12.0436 Precedent and availability of orders

The MSAPA contains a section addressing agency precedent in contested cases.[130] Before an agency may rely on a final order as precedent, the order must be designated as precedent, and indexed, published, and made available for public inspection, unless the order is exempt, privileged, or otherwise confidential.[131] The federal APA does not require an agency to follow its own precedent, so long as the presiding officer justifies the deviation in the order.[132] The MSAPA, like the federal APA, makes all orders available for public inspection and copying.[133]

---

125. 2010 MSAPA § 403(*l*).
126. *Id.* § 416.
127. *Id.* § 417.
128. Although the federal APA does not provide for stays, the drafters based part of the MSAPA language on stays from 5 U.S.C. § 705. *See* 2010 MSAPA § 417 cmt.
129. 2010 MSAPA § 204; APA § 554(e).
130. 2010 MSAPA § 418. For more information on agency precedent, see *Illuminating a Bureaucratic Shadow World: Precedent Decisions Under California's Revised Administrative Procedure Act*, 21 J. NAT'L ASS'N ADMIN. L. JUDGES 247 n.68 (2001). *See also* SEC v. Chenery Corp., 332 U.S. 194, 199–211 (1947) (discussing precedent as it relates to the agency's decision).
131. 2010 MSAPA § 418(c). This provision prevents prior agency decisions known only to agency personnel from constituting the basis for a decision in a contested case. If an agency intends to use a case as precedent in the future, it must make the order and decision in that case available to the public. It makes clear that the choice between rulemaking and adjudication is entirely at the discretion of the agency.
132. *See* Chapter 6, § 6.023 (indicating that if the presiding officer does not explain the deviation from precedent, reviewing courts presume that the presiding officer failed to engage in reasoned decisionmaking).
133. 2010 MSAPA § 418.

12.05 INTEGRITY OF DECISIONMAKING PROCESS

12.051 Presiding officer

The MSAPA defines a presiding officer as "an individual who presides over the evidentiary hearing in a contested case."[134] The MSAPA follows most of the federal APA as it relates to the roles and responsibilities of presiding officers. For example, an agency employee may not preside over a contested case if the employee engaged in any investigation or prosecution of a factually related case.[135] The presiding officer must make a reasonable inquiry and disclose any grounds for disqualification material to the presiding officer's impartiality.[136] The MSAPA and federal APA have similar requirements on a party petitioning for disqualification. Under the MSAPA, the party must "state with particularity the ground on which it is claimed that a fair and impartial hearing cannot be accorded or the applicable rule or canon of practice or ethics that requires disqualification."[137] The federal APA requires a "sufficient affidavit of personal bias or other disqualification."[138] Both acts require the presiding officer whose disqualification is sought to consider and rule on the petition.[139] If a new presiding officer must be assigned to a hearing, the MSAPA looks for a substitute to be appointed as required by law.[140] Finally, as followed by the federal APA, the MSAPA codifies the rule of necessity, which foregoes disqualification of the agency head as presiding officer if the agency head is necessary to allow the agency to take action.[141]

---

134. *Id.* § 101(26).
135. APA § 554(d); 2010 MSAPA § 402(b). *See also* APA § 554(d) (stating that the prohibitions "do[ ] not apply in determining applications for initial licenses; to proceedings involving the validity or application of rates, facilities, or practices of public utilities or carriers; or to the agency or a member or members of the body comprising the agency").
136. 2010 MSAPA § 402(e) cmt. Disclosure duties are based in part on state ethics codes for judges, the 2000 Uniform Arbitration Act section 12, and state laws for government officials and employees.
137. 2010 MSAPA § 402(d).
138. APA § 556(b). *See* Chapter 7, § 7.02021.
139. 2010 MSAPA § 402(e); APA § 556(b).
140. 2010 MSAPA § 402(f). Specifically, the MSAPA grants authority to appoint a new presiding officer to the governor (if the original presiding officer is an elected official) or to the appointing authority (if the original presiding officer is an appointed official).
141. *Id.* § 402(g).

12.052 Ex parte communications

Like the federal APA,[142] the MSAPA contains a general prohibition against ex parte communications when a contested case is pending.[143] An important distinction, though, is that the MSAPA restricts "any communication concerning the case" from or to "any person" while the case is pending, with four exceptions.[144] First, a presiding officer may communicate with any person if necessary to dispose of ex parte matters authorized by statute or concerning an uncontested procedural issue.[145] Second, a presiding officer may obtain legal advice if the individual providing legal advice has not served as investigator, prosecutor, or advocate at any stage of the case and if the communication does not augment, diminish, or modify the evidence in the record.[146] Third, a presiding officer who is also the agency head may communicate with an employee or representative of the agency who has not served as investigator, prosecutor, or advocate at any stage of the case and who has not communicated with others about the case.[147] That communication may explain agency precedent, policy, or procedures—it must not augment, diminish, or modify the evidence in the hearing record, nor address the quality, sufficiency, or weight that should be given, or the credibility of witnesses, and it is limited to an explanation of the technical or scientific basis or terms in the record.[148] Fourth, a presiding officer who is a member of a multimember

---

142. *See* Chapter 7, §§ 7.04, 7.049 (discussing that ex parte communication in a federal informal proceeding might deprive a party of procedural due process).

143. 2010 MSAPA § 408(b).

144. *Id.* The federal APA restricts a "communication relevant to the merits of the proceeding" from or to an "interested person." APA § 557(d)(1). An "interested person" is understood to have a broad and inclusive meaning. *See* Chapter 7, § 7.0431.

145. 2010 MSAPA § 408(c).

146. *Id.* § 408(d).

147. *Id.* § 408(e)(1).

148. *Id.* § 408(e)(2). For a lively debate on subsection § 408(e)(2)(C), *see* Michael Asimow, *Staff Advice to Decision Makers Under the 2010 MSAPA*, 36 ADMIN. & REG. L. NEWS 6 (Winter 2011), and Ann Marshall Young, *Ex Parte Communications and the Exclusive Record Provision of the 2010 MSAPA*, 36 ADMIN. & REG. L. NEWS 8 (Winter 2011). Professor Asimow argues that the prohibition against an agency head who is the presiding officer or final decisionmaker communicating with agency staff about the quality, sufficiency, or weight of evidence in a record or the credibility of a witness would not allow the agency head to get needed advice. Administrative

body that is the agency head may communicate with the other members of the body.[149]

The third exception is a compromise to differing positions by the National Conference of Administrative Law Judiciary, a section of the Judicial Division of the American Bar Association, and the ABA Section of Administrative Law and Regulatory Practice. The compromise departs from the federal APA, which allows a presiding officer to communicate with agency staff.[150]

Finally, under the MSAPA, the presiding officer must notify all parties of a prohibited ex parte communication and provide the parties with an opportunity to respond.[151] To eliminate the effect of an ex parte communication, the MSAPA allows for disqualification of the presiding officer or final decisionmaker, sealing of those portions of the hearing record containing the ex parte communication, or other appropriate relief, including an adverse ruling.[152]

Judge Young, on the other hand, points out the prohibition is necessary to avoid violation of the exclusive record rule by preventing communications of information that should be put on the record. The articles are available through: http://www.americanbar.org/groups/administrative_law/publications/administrativeandregulatorylawnews.html (last visited Feb. 22, 2012).

149. 2010 MSAPA § 408(h).
150. *See* Chapter 7, § 7.0633 (discussing separation of nonadversary staff persons from decisionmaking in federal adjudications).
151. 2010 MSAPA § 408(g).
152. *Id.* § 408(i).

Appendix A

A BLACKLETTER STATEMENT OF FEDERAL ADMINISTRATIVE LAW*

PREPARED BY THE SECTION OF ADMINISTRATIVE LAW AND
REGULATORY PRACTICE OF THE AMERICAN BAR ASSOCIATION
ORIGINALLY APPROVED BY THE SECTION COUNCIL, NOVEMBER 3, 2001
APPROVED AS AMENDED BY THE SECTION COUNCIL, FEBRUARY 5, 2012

I. DUE PROCESS REQUIREMENTS FOR A HEARING
II. RIGHT TO A HEARING UNDER THE ADMINISTRATIVE
  PROCEDURE ACT
III. PROCEDURAL REQUIREMENTS FOR FORMAL HEARINGS
  UNDER THE ADMINISTRATIVE PROCEDURE ACT
IV. INTEGRITY OF DECISIONMAKING PROCESS
V. ADMINISTRATIVE LAW JUDGES UNDER THE FEDERAL
  ADMINISTRATIVE PROCEDURE ACT
VI. POST-HEARING REQUIREMENTS
VII. INFORMAL ADJUDICATION

ADJUDICATION

Adjudication is the agency process for issuing an order which resolves particular rights or duties. It would be impracticable to canvass the entire subject of administrative adjudication throughout the range of its uses. The present treatment is bounded in two respects: it deals only with federal administrative law, and it deals only with fundamental elements, as specified by constitutional due process and by the Administrative Procedure Act (APA).

---

* The original blackletter statement was published in 54 Administrative Law Review 1 (2002); it is largely unchanged and thus reprinted here with the permission of the Administrative Law Review.

I. DUE PROCESS REQUIREMENTS FOR A HEARING

A. Basic Principles

Due process analysis requires, first, a determination that there exists a constitutionally protected interest within the meaning of the constitutional Due Process Clauses; second, it requires a determination that there has been a "deprivation" of one of those interests; third, it requires a determination of what process is due in order to protect those interests. Due process attaches only to "state action."

B. Protected Interest

Procedural due process requires a "substantive predicate," which is a substantive right to "life, liberty or property." The substantive rights that are protected by due process must be independently determined, apart from the demand for procedural protection itself.

Substantive rights may be derived from a variety of sources. In the case of property, the right or entitlement must be grounded outside the federal Constitution, which presupposes but does not itself create property rights. An entitlement requires the presence of substantive standards that constrain the discretion of a governmental decisionmaker. Protected property rights are established by state or federal law, including both statutory and common law. Liberty interests may be based on state or federal law, or on the federal Constitution, including the due process clause itself.

C. Deprivation

To constitute a deprivation for due process purposes, government action must adversely affect a protected interest. Negligent actions, however, even if tortious, do not amount to a deprivation for due process purposes.

D. Process Due

Determining the procedures required by due process involves consideration of three factors: (1) the strength of the private interest, (2) the risk of error and the probable value of additional or substitute procedural safeguards to avoid error, and (3) the strength of the government's interest. These considerations govern both the adequacy and timing of the procedures required. The requirements of due process vary with the particulars of the proceeding. While in some circumstances an individualized adjudicatory hearing is required, in other cases notice of the subjects of the agency proceeding and the opportunity to submit written comments or oral comments at a legislative-type hearing may be sufficient.

E. Legislative-type determinations

An adjudicatory hearing is not required, as a matter of constitutional due process, when agency action is legislative in character rather than adjudicatory.

II. RIGHT TO A HEARING UNDER THE ADMINISTRATIVE PROCEDURE ACT

A. Formal Hearings Under the APA

Subject to the set of exceptions set forth in § 554(a) (see discussion exceptions in Subpart B), a formal hearing is required by the APA in "every case of adjudication required by statute to be determined on the record after opportunity for an agency hearing." Where a federal statute requires such an on-the-record hearing, the hearing must comply with the provisions of §§ 554, 556, and 557 of the APA.

Determining whether a statute that calls for a hearing (but does not use the words "on the record") triggers the formal adjudication requirements of the APA is a matter of statutory interpretation. The prevailing view is that courts will defer to a reasonable agency interpretation that such a statute does not trigger the APA's formal adjudication provisions.

B. Agency Action Excepted from Adjudication Requirements

The APA does not require a formal hearing to the extent that there is involved a matter subject to a subsequent trial de novo in a court; the selection or tenure of an employee; proceedings in which decisions rest solely on inspections, tests, or elections; the conduct of military or foreign affairs functions; cases in which an agency is acting as an agent for a court; or the certification of worker representatives.

III. PROCEDURAL REQUIREMENTS FOR FORMAL HEARINGS UNDER THE ADMINISTRATIVE PROCEDURE ACT

A. Basic Requirements

Hearings required to be conducted under the APA must follow the procedures required by § 556 of the APA.

B. Openness

Although § 556 of the APA does not specifically state that hearings must be open, the very concept of a hearing comparable to a judicial proceeding entails norms of openness. Thus, agency hearings generally must be open to the public.

Notwithstanding the general policy favoring open hearings, agencies may close hearings for reasons of confidentiality or to protect potential spectators, witnesses, or parties to a hearing. In such circumstances, the presiding administrative law judge (ALJ) "may take only the most limited action necessary to sufficiently protect the interest perceived to be paramount to the interest of the public in an open hearing."

C. Burden of Proof

Section 556(d) requires that, unless another statute provides authority for a different allocation for the burden of proof, the burden of proof with respect to any decision rests with the proponent of that decision. For purposes of § 556(d), the term "burden of proof" means the burden of persuasion. Unless a statute or rule specifies otherwise, the standard of proof in agency adjudication is the familiar "preponderance of the evidence" standard.

D. Rules of Evidence

The APA requires that formal adjudicatory decisions be "supported by and in accordance with the reliable, probative, and substantial evidence." Agency adjudications need not conform to the Federal Rules of Evidence, and agency adjudicators may consider evidence, such as hearsay, that would be inadmissible in federal courts. Such evidence may form the sole basis for agency decisions. Under § 556 of the APA, agency adjudicators must "provide for the exclusion of irrelevant, immaterial, or unduly repetitious evidence." Subject to that requirement, agencies have power to prescribe their own rules of evidence, provided that those rules are consistent with constitutional standards of due process.

Though agency adjudications are not governed by the Federal Rules of Evidence as a general matter, the attorney-client privilege and like privileges may be asserted in an agency proceeding. Agencies may take official notice of facts not supported by record evidence. Where an agency has taken official notice of a material fact, parties to the proceeding are entitled to an opportunity to demonstrate the contrary.

E. Oral Evidence and Cross Examination

Parties to formal adjudications are entitled under § 556(d) of the APA to present their case or their defense "by oral or documentary evidence." The right to present oral evidence does not apply, however, in formal rule-makings, determinations relating to claims for money or benefits, and applications for initial licenses if the agency has adopted procedures for submitting all evidence in written form, to the extent that the parties are not prejudiced by those procedures. Also the agency may require a party seeking a hearing to request the hearing and to make a threshold show-ing that a hearing would serve its purpose. The agency may deny a hear-ing if no issues of material fact are in dispute.

Parties to formal adjudications are entitled under § 556(d) "to conduct such cross-examination as may be required for a full and true disclosure of the facts."

IV. INTEGRITY OF DECISIONMAKING PROCESS

A. Bias or Prejudgment of Adjudicatory Decisionmakers

A decision by a biased decisionmaker may violate due process as well as the APA.

Because some agency adjudicators, particularly agency heads, have responsibilities broader than simply adjudicating, the rules relating to disqualification of those administrative adjudicators for bias do not entirely parallel the rules relating to judges

An adjudicative decisionmaker must disqualify him or herself, or be disqualified, from deciding any case in which the decisionmaker is biased. If a party fails to make a timely motion for disqualification, the party has waived the right to do so.

Bias or prejudgment exists when the decisionmaker has a pecuniary or other personal interest in the case, has prejudged the facts against a party or, prior to the commencement of the hearing, had developed personal animus against a party, witness, or counsel or a group to which they belong. Bias is not established merely because the decisionmaker has rejected the claims or the testimony of a party or because the decisionmaker has fixed views about law, policy, or factual propositions not related to specific parties.

If a single member of a multimember agency was biased and was not disqualified from deciding the case, the agency's decision should be reversed, even though the biased member's vote was not necessary to the decision.

B. Personal Responsibility of Decisionmakers

An agency decisionmaker who did not hear the presentation of evidence must become personally familiar with the issues in the case prior to rendering a decision. The decisionmaker can comply with this requirement by reading portions of the transcript and briefs; hearing oral argument; reading a report of lower-level decisionmakers; reading summaries prepared by staff members; or receiving a briefing by staff members. An agency decisionmaker may also delegate the decision to a lower-level official if such delegation is permitted by law.

Agency decisionmakers are presumed to be personally familiar with the issues of a case prior to rendering their decision. Absent evidence suggesting the decisionmaker was not familiar with the issues, it is improper to conduct discovery on the extent to which a decisionmaker familiarized him or herself with the issues or the manner in which this occurred.

C. Prohibition on Ex Parte Communications

Interested persons outside the agency may not make, or cause to be made, an ex parte communication to an agency decisionmaker that is relevant to the merits of a formal adjudication in which they are interested. If prohibited communications occur, they must be disclosed.

"Interested person" means a person whose interest in the matter is more specific than the general interest of a member of the public.

The phrase "relevant to the merits of the proceeding" is broader than the term "fact in issue" under APA §554(d)(1). However, requests for status reports are not relevant to the merits.

The prohibition on ex parte communication covers members of the body comprising the agency (so-called agency heads), administrative law judges, or any "other employee who is or may reasonably be expected to be involved in the decisional process of the proceeding."

APA §557(d) applies only to communications from persons "outside the agency." Communications to decisionmakers from staff members inside the agency are covered by the provision on separation of functions. The President is considered to be "outside the agency" even though the agency is in the executive branch.

The APA section on ex parte communications does not constitute authority to withhold information from Congress. Nor does it extend to "disposition of ex parte matters authorized by law."

The prohibition on ex parte communication goes into effect at the earliest of the following times: (1) when the person responsible for the communication acquires knowledge that a hearing will be noticed; (2) when the proceeding is noticed for a hearing; or (3) at such time as the agency shall designate.

If an adjudicatory decisionmaker makes or receives a prohibited ex parte communication, the decisionmaker shall place in the record the prohibited ex parte communication if the communication was written, or, if it was oral, a memorandum stating the substance of the communication. In addition, the decisionmaker shall place on the record all written responses, and memoranda stating the substance of all oral responses, to such communications.

Adjudicatory decisionmakers may, consistent with the interests of justice and the policy of underlying statutes, require a party who makes or causes to be made a prohibited communication to show cause why his claim or interest in the proceeding should not be dismissed, denied, disregarded, or otherwise adversely affected on account of such violation. Moreover, the agency may, to the extent consistent with the interests of justice and the policy of the underlying statutes, consider a violation of the section sufficient grounds for a decision adverse to a party who knowingly violated it.

Decisions tainted by ex parte communications are voidable rather than void. A reviewing court must decide whether the agency's decisionmaking process makes the ultimate judgment of the agency unfair either to any party or to the public interest.

The APA's limitations on ex parte communications are inapplicable to informal adjudications. A court reviewing an informal adjudication should not overturn the agency action on the basis of ex parte communications unless the communications violated restrictions in a statute other than the APA or deprived a party of procedural due process under the Constitution.

D. Legislative Interference with Adjudication

Legislative pressure on adjudicators may violate the APA prohibition on ex parte contacts and may also deprive parties of their constitutional rights to due process. Claims of such violations are most likely to succeed where the congressional pressure probably influenced the decision of the adjudicators, the communication concerned disputed facts as opposed to issues of law or policy, and the particular application of pressure served no legitimate purpose such as statutory revision or congressional oversight of administration.

E. Separation of Functions: General Rule

An agency staff member who has engaged in an adversary function in a case may not participate or advise in an adjudicatory decision in that case or a factually related adjudication. Engagement means significant and personal participation in the functions of prosecution, investigation, or advocacy.

The separation of functions requirement does not preclude agency decisionmakers from taking part in a determination to launch an investigation or issue a complaint, or similar preliminary decision, and later serving as a decisionmaker in the same case.

Under the APA, separation of functions does not apply in determining applications for initial licenses or to proceedings involving the validity or application of rates, facilities, or practices of public utilities or carriers.

The requirement of separation of functions does not prohibit agency heads, including members of multimember commissions, from personally engaging in an adversary function and later participating in an adjudicatory decision in the same or a factually related case. However, the individual must be an agency head both at the time of investigation and decision.

F. Separation of Functions and Administrative Law Judges

An ALJ is not permitted to consult off-the-record with any person, inside or outside of the agency, concerning a fact in issue.

An ALJ may not be responsible to or subject to the supervision or direction of an agency staff member who is contemporaneously performing investigative or prosecutorial functions.

The APA's separation of functions restrictions do not apply in determining applications for initial licenses or to proceedings involving the validity or application of rates, facilities, or practices of public utilities or carriers.

G. The Rule of Necessity

If disqualifying one or more decisionmakers would render the agency incapable of acting, those decisionmakers should not be disqualified.

V. ADMINISTRATIVE LAW JUDGES UNDER THE FEDERAL ADMINISTRATIVE PROCEDURE ACT

A. ALJ Powers and Duties

The APA confers substantial powers on ALJs in the course of presiding at hearings, including the powers to issue subpoenas and take depositions as authorized by law, administer oaths, receive relevant evidence, and regulate the course of the hearing. These powers arise from the APA without the necessity of express agency delegation, and agencies are "without power to withhold [them]." They must be exercised subject to the published rules of the agency.

B. The Selection Process

The Office of Personnel Management (OPM), the central personnel agency of the federal government, holds periodic competitions for positions as ALJs. The OPM has broad discretion in determining the method of selection; the creation and modification of these standards can be declared invalid if the OPM's actions are arbitrary and unreasonable.

C. Inconsistent Functions

An agency cannot assign an ALJ to perform duties inconsistent with the duties and responsibilities of ALJs.

D. Tenure

The position of ALJ is a tenured position, and one holding this position may be removed or disciplined only for good cause established by the Merit Systems Protection Board (MSPB) after opportunity of hearing before the Board. The MSPB itself has no authority to take action against an ALJ; it determines whether there is good cause for the particular agency to take action and, if so, what particular action the agency is allowed to take.

Actions by an ALJ that are inconsistent with the primary purpose of the APA in that they undermine confidence in the administrative adjudicatory process constitute good cause for disciplinary action. Thus, good cause for disciplinary action may include instances of bias, misconduct, incompetence, failure to perform duties, insubordination, physical incapacity, violations of statutory law or agency rules, or a refusal to follow settled precedents.

If a disciplinary action by an agency is arbitrary, politically motivated, or otherwise based on reasons that constitute an improper interference with the performance by an ALJ of his or her judicial functions, the charge cannot constitute good cause.

Disciplinary action against an ALJ may include removal or suspension.

E. Compensation

Compensation of ALJs is set by the OPM at designated levels independent of agency recommendations and ratings. The OPM has the right to determine the pay level at which each ALJ is placed and the qualifications required for appointment to each level. Once an ALJ is appointed to a designated level, the method of advancement is governed by the provisions of 5 U.S.C. § 5372.

In promoting ALJs, the hiring agency decides if there is a vacancy for an ALJ and if the vacancy should be filled by promotion of a current ALJ. The OPM then decides which ALJ shall receive the promotion. However, in cases of promoting an incumbent ALJ to Chief ALJ, the power to select is vested in the employing agency.

F. Rotation

ALJs shall be assigned to cases in rotation so far as practicable. The phrase "so far as practicable" permits a practice of categorizing cases according to level of difficulty and assigning ALJs in rotation among the categories in which they qualified. The assignment of ALJs cannot be made with the intent or effect of interfering with ALJ independence or otherwise depriving a party of a fair hearing.

G. ALJ Performance

Under OPM regulations, an agency shall not rate the performance of an ALJ. An agency may, however, introduce managerial programs to increase the quality and production of case decisions, so long as these programs do not interfere with the decisional independence of the ALJ. Agencies may institute programs for reviewing ALJ decisions outside of the normal administrative appeal process. Agencies may also set reasonable production goals for ALJs.

H. The Savings Clause

When a hearing is required by the APA for adjudication and the hearing is not held before the agency itself or one or more members of the body which comprises the agency, an ALJ must preside over the hearing unless the hearing is conducted "by or before boards or other employees specially provided for by or designated under statute." A statutory provision that relies on this "savings clause" to except a case from the scope of the APA must be express and clear.

VI. POST-HEARING REQUIREMENTS

A. Findings of Fact and Conclusions of Law

Agency decisions in formal adjudications shall include agency findings and conclusions, and the reasons underlying those findings and conclusions, on all material issues of fact, law, or agency discretion presented in the adjudication record. An agency need not provide a detailed and explicit weighing of each relevant consideration to accomplish these purposes. It is sufficient if the bases of its decision are reasonably discernible and a reviewing court can satisfy itself that the agency gave a "hard look" at the relevant issues. An agency's departure from its own prior decisions in a similar case or cases must be accompanied by an explanation for that departure.

B. Administrative Review

Most agencies have at least one level of internal administrative review. Such review, however, is not a constitutional right. Because constitutional due process does not require administrative review, its specification is determined by an agency's enabling act and its rules. The agency has a duty to inform disappointed parties of the means for seeking administrative review of an initial decision.

Parties seeking administrative review generally must satisfy the same conditions imposed on judicial review: they must exhaust nonappeal processes and the decision appealed must be final; they must present the administrative review authority with all of their objections to the decision below, must note all available evidence and issues in the prior proceeding, and preserve issues for review. However, in an appropriate case the administrative review authority may consider an issue sua sponte even though the issue was not raised by a party.

The adjudicatory authority of the agency resides with the agency head or heads unless it has been delegated by statute or agency regulation to another or subordinate decisionmaker. Except where an ALJ decision has become final under § 557(b) (an initial decision not timely appealed), it becomes part of the record underlying the agency's decision. Where an initial decision is appealed within an agency, the decision of the final appellate authority within the agency constitutes the agency's decision for purposes of judicial review.

An agency may adopt an initial decision by an ALJ without making independent findings or reasons.

On appeal from an initial decision, the agency has all the powers which it would have in making the initial decision, unless a statute or the agency's own rules provide otherwise. Absent such a provision, an agency owes no deference to initial decisions by an ALJ. Where the agency and ALJ disagree on the facts, the court will review the agency's not the ALJ's findings, unless otherwise provided by the agency's enabling statute or regulations. However, the initial decision of an ALJ is part of the record for purposes of judicial review, and a reviewing court will take it into account in judging whether the agency's decision is adequately reasoned and supported by substantial evidence.

VII. INFORMAL ADJUDICATION

A. Basic Principles

Informal adjudication is the name used to denote various procedures for issuing orders when formal adjudication is not required. As discussed in Part II.A, *supra,* formal adjudication is required when an agency issues an order under a statute that requires an "on the record" agency hearing.

B. Informal Adjudication Procedures

Informal adjudication comprises a wide variety of agency procedures, some resembling what is traditionally thought of as adjudication and others not resembling adjudication at all. The APA contains little in the way of procedural requirements specifically targeted to informal adjudication. However, §§ 555 and 558 prescribe a number of general procedural requirements that are pertinent to informal and formal adjudication. Section 555 governs the mechanics of agency process, including the issuance of administrative subpoenas, the rights of representation to be afforded before an agency, an agency's obligations to provide transcripts, notices of denial, and statements of reasons. Section 558 imposes certain minimal requirements on licensing proceedings and requires that all agency orders and sanctions be authorized by law. More detailed procedures for informal adjudication are typically found in particular agency statutes and agency rules and may also be required by due process.

C. Departures from Formal Proceedings

Informal adjudication procedures depart from the formal adjudicatory model in many respects. Subject to possible constraints imposed by due process, informal adjudication may include informal conferences, ex parte contacts, active involvement by the decisionmaker in the investigation and prosecution of the agency's case, lack of representation by counsel if there are no hearings before the agency, limited evidentiary requirements, and generally a relaxation of the formalities associated with formal adjudication. There also may be no provision for confrontation of evidence and witnesses, and there may be no discovery or transcript of the proceedings. Some informal adjudications employ procedures similar to those used in notice and comment rulemaking, for example by giving interested parties notice of the agency's proposed order and allowing written or oral comments without formal adjudicatory procedures.

If an agency employs notice and comment procedures in informal adjudication, comments may be accepted from interested persons not party to the proceedings. If the agency chooses (or is required by statute or regulation) to hold public hearings, these may actually be open meetings at which all interested persons can express their views on the matter without cross examination or formal consideration of evidence.

D. The *Vermont Yankee* Rule in Informal Adjudication

The *Vermont Yankee* rule prohibiting courts from imposing procedures not required by any statute, rule, or the Constitution on agencies applies to informal adjudication. Absent constitutional concerns, federal courts may not require agencies engaged in informal adjudication to add to the procedures required by applicable statutes and rules such as APA §§ 555 and 558.

E. Judicial Review of Informal Adjudication

Judicial review of final agency action in cases of informal adjudication generally is available. Unless a statute or the Constitution requires otherwise, the standard of review of fact findings underlying orders issued after informal adjudication is "arbitrary, capricious, an abuse of discretion, or otherwise not in accordance with law."

TABLE OF CASES

O

INDEX

A

adjudication. *See also specific types of proceedings such as* employment proceedings

administrative law judges in (*see* administrative law judges)

agency actions excepted from, 47–48, 263, 271

alternative dispute resolution in, 163–174, 244n74

APA on (*see* Administrative Procedure Act *entries*)

attorneys' fees for, 32, 41n1, 219–234

bias of adjudicatory decisionmakers, 121–131, 258–259, 265–266

defined, 6–9, 239, 261

electronic technology use in, 9–10, 35–36, 249

emergency, 241–242

evidence in (*see* evidence)

ex parte communications related to, 3–4, 82n3, 84, 133–143, 178n15, 217, 251, 259–260, 266–267

hearings for (*see* hearings)

informal, 41n2, 142–143, 176–196, 222–224, 239, 247n70, 249, 272–274

integrity of decisionmaking process in, 119–161, 258–260, 265–268

legislative interference with, 143–148, 267

licensing as, 6, 7–9, 40, 43, 191n69

notice of (*see* notice)

procedural due process in (*see* procedural due process)

quasi-legislative action *vs.*, 37–40

rulemaking *vs.*, 6–9, 37–38, 240

separation of functions in, 148–159, 268

subpoenas in, 33, 59–60, 60–72, 185, 247

Administrative Conference of the United States (ACUS), 6n30, 9–10, 164

Administrative Dispute Resolution Act (ADRA), 163–164, 166, 169–170n25, 170–172

administrative law judges (ALJs)

administrative review of ALJ decisions, 110–118, 255–256, 271–272

alternative dispute resolution by, 174

attorneys' absence impacting duty of, 99, 203

bias of, 121–131, 258–259, 265–266

command or supervisory influence over, 3, 158–159, 217, 268

compensation of, 212–213, 270

examination of, 202

exclusive record rule for, 160–161

ex parte communications prohibition for, 3–4, 82n3, 84, 133–143, 178n15, 217, 251, 259–260, 266–267

hearing requirements for presiding, 82, 83

inconsistent functions of, 203, 269

insubordination of, 206–207

integrity issues facing (*see* integrity of decisionmaking process)

interference with independence of, 143–148, 209, 267

legislative interference with, 143–148, 267

misconduct or incompetence of, 205–206

Model Code of Judicial Conduct for, 120–121, 124, 134n45, 150, 178n15, 204

nonconsultation rule for, 156–158